MEDIA AGENDA-SETTING IN A PRESIDENTIAL ELECTION

Issues, Images, and Interest

David H. Weaver
Doris A. Graber
Maxwell E. McCombs
Chaim H. Eyal

PRAEGER SPECIAL STUDIES • PRAEGER SCIENTIFIC

Library of Congress Cataloging in Publication Data

Main entry under title:

Media agenda-setting in a Presidential election.

   Bibliography: p.
   Includes index.
   1. Presidents--United States--Election--1976.
2. Press and politics--United States. I. Weaver,
David H., 1935-   .
E868.M42   324.7'3'0973   80-39685
ISBN 0-03-059066-3

To Dad and the Memory of My Mother
—DHW

To Better News and Better Presidents
—DAG

To Zoe, Molly, Leslie, and Dody
—MEM

To My Mother

—CHE

Published in 1981 by Praeger Publishers
CBS Educational and Professional Publishing
A Division of CBS, Inc.
521 Fifth Avenue, New York, New York 10175 U.S.A.

© 1981 by Praeger Publishers

123456789   145   987654321

Printed in the United States of America

PREFACE
AND ACKNOWLEDGMENTS

Planning for this yearlong study of the 1976 election began in the spring of 1975 at the annual meeting of the International Communication Association held in Chicago. There David Weaver, Doris Graber, Maxwell McCombs, and several other persons met to discuss the need for a study of media agenda-setting that would be far more comprehensive and intensive than earlier studies.

Previous media agenda-setting studies had shown that learning of issue saliences takes place over lengthy periods of time and that things besides issue importance are learned from the mass media's coverage of an election campaign. Therefore we set out to design a study that would enable us to look at political learning during an entire presidential election year (1976). Taking advantage of our geographical dispersion, we decided to include more than one kind of community in the study so as to check on the effects of different settings on voters' learning from newspapers and television. We chose a large metropolitan area (Indianapolis, Indiana), a smaller suburban community (Evanston, Illinois), and a fairly small town in the state with the first presidential primary (Lebanon, New Hampshire). Each of the three sites is within a day's drive of the professional home of Weaver, Graber, or McCombs.

McCombs of Syracuse University served as the project coordinator. He proposed the basic questionnaire design, after consultation with Graber and Weaver. Except for one intensively studied panel in Evanston, coding and key punching of the voters' responses were handled at Syracuse University. The authors owe a debt of gratitude to the staff of the Communications Research Center in the S.I. Newhouse School of Public Communications for its courteous and efficient processing of each round of questionnaires. In addition, the Communications Research Center at Syracuse University generously provided the bulk of funding to pay each voter in our study for his or her participation throughout the year. Interviews and diaries furnished by the special Evanston panel were paid for by the Center for Research in Criminal Justice at the University of Illinois at Chicago Circle, in connection with another phase of this project.

The content analysis of the newspapers in each community was done primarily by research assistants employed at each of the three universities, using code books designed by Graber. The bulk of the analysis of the content of the three television network evening news programs was handled at the University of Illinois at Chicago Circle.

The organization of this book reflects, in part, the division of labor among the authors in analyzing this huge set of survey and content data. McCombs, because of his role in the original conception and empirical study of media agenda-setting, was primarily responsible for the introductory chapters, the research design chapter, and the chapter on political interest. Graber, due to her interest in political learning from the media, was primarily responsible for Chapter 3 on political learning and agenda-setting, and she collaborated with Weaver on the final chapter of the book. Weaver, the central coordinator of the book, was primarily responsible for Chapters 6-8 on issue agenda-setting. He also collaborated with Chaim Eyal, who was then at Syracuse University, on Chapters 4 and 9. Each author contributed commentary and often entire sections to chapters drafted by other collaborators. This book therefore represents a genuine merger of ideas and expressions.

The first part of the book—The Context for Agenda-Setting Studies—provides an introduction and theoretical overview for the idea of media agenda-setting. It includes a review of the major findings of many of the earlier studies and discussion of many of the chief issues and developments in agenda-setting research since McCombs and Shaw's original study of the 1968 presidential election, which was published in *Public Opinion Quarterly* in 1972. The second part of the book—Interest, Issue, and Image Agenda-Setting—concentrates in detail on the role of newspapers and television in setting interest, issue, and image agendas throughout the election year. In doing so, it broadens the focus of media agenda-setting beyond its customary concentration on issues and it extends the time period for agenda-setting effects from a few weeks or months to an entire election year.

Naturally, any study of this magnitude would not have been possible without the assistance of many other people. At Indiana University, Dr. Richard Gray, director of the School of Journalism, provided continued support and the funding to hire interviewers and research assistants to code the Indianapolis *Star* and *News*. Graduate students Douglas Dietsch, Brian Werth, and Frederick Ficu were especially helpful in analyzing both content and survey data. Inez Woodley, editorial assistant of the Bureau of Media Research in the School of Journalism, provided critical guidance on writing style. Her expert administrative and typing abilities were indispensable in producing the entire manuscript. Jeff Black also assisted with the typing and proofreading of much of the manuscript and managed to keep all of us smiling most of the time. Colleagues G. Cleveland Wilhoit, Walter Jaehnig, David Nord, and Eric Fredin listened patiently to lengthy descriptions of the problems and progress of the study, and Gail and Quinn Weaver helped David Weaver maintain some sense of perspective about the whole project. Finally, Professor John Schweitzer suggested some of the lifestyle measures used in several of the questionnaires.

At the University of Illinois, Chicago Circle, Jim Marek supervised and assisted with coding and computer operations. Roger Sanders initiated the computer programs and David Mongan viewed and coded television news. Dr. Young Yun Kim prepared most of the media code books and coded all the interviews for the special Evanston panel. Anne Spray prepared the index and assisted in a number of editorial tasks. We also acknowledge with gratitude the financial contributions of the Center for Research in Criminal Justice and the support of the Computer Center at the University of Illinois at Chicago Circle.

At Syracuse, the continual interviewing of voters in New Hampshire and the coding of data from all three survey sites required the participation of literally dozens of people in the Communications Research Center between December 1975 and the late fall of 1976. Among our key lieutenants and support staff, several are due special thanks. Paula Poindexter and Bob Burnham interviewed our New Hampshire panel across 1976. This involved many hours on the telephone and several trips to Lebanon. David Nicholas, dubbed with the Gilbert and Sullivan-esque title of "Coder General," patiently spent months devising coding schemes and overseeing the coding and key punching of the immense amount of survey data generated by a year of interviewing. While on the Syracuse faculty, Lee Becker contributed helpful ideas and many hours to the development of the voter interviews. Two administrative services managers in the Communication Research Center, Kathy Pious and Jo-Anne Sliva, kept the entire operation humming smoothly. Special appreciation is due Henry F. Schulte, dean of the School of Public Communication at Syracuse University during the time of this project, and to the Newhouse and Snow research endowments for establishing the conditions and environment conducive to this longitudinal theoretical contribution to our understanding of the political role of mass communication.

CONTENTS

LIST OF TABLES

LIST OF FIGURES

I

THE CONTEXT FOR
AGENDA-SETTING STUDIES

one

A SKETCH OF REALITY

An election campaign exists in the public consciousness largely the way it exists in mass media presentation of campaign events.

John Carey

MEDIA IMAGES OF REALITY

Most of the world we talk about and think about is out of sight and never directly experienced. The news media, therefore, have been described as our intellectual windows on the world. In a similar vein, the task of the news media also has been described as holding a mirror up to reality. Both metaphors imply that the proper role of the press is to serve as a conduit between its audiences and the vast current history of the world.

But the press does not serve as a simple conduit passing along bits of information on everything out there. As Walter Lippmann observed long ago, the capacity of the press to report the world around us is quite limited. There are not a great many reporters. Indeed, if it were not for the professional news values of journalism, a traditional set of criteria defining what is news and what is not, these few reporters could not cover as much as they do.

These values guide journalists to the key newsworthy events, personalities, and situations of the day. Looked at another way, this means that these news values shape the prism through which we view much of volume in a series of mass communication studies dating from the benchmark 1940 Erie County study. Among its major contributions are sets of data covering the entire election year of 1976 and a particularly intensive focus on the agenda-setting role of the press through the use of both survey and content-analysis data.

Since the agenda-setting process involves learning over a considerable period of time, our study of voters and mass communication during 1976 set out to observe a number of voters from the early weeks of the year right through to the postelection weeks. Following the tradition established by other studies of the agenda-setting role of the press, we also content-analyzed the major newspapers and television newscasts used by these voters to learn about and follow the political events, issues, and personalities of 1976.

Like *The Emergence of American Political Issues*,[3] which was based on data from a 1972 panel study in Charlotte, N.C., and most previous studies of agenda-setting, this yearlong investigation set its primary focus on the issues of the election year, those topics that concerned voters and that they talked about with others. The first necessary step was to match this voter agenda with the press agenda in order to retest the basic hypothesis of agenda-setting that the priorities of the press become in time the priorities of the public.

The more important role of this 1976 research, however, was to specify the circumstances under which this transfer of saliences takes place. Over what period of time does this happen, and during which parts of the political year? Are newspapers and television equal partners in the process, or does each have a specialty role to play? What about differences among voters and among issues? No one contends that agenda-setting is a universal influence process affecting all voters on all issues. This book extends our understanding of which voters are influenced on which issues.

This is not the only area of advance. Two other key political elements—images of the candidates and general interest in politics—also are susceptible to analysis in agenda-setting terms. In 1976 our analysis of mass communication and voter behavior expanded the domain of the agenda-setting concept to include these elements.

One of the attractive features of the idea of an agenda-setting role of mass communication is its application to a number of topics formerly considered quite discrete and separate by analysts of mass communication. In the abstract, agenda-setting is concerned with the salience of an object or a set of objects. In most studies, the set of objects has been public issues of major concern at the moment. Of course, each of these objects also has a wide variety of attributes that can be rated, or even rank-ordered, in terms of their prominence in the news media or in the minds of the audience.

One key set of objects in the early months of 1976 was the large number of contenders for the Democratic nomination. How did Jimmy Carter emerge from this pack to secure the nomination? Especially important, since he was a newcomer to national politics, what kind of image of Carter emerged in the public mind? Where did it come from? Since most voters never see presidential hopefuls in person, to what extent did the descriptions in the news media become translated into voters' pictures of these candidates?

Just as we can conceive of various agendas of political elements, issues, candidates, candidate characteristics, or whatever, it is also possible to think of a larger agenda of concerns for each voter in which politics is only one item. For most people most of the time, politics is a very minor item on one's personal agenda. However, every four years there is an upsurge in political interest as Americans prepare to select a president. Since the mass media, especially newspapers and television, are the dominant source of political information, one of their key roles in a presidential election year may be to restore politics to a prominent position on the agendas of America's voters. This role of stimulating renewed interest in learning about politics may be the ultimate agenda-setting influence of the media.

In sum, this book continues the exploration of the agenda-setting role of mass communication, an exploration that began with an original empirical study by McCombs and Shaw during the 1968 presidential election[4] and continued with the Charlotte study during the 1972 election.[5] These three successive benchmarks in agenda-setting research denote the continuing exploration of the domains in which this idea of an agenda-setting role of mass communication applies within national political campaigns. The original 1968 study focused on the issue orientations of undecided voters. In 1972 additional aspects of the issue orientations of a general population of voters were explored. This book continues and expands this exploration of issue orientation among voters while also broadening the inquiry into two new domains, candidate images and interest in politics.

NOTES

[1]G. Ray Funkhouser, "Trends in Media Coverage of the Issues of the '60s," *Journalism Quarterly* 50 (Autumn 1973): 533–38.

[2]Charles Wright, "Functional Analysis and Mass Communication," *Public Opinion Quarterly* 24 (Winter 1960): 608.

[3]Donald L. Shaw and Maxwell E. McCombs, *The Emergence of American Political Issues: The Agenda-Setting Function of the Press* (St. Paul: West, 1977).

[4]Maxwell E. McCombs and Donald L. Shaw, "The Agenda-Setting Function of Mass Media," *Public Opinion Quarterly* 36 (Summer 1972): 176–87.

[5]Shaw and McCombs, *The Emergence of American Political Issues*.

two

RESEARCH DESIGN:
A HYBRID METHODOLOGY

Most studies of the agenda-setting role of mass communication use traditional survey research procedures to measure the public agenda. Both the original agenda-setting study in Chapel Hill, N.C., during the 1968 presidential election and the follow-up study in Charlotte, N.C., during the 1972 presidential election followed this tradition.[1] However, in this study of the 1976 presidential election the traditional large-sample survey was abandoned and a new hybrid that represents the interface of traditional large-scale survey research and participant observation was used.

RATIONALE FOR A NEW DESIGN

Before describing this 1976 departure in the study of voters' agendas, it is important to understand why tradition was not followed. Basically, two reasons account for a new approach in this election study. First, at this stage in the study of the agenda-setting of mass communication there is an obvious need to go beyond description of the agenda-setting phenomenon per se. There is a need to probe and understand the public-opinion process and agenda-setting more intimately than is possible with the usual standardized questionnaire. Research procedures must provide greater depth and breadth, including consideration of the personal and political context in which respondents find themselves at interview time.

Part of this increased depth also must come from study over longer spans of time. It is quite clear that agenda-setting is not an instantaneous or even short-term effect of the mass media. Audience perceptions rarely change precipitously. Since news impact is cumulative, news flow and its effects must be observed over extended periods of time. Changes cannot be assessed adequately without knowing prior conditions.

While panel designs can be used to extend traditional survey research across long periods of time, the logistics and costs of interviewing a large sample over and over again—while also striving for the necessary depth—dictate a different approach. There is a need for logistical parsimony in tracking voters across the full length of the election year. So traditional research procedures were modified to yield a hybrid version of survey research that brought it closer in quality and duration of contact to clinical, in-depth interviewing.

SURVEY PROCEDURES

The starting point in the procedure was identical to the 1972 study of Charlotte voters reported in *The Emergence of American Political Issues*. A random sample of people was selected from the voter registration lists of three communities.[2] However, rather than beginning with a full interview and just reappearing several more times during the election year, we told the final sample of voters chosen in each community that they were being recruited as participants in a yearlong in-depth public opinion survey. This final sample of voters was purposively chosen from the larger random samples to ensure that each voter in our study regularly used newspapers, television, or both for political news. Those voters not regularly using newspapers or television for political information were eliminated from the panel because we reasoned that they could not be *directly* affected by political messages from these media.[3]

While this selection procedure disturbed the randomness of the samples, it was necessary. Both our need to become closely acquainted with their feelings and behaviors in the course of nine interviews and conversations and our logistical need to keep the number of participants and mass media to be content-analyzed within manageable limits dictated a fairly small sample. In turn, a small sample made it important to screen participants to ensure a sample of voters who used the same newspapers and television news programs but who, at the same time, exhibited a fairly wide range of media use patterns and interest in politics.

Our final decision was to recruit about 50 voters in each of three geographic sites: Lebanon, New Hampshire, a small town in the state with the earliest primary election, where the interviewing was handled by

McCombs and his associates at Syracuse University; Indianapolis, Indiana, a fairly large and heterogeneous city, where the interviewing was handled by Weaver and his associates at Indiana University; and Evanston, Illinois, a suburban satellite of Chicago, where the interviewing was handled by Graber and her associates at the University of Illinois at Chicago Circle. Each member of the final sample was offered a $50 cash payment ($25 during the summer of 1976 and $25 at the end of the year) for his or her participation in the yearlong study.

The median age of our panel members was in the thirties, and there were no significant differences in the age distributions in the three communities. In all three, from one-fifth to one-fourth of the panel members were 18 to 29 years old, from 34 percent to 40 percent were 30 to 49 years old, and from 37 percent to 46 percent were 50 or older. Likewise, there were no significant differences in the proportions of men and women in the three samples (from 44 percent to 60 percent male), nor were there any significant differences in average annual family income (from 50 percent to 69 percent made $15,000 or more a year). All three samples consisted of predominantly white-collar workers, though this was more true of Evanston (84 percent) than of Indianapolis (61 percent) or of Lebanon (57.5 percent). Conversely, there were considerably greater proportions of blue-collar workers in Indianapolis (27 percent) and in Lebanon (15 percent) than in Evanston (5 percent). Also, more people in the Evanston sample (65 percent) had graduated from college than in Indianapolis (28 percent) or in Lebanon (31 percent). Taken as a whole, then, the samples from the three communities did not differ substantially in age, sex, or income, but they did differ in education and occupation.

The actual sizes of the voter samples and the dates of the nine interviews across 1976 are shown in Table 2–1. Here one begins to sense the shift toward in-depth interviewing, using the basic data collection procedures of survey research to complete 1,133 interviews during the year.

One substantial advantage of these small samples is that one or two interviewers can telephone all the members of the panel at one site within a short period of time. All of the interviews except the one in July and the last wave were conducted by telephone. Because the same interviewers were used for a number of waves, an additional feedback loop was created beyond that available from formal coding and analysis of the data. On the basis of this feedback, plus continuing theoretical reflections on the nature of the agenda-setting role of the press in a presidential election, questions were assembled at Syracuse University in preparation for each new wave of interviewing. These questions ranged from open-ended probes into the voters' views on the major public issues and their reactions to the full

TABLE 2–1

1976 Voter Survey Interviews

Wave Dates	New Hampshire	Indiana	Illinois	Total Interviews
1 February 4–27	43	48	48	139
2 March 17–28	44	46	44	134
3 May 15–19	44	46	43	133
4 July 14–23	43	38	45	126
5 August 18–31	43	45	42	130
6 September 13–22	43	40	42	125
7 October 26–November 1	41	41	33	115
8 November 3–18	42	43	42	127
9 December/January 1977	40	38	26	104
Total	383	385	365	1,133

Source: Compiled by authors.

spectrum of political news and information in the mass media to a variety of measurement scales on political topics, media use, and personal background information on each voter.[4]

The broad range of questions permitted us to go beyond the assessment of the causal links between media emphasis and media audience saliences to investigate the effects of antecedent and intervening variables on agenda-setting. These include such antecedent factors as age, education, interest, past knowledge, and party affiliation and such intervening factors as reading or viewing habits, discussions with others, information needs dictated by one's social and occupational setting, and the quality and presentation of media stories.

In addition to the three panels or sample groups in Table 2–1, a "core panel" of 21 respondents in Evanston furnished taped in-depth interviews and completed daily diaries recording news stories that had come to their attention. These panelists were selected in the same manner as the others. To provide a broad range of explanatory information to supplement our survey data, these respondents were questioned far more intensively about their past and current lifestyles and media use patterns, about their attention to specific news stories, and about their knowledge of the election and other current events.

Ten interviews, each averaging two hours in length, were completed with each member of the core panel. Panelists received $5 for each interview and $1 for each day for which they completed diaries reporting the source and substance of remembered news stories and their reactions to these stories. On an average, core panel members completed diaries for five days of the week, with four hours or more elapsing between reception of the story and diary recording. Respondents who preferred to dictate their diary entries were contacted daily by a telephone interviewer who recorded the information. No differences were detected between personally recorded and telephoned diaries. The average number of diary stories per person was 533, with a range from 351 to 969.

The other portion of the data presented in this book, descriptions of the mass communication messages available to our voter panels during the course of 1976, came from the content analyses of four newspapers and of the early evening news broadcasts of the three national television networks as well as of the 5 p.m. NBC and 10 p.m. Chicago local news broadcasts.

The *Valley News* and the Chicago *Tribune*, the principal newspapers used by our panel members in Lebanon and Evanston respectively, were content-analyzed on a daily basis for the entire year of 1976. This permitted us to capture the daily flow of news to which our panel members were actually exposed and to assess its completeness and cumulative impact. This also prevented sampling problems from arising due to the fact that major news events are not randomly distributed. In Indianapolis it was necessary to code both the *News* and the *Star* because each serves a distinct portion of the city's population. A sample was constructed from every fourth issue of each of these two newspapers across the entire year of 1976.

The coding unit used in all these content analyses was the individual story. Its subject matter was coded with particular attention to the availability of information presumably important to the appraisal of presidential candidates. This included news about candidates' personal and professional qualifications and about the major issues facing the nation, the merits of the candidates' positions on these issues, and their capabilities to deal with them. We also recorded placement and emphasis given to various types of stories because prominent displays generally attract audience attention.[5] Since political news in general and election news in particular are part of a larger supply of news that competes for the audience attention, we coded all news content to assess the treatment of election stories in relation to other types of stories. This puts election stories into a more realistic perspective.

The television network news for 1976 was content analyzed in a similar manner, using the abstracts prepared by the Vanderbilt University Library Archives for national newscasts and the actual broadcasts for local newscasts. Comparisons of coding national news directly from broadcasts with coding from abstracts showed only minor differences for the information required for this study. The one major exception was coding of candidate images, which was fruitful only when both sound and pictures were analyzed in full.

The reliability of coding for the content analyses was carefully controlled. It is difficult to report a single reliability figure since many different coders were involved in this project. The same coding supervisor checked and recoded a portion of each coder's work following the initial training period and at various times thereafter. Excluding simple identification categories, such as newspaper or station name and date, which might inflate reliability figures, intercoder reliability averaged 85 percent and intracoder reliability averaged 90 percent, using the ratio of coding agreements to the total number of coding decisions. Considering the complexity of coding, these are good results.[6]

ASSESSING THE INTERVIEW METHODOLOGY

One of the major advantages of in-depth interviewing is the close relationship between the observer and those persons whose behavior is under scrutiny. It was the desire for this quality that led to the hybrid survey methodology used. Repeated interviews of small panels by a few interviewers accomplished this purpose.

The voters in each panel knew from the outset that they were participating in a long-term study of political learning during a presidential year. They also knew that Syracuse University was going to pay them $50 for their participation. Their involvement in the project and in responding to the interviewers' questions was therefore qualitatively different from the involvement of the typical survey respondent in an unsolicited, unanticipated interview with a stranger.

Familiarity with individual respondents permitted interviewers to sense when questions required further explanations to make them meaningful to the respondent. This was particularly important for respondents with little education or experience in political matters. But even with politically sophisticated respondents, a surprisingly large number of questions brought forth requests for clarification of contingencies and standards. For instance, when rating debate performance of presidential candidates, respondents wanted to know whether ratings should be absolute or based on comparisons of the candidates or on comparisons with debates of prior years. Each contingency required a different rating. Meaningful interpretation of survey results is impossible without ascertaining the contingencies on which the answers are predicated.

The degree of rapport was usually high between respondents and interviewers in this study. Personal interviews plus a continuing series of telephone calls established sufficiently intimate relationships to permit construction of panel member profiles that helped to explain member interactions with mass media information. These profiles go beyond the formal material available from the questionnaires. A Lebanon interviewer noted, for example:

Respondent #6, age 57, works long hours as a garage mechanic and spends a good part of what leisure time he has tending his garden. He espouses minimal interest in politics and did not vote in the New Hampshire primary because he "was working." He opines that the government and U.S. foreign affairs are "a mess" but keeps these views pretty much to himself, rarely discussing politics with either family or friends. A man of few words, he seldom provides elaborate answers to open-ended survey questions. Although agreeable to being interviewed, he maintains a high regard for privacy and declines to declare even his political affiliation.

The interviewer also noted:

A witty 36-year-old administrative secretary, respondent #11 expresses a consistent concern over the national economy and unemployment and their impact on New Hampshire residents. "Everyone has found it difficult to live in New Hampshire this year," she noted in an early interview. "Employment is down and prices are up." An ardent independent, respondent #11 finds a greater hope in the Democratic candidates than the Republican. She did not, however, vote in the state primary.

RAPPORT AND SENSITIZATION

The unusually high degree of rapport in this set of interviews resulted in a high degree of receptiveness to the interview questions. Respondents enjoyed the interviews and often went to great lengths to explain how and why they had formed their answers. Another way of phrasing this receptiveness is to state that the respondents were sensitized to the general purpose of the interviews. Negatively, this could have resulted in respondents being primed for each interview, much as students are primed for an examination. While there was sensitization, it did not systematically bias the information obtained. Respondents knew that the interviewer would be calling again, but they were never told what the schedule of interviews was. They did not know whether the next call would come in four weeks, six weeks, eight weeks, or whenever. For example, at the conclusion of the March interview, respondents were told,

"Thank you. We'll be talking with you again in the spring." It was not until May that they received another call.

In the final group sessions held at the end of 1976, a number of respondents remarked that the thought had indeed occurred to them to be better informed for the next interview, but they said that the pressures of everyday activities and the uncertainty as to when the next call would come and what topics it would cover usually eliminated any implementation of that passing thought.

Two simple checks conducted during the year support these impressions. A matching group of respondents, chosen as were our panelists but not included in the panels, were questioned about recall of specific news stories about which core panel members had been questioned as well. Story recall was scored on a four-point scale, ranging from 1 for "none" to 4 for "a lot." The latter rating was awarded whenever respondents could spontaneously relate three or more major aspects of a news story. Comparisons of the mean recall scores showed no significant differences ($p < 0.05$) between the panel members ($\bar{X} = 2.3$ points) and the control group ($\bar{X} = 2.4$ points). If our panelists had been sensitized, one would have expected a higher rate of recall from them.

The final group sessions, held in the months following the elections, marked a high point in the methodology. During the formal November interview immediately after Election Day, panel members were asked if they would like to meet with other panel members in their community in small groups to discuss the election year and their participation in the study. Most were extremely enthusiastic about the chance to meet and talk with others who shared their yearlong experience. Even in Evanston, where the final interview period coincided with record-breaking blizzards, storms, and subzero temperatures, more than half of the respondents ventured out at night to attend the group sessions.

While the moderators of these sessions had received a set of especially prepared questions, they were not essential. Panel members were eager to talk and had much to say. The group setting eased the difficulty of formulating ideas often experienced by individuals. It also reduced inhibitions to express ideas that might be threatening to the interviewer but acceptable to the group. The rapport built up during the year was a major asset for these focused group sessions.

What positive results did this high level of rapport yield? Browsing through the questionnaires and the code book, one comes away with the strong feeling that the quality of answers across 1976 is better than in the typical one-shot survey. There is more information and detail than usual, and the amount of information and detail improves throughout the year. Most likely this is an interaction of repeated interviewing, the dedication of respondents who had signed on for a year's voyage, and the natural rise in political interest during the course of a presidential election year.

Some of these changes are apparent across relatively short spans of time. For example, for July the codebook lists 13 categories for people's explanations in their own words of the reasons for paying a specified amount of attention to the broadcast coverage of the Democratic national convention. In August, when the same question was asked about the Republican convention it took 18 additional categories to code the answers.

Similar comparisons can be made of other open-ended material in the interviews. The respondents in Lebanon, Indianapolis, and Evanston provided a rich lode of data about their use of mass communication and their varied reactions to politics and public issues as the election year progressed. Beyond these qualitative contributions of the methodology to the purposes of the study, there is also an important practical, logistical consideration. This lode was mined at considerably less than the cost of large-scale survey research.

STATISTICAL CONSIDERATIONS

There are, of course, statistical limitations in a small sample. The likelihood of accepting the null hypothesis even when a true relationship exists is indeed higher for the small sample here than it would be for the larger sample typical of traditional survey research. A small sample means that formal statistical analysis of the data must remain largely exploratory and in the *hypothesis formation* stage. It also means that the analysis provides illustrative supportive evidence rather than rigorous testing of hypotheses with substantial controls. But then, to one degree or another, that is always our fate with any kind of data. The possiblity of spuriousness always looms on the horizon.

Since elaboration of both the basic agenda-setting concept and an extended theory linking agenda-setting to its antecedents and consequences is still in the formative stages of development, these limitations on the statistical analysis of the data gathered in Lebanon, Indianapolis, and Evanston during 1976 are not unduly restrictive. The availability of nine waves of data stretching across an entire year for a group of voters well known to their interviewers adds far more to our enterprise than the small sample subtracts. This close contact with voters' views of the major public issues and their use of mass communication in the formation and modification of those views takes us beyond the limited scope of a cross-sectional survey, or even the usual panel design. It brings to our attention a more holistic and detailed picture of voters and the agenda-setting role of the mass media during an election year.

Furthermore, a comparison of responses by our panelists with equivalent responses by Gallup and Roper poll interviewees throughout 1976 shows no significant discrepancies. This gives us confidence that our respondents did not differ significantly in their political learning behavior from general population samples. Intensive study of their political learning patterns should provide clues to the general learning patterns found commonly among voters in similar circumstances.[7]

NOTES

[1]For reports of these studies, see Maxwell E. McCombs and Donald L. Shaw, "The Agenda-Setting Function of Mass Media," *Public Opinion Quarterly* 36 (Summer 1972): 176–87 and Donald L. Shaw and Maxwell E. McCombs, *The Emergence of American Political Issues: The Agenda-Setting Function of the Press* (St. Paul: West, 1977).

[2]See Shaw and McCombs, ibid., for more detailed description of the sampling methods employed in the Charlotte, N.C., study. The probability samples in the 1976 election study, from which our panel members were recruited, were drawn randomly from the voter registration lists in Lebanon, Indianapolis and Evanston. Participation rates were good. In Evanston, for instance, 84 percent of the people contacted agreed to take part in our study. And more than 90 percent of all panel members from all three locations participated in the study for the full campaign period. Because our panel members were recruited from random samples of registered voters, the results of the study are generalizable mainly to registered voters rather than to the general public. But see the end of this chapter and footnote 7 for qualification of this point.

[3]This procedure of limiting our panel to randomly selected registered voters who used newspapers and/or television for political information probably produced a sample of more politically interested and higher socioeconomic status persons than would have been obtained using conventional random sampling procedures. We were not sure what effect this "elite status" had on our panel members' perceptions of campaign issues and candidate images during the 1976 presidential election year. As we point out at the end of this chapter, our panel's perceptions were not far off from the perceptions of nationwide samples used by the Gallup and Roper polling organization. See footnote 7.

[4]Write to David Weaver, School of Journalism, Ernie Pyle Hall, Indiana University, Bloomington, Indiana 47405 for the actual questions and the frequency of their use in the nine interviews conducted throughout the year.

[5]See Percy H. Tannenbaum, "The Indexing Process in Communication," in *The Process and Effects of Mass Communication*, eds. Wilbur Schramm and Donald F. Roberts (Urbana: University of Illinois Press, 1971), pp. 313–25. "Stories" for newspapers were defined as including editorials, letters to the editor, and features and cartoons as well as ordinary news reports, but excluding advertisements, obituaries, puzzles, radio and television listings, and similar announcements. For television, stories encompassed all information conveyed during regularly scheduled newscasts. In addition to date, page location, size of story (or time devoted to it), and other descriptive measures, each newspaper or television story was coded into one, two, or three of the 73 general subject matter categories (e.g. foreign affairs), and into one, two, or three of 65 specific issue categories (e.g., Panama Canal). More than one

subject matter or issue category was used only if coders decided that a given story equally emphasized more than one issue or was about more than one subject.

[6]Write to Doris Graber, Department of Political Science, University of Illinois at Chicago Circle, Box 4348, Chicago, Illinois 60680 for newspaper and television coding instructions.

[7]Many studies provide evidence that generalizable findings about human behavior can be produced from intensive studies of small numbers of people, given proper controls. Examples include Steven R. Brown, "Intensive Analysis in Political Research," *Political Methodology* 1(1974): 1–25; Robert E. Lane, *Political Ideology: Why the American Common Man Believes What He Does* (New York: The Free Press, 1962), pp. 1–11; and Karl A. Lamb, *As Orange Goes: Twelve California Families and the Future of American Politics* (New York: W.W. Norton, 1975), pp. vii–xiii, 3–23.

three

POLITICAL LEARNING AND MEDIA AGENDA-SETTING

Agenda-setting involves a learning process. People familiarize themselves with mass media images of the political world and learn through a variety of cues how important particular stories are deemed by the media. Learning story content and internalizing salience appear to be neither automatic nor uniform for different people or different subject matter, or in different contexts. To fully understand agenda-setting, we need to know the scope of these variations. We also should know whether agenda-learning involves considerable thought and evaluation, or whether it is a comparatively mindless form of rote learning whereby people memorize media priorities and emphases without absorbing much of the information on which these priorities are based.

In this chapter, we will try to shed light on these questions, using primarily data gathered from the core panel interviews, recall tests, and diaries. As described earlier, core panel members kept daily diaries of newspaper and television stories that had come to their attention in the course of the day. They were also asked during each interview about their recall of some 20 to 30 prominent news stories.

Using this extensive store of information, we will examine the factors that have a bearing on the substance, quality, and quantity of learning about the presidential candidates and public policy issues involved in the campaign. First, we shall focus on the depth and breadth of learning about the issues and candidate qualities and qualifications. This will be an indication of the knowledge base on which the formation of priorities rests. Next, we shall take a brief look at differences between learning about issues and learning about candidate images to explain why some subjects are more readily absorbed from the media than others. Finally, we shall explore some of the inherent and environmental factors that explain individual variations in learning. Demographic as well as motivational differences will be considered. Since exposure and learning are matters of free choice, people's predispositions and preferences are likely to be important aspects of learning behavior.[1]

LEVELS OF LEARNING

To test the extent of knowledge transmitted by the media, we asked the core panelists what they knew about issues and candidate qualities that they or the media had previously mentioned as important. Four levels of knowledge could be indentified. The first was "awareness" of issues and candidate images. At this lowest level of learning, respondents remembered mention of issues or qualities, but could not spontaneously recall any facts about them. A second level was "recall with facts." At that level, respondents could give facts to identify the issue or give examples of the presidential candidates' qualities as well as reasons for deeming them important. The extent of factual knowledge was then scored to indicate whether the respondent could provide one, two, or three or more facts. If respondents lacked facts but had issue and image priorities nonetheless, questions about the thoughtfulness of their choices were, of course, raised. A third level of knowledge was "recall with facts and knowledge of one candidate's position or qualities." Here respondents were able to specify some dimensions of the issues or qualities and link them to one of the candidates. A fourth level was "recall with facts and two candidates' positions." This of course is the only level of knowledge that is fully adequate for making bonafide issue- or image-based choices between two candidates.

We tested for these discrete knowledge levels at various stages of the campaign, including the heavily publicized presidential debates that occurred during the last weeks of the 1976 contest. At that stage, knowledge levels ordinarily are at a peak. We asked, "What specific things about Ford/Carter did you learn from the debate?" and "What specific knowledge did you gain in terms of each candidate's issue stands?" The learning scores were meager.

Content analysis of the debates shows that 166 questions were asked altogether. Counting repetitions, various issues were mentioned 297 times. Less than two weeks later, the average issue recall amounted to a total of barely two statements. This score masks the fact that well over half of the core panel could not make a single statement about any of the issues. If one assumes that the answers to each of the 166 questions provided a separate opportunity to appraise each candidate, there were a total of 332 opportunities to learn about qualities. Yet half of the panelists could recall no information about Ford's or Dole's qualities as candidates, and slightly less than half were similarly blank about Carter and Mondale.

Issue knowledge extended little beyond sheer awareness. Barely 2 percent of the answers provided three or more facts about either issues or candidates' qualities. Only 10 percent of the responses involved recall of two facts. The bulk of respondents, if they learned any facts at all, had only a single item of information about a specific issue or quality.

A probe to assess the ability to link issue information to the positions of the candidates produced even less impressive results. We asked Ford's and Carter's positions on six issues that had been widely discussed and that we knew to be very important to most respondents. The issues were unemployment, taxation, amnesty for draft evaders, policy toward Africa, policy toward the Soviet Union, and defense policy in general.

Except for information on President Ford's African policy, three out of four respondents could not identify Ford's stands on the issues. In Governor Carter's case, leaving aside his political proposals about Africa and the Soviet Union, about which a large majority of the respondents were well-informed, two out of three panelists were ignorant about his positions on the remaining four issues. It is ironic that the panel members, who so often echoed the media complaints that Carter was "fuzzy" on the issues, could recall more of his issue positions than those of Ford. It was a rare respondent who knew the stands of both candidates on all six issues. The positions of both candidates were familiar to more than half of the panelists on only two issues: amnesty for draft evaders and national defense policies.

This lack of important information about the very issues that many respondents had included as high-priority items on their agendas may indicate that much agenda-setting involves only minimal learning beyond rote memorization of salience cues. However, it is possible that information that cannot be explicitly recalled has nonetheless become part of the judgmental process underlying generalized assessments. When people say, for instance, "I just don't like the candidate; there is something about him; I can't put my finger on it," they may be reciting conclusions based on forgotten clues. There may thus be submerged learning that is not discoverable by the usual open-ended questions. This possibility is underscored by the fact that "aided recall," which calls for verification of a stated fact, produces more plentiful responses than do open-ended questions that necessitate spontaneous, unaided recall.

Table 3–1 gives two examples of the amount of specific information that core panelists learned about Ford and Carter positions on the key

TABLE 3–1

Recall of Specific Information—Sex and Age Distinctions (in percentages)

Responses	Ford		Carter		Ford		Carter	
	Women	Men	Women	Men	Older	Younger	Older	Younger
Unemployment								
Statistics	0	1	2	6	1	0	7	1
Policy data	10	10	3	4	12	8	4	3
General information	40	44	42	43	42	42	40	45
Don't know	50	45	52	47	45	50	50	50
Inflation								
Statistics	0	0	0	0	0	0	0	0
Policy data	1	1	2	6	0	2	4	5
General information	37	40	32	28	40	37	31	29
Don't know	61	58	66	65	59	61	65	66

Notes: Statistics means ability to cite precise figures; *policy data* means ability to refer to precise candidate proposals, but lacking statistics; *general information* means knowledge of general trends of the problem and awareness of planned action; *don't know* means inability to discuss problems in general terms and unawareness of planned action.

Older respondents were over 40 years of age; *Younger* respondents were 40 and younger.

N = 1,716 responses by core panelists. N's for women's and older panelists' responses were 210 each; N's for men's and younger panelists' responses were 219 each.

Some percentages in this and other tables do not total to exactly 100.0 percent because of rounding error.
Source: Compiled by authors.

23

issues of inflation and unemployment during the 1976 campaign. The positions of both candidates on these issues had received a good deal of media coverage. The issues had also been repeatedly mentioned by our respondents as matters of high concern to them. The data, which entail responses to questions from successive interviews, have been arranged by respondents' sex and age to highlight differences along these dimensions.

The most striking fact revealed in Table 3-1 is that half or over of the responses were "don't knows," with greater ignorance about inflation than about unemployment, even though inflation touches a larger number of people directly. Another striking fact is the scarcity of responses containing statistical or policy information, even though unemployment and inflation data were featured and repeated frequently by the media. Obviously, even for issues that were near the top of the public's agenda during much of 1976, learning of specific information was quite limited.

Men held a slight edge in knowledge over women, with 5 percent more women drawing blanks on unemployment policies for both Ford and Carter, and men knowing more statistics. On knowledge about inflation, the spread between men and women was smaller, suggesting that the nature of the issue may be a factor in knowledge differences between men and women. The identity of the candidates may also produce learning differences, judging from the fact that "don't know" answers for these two issues were slightly more plentiful for Carter, the newcomer, than for Ford, the incumbent president.

Age differences were minor. However, one can say generally that, compared with their younger colleagues, fewer older respondents gave "don't know" answers and more of them had specific facts and figures and policy information at their fingertips for unemployment. In part, these knowledge differences may reflect differences in newspaper use. Nine percent more men than women and 9 percent more older people than younger people reported using newspapers a great deal for political news.[2] Differences in the use of television for political news werre minor.

To check whether low knowledge levels were due to overlooking news stories entirely, rather than paying only cursory attention to them or engaging in superficial and fleeting learning, we asked the core panelists how frequently they had noticed stories on specific topics during the course of the election year. Table 3–2, which has been arranged to show age and sex distinctions, indicates that both factors were at work. Many stories had been overlooked or quickly forgotten. But even when most respondents agreed that certain topics had been frequently reported, they still lacked factual knowledge about them.

All of the issues included in Table 3–2 had been heavily covered by the media. Yet, more often than not, more than half of the panelists reported that there had been only "some" coverage or "none." Interest-

TABLE 3–2

Memory of Frequency of Media Coverage of Selected Issues—Sex and Age Distinctions

(in percentages)

Issues	Frequency	Women	Men	Older	Younger
Foreign Affairs, Defense	A lot	43	43	44	42
	Some	50	36	47	40
	None	8	20	8	19
Government credibility	A lot	50	64	11	92
	Some	30	27	56	8
	None	20	9	33	0
Crime	A lot	30	36	44	25
	Some	60	55	56	58
	None	10	9	0	17
Social problems	A lot	36	20	31	25
	Some	46	55	42	57
	None	18	25	27	18
General economy	A lot	50	50	44	54
	Some	25	18	17	25
	None	25	32	39	21
Environment and energy	A lot	17	15	15	17
	Some	43	36	44	36
	None	40	48	41	47
Government spending and size	A lot	60	45	44	50
	Some	15	45	44	25
	None	25	9	11	25
Race relations and busing	A lot	45	55	61	42
	Some	50	27	28	46
	None	5	18	11	13
Taxes	A lot	50	36	22	58
	Some	40	55	78	25
	None	10	9	0	17
Unemployment	A lot	80	55	56	75
	Some	20	45	44	25
	None	0	0	0	0
Inflation	A lot	50	55	33	67
	Some	40	45	56	33
	None	10	0	11	0

Notes: N = 443 responses by core panelists; some answers represent combinations of subissues.

Older respondents were over 40 years of age.

Source: Compiled by authors.

ingly, even though the panelists had used the same media sources, they varied widely in their perceptions of how often key topics had been reported. Discrepancies in perception, on the whole, were greater by age than by sex. Half or more of all men and women agreed that there had been a lot of coverage of four of the eleven topics—government credibility, the general economy, unemployment, and inflation. A majority of the women, but not of the men, noted a lot of coverage of government spending size and taxes. A majority of men, on the other hand, thought that there had been a lot of coverage of busing and race relations.

Twenty-five percent or more of the women claimed that there had been no mention of three topics—the general economy, environment and energy, and government spending and size, making it somewhat unlikely that media agenda-setting would be potent for them on these issues. For men, the array of issues that failed to draw attention of 25 percent or more also included the general economy and environment and energy, but social problems were substituted for government spending and size.

When older and younger respondents are compared, the younger group appears more attentive to news and hence more exposed to opportunities for media agenda-setting. Table 3–2 indicates that six issues were mentioned by more than half of the younger group as receiving a lot of coverage. The list starts with government credibility, mentioned by 92 percent (compared with 11 percent for the older group) and includes the general economy, government spending and size, taxes, unemployment, and inflation. For the older group, only two issues were mentioned by more than half as receiving a lot of coverage—race relations/busing and unemployment. Twenty-five percent or more of the older group failed to note coverage of four issues—government credibility, social problems, the general economy, and environment and energy. The younger group failed to report a lot of coverage on only two issues: environment/energy and unemployment.

REASONS FOR REMEMBERING AND FORGETTING

When people report missing out on information to which, in all likelihood, they were exposed, the question arises whether the information was noted at the time and later forgotten or whether it was skipped entirely. To shed light on the process of remembering and forgetting and to examine it for clues about the types of media images likely to leave a mark and the types likely to be transient, we asked our panelists to record their reasons for remembering and forgetting stories.

Reasons for remembering were reported during the regular story recall test and in the diaries of the core panel members. Panelists could give an unlimited number of reasons of their free choice or select by number from a sample list of ten commonly named reasons. When asked why specific stories had been remembered, the most prevalent reason, given nearly half of the time (49 percent), was general interest in the story. Human interest aspects of the story were second (18 percent), followed by general significance (10 percent), respondents' special interests (7 percent), entertainment value (7 percent), and personal importance of the story (6 percent). Less frequently mentioned reasons were the appealing format of the story, its usefulness for one's job or social life, and pure chance.

What this tells us is that general significance is a minor reason for remembering a story. Even personal importance of the story or its usefulness for one's job or social life were comparatively minor reasons for selecting it, despite the fact that they were specifically included in the sample list of choices. Rather, our panelists appeared to pay attention to stories primarily for personal pleasure. General, special, and human interest aspects of the story accounted for nearly three-quarters of the motives (74 percent). A check of the actual stories recorded in the diaries supports the accuracy of this self-assessment. Diary stories ran the gamut of topics with heaviest, though by no means predominant, emphasis on stories about crimes and accidents, health care, sports and entertainment, celebrities, and other stories with human interest elements.

When reasons for forgetting stories were probed, the panelists reported in 31 percent of the cases that they had been skeptical about the truth of the story or skeptical about the media's accuracy in presenting it. Twenty-three percent of the forgotten stories were deemed too complex by the panelists and another 23 percent were described as too boring or uninteresting to the respondents to be remembered. Nine percent of the stories were forgotten because they did not seem important to the panelists, despite the prominence that the media had bestowed on them. For 14 percent of the stories, forgetting was unexplained.

Again, the message that is conveyed is that, to be remembered, stories must be interesting and appealing to audience members, simple to understand, and believable. Their general social significance is a minor factor. The interest element is partly inherent in the story and partly linked to the timing and context. For example, similar election stories were found more interesting and were remembered at a steeply higher rate (60 percent compared with 40 percent) when they were presented during high points of the campaign rather than at interludes. Story appeal and comparative simplicity also provide good explanations for the long-standing distinctive recall patterns. Panelists remembered and mentioned the personal qualities of the presidential candidates more frequently than was true for public policy issues.[3]

ISSUE AND IMAGE LEARNING COMPARED

Comparisons of recall of images—defined as the sum total of presidential qualities and qualifications—with recall of issues show that respondents claimed to remember a substantially higher number of images for the two candidates during all phases of the campaign. In the wake of the presidential debates, the rate for image recall was more than double the issue rate—3.6 qualities per respondent compared with 1.6 issues.

Whenever the panelists discussed the qualities of the presidential candidates, they dwelled more heavily on personality traits and appearance factors than on the candidates' job competence and political philosophies. Mention of the personality traits and style factors took up an average of 70 percent of all remarks about candidates, leaving 30 percent for characteristics that are more directly related to the professional aspects of the presidency. The corresponding distribution for image qualities in Chicago *Tribune* election stories was 62 percent and 38 percent. There was a high degree of similarity between the types of qualities emphasized by the media and those emphasized by the panelists. As discussed more fully in Chapter 9, this indicates that the media may be even more important for setting image agendas than for setting issue agendas.

What explains the more plentiful learning about images compared with issues, in the face of social pressures that convey the message that "intelligent" choices are issue-based choices? There are many reasons. The importance accorded to personality factors is one of them. As one respondent phrased it:

What people are voting on is not the issues. The real issue is what kind of guy will be running the country, how will he handle the problems that come up. I don't think people believe in promises any more. They believe more in the kind of person that's there. What kind of integrity. How he's going to react in situations that will come up. What kind of stuff he is made of, essentially. That's *the* issue for the people.

We have already noted that learning is easier when stories have human interest appeal. Information about candidates as people, particularly when it deals with their personal qualities, has such appeal. Most issue stories do not. Moreover, the average person, through daily life experiences, has learned to make judgments about other individuals and knows how to translate evaluations about personal qualities, such as trustworthiness, into choices about the quality of service that may be expected from others.

Audiences can learn that a candidate is trustworthy and experienced through personal or media appraisals and then use subsequent candidate actions and policy pronouncements to reinforce or weaken these judgments. The supporting information need not be committed to memory, avoiding the necessity to digest complex and unfamiliar data. Judgments about personal qualities, distilled from the information stream, appear to be remembered more readily than straight recall of factual information.

The audience's predilection for recalling personality judgments is augmented and encouraged by what the candidates do and what the media report. For instance, during the presidential debates, the candidates obviously used their answers to convey impressions about their competence to perform the job, their sensitivity to human needs, their poise, and their credibility as well as the lack of these qualities in the opponent. The audience readily absorbed these messages. Similar interpretations were made by the media. Media coverage following the debates typically concentrated heavily on the performance of the candidates as winners or losers. Three out of four postdebate stories stressed this aspect, as did a series of public opinion polls reported in the wake of each debate.

Compared with the simplicity of learning about human qualities, learning about issues is difficult. The average voter is baffled when candidates argue whether wage and price controls are necessary to stop inflation, whether taxes can be cut without cutting essential budget items, or whether zero-based budgeting is sound. People have no way to determine whether U.S. defenses are sufficiently strong to cope with potential enemies, whether U.S. prestige in the world is continuing to plunge or is on the rise, and whether human rights can be protected without endangering relations with other countries.

Learning candidate positions is made more difficult because, in most cases, they are not diametrically opposed. Rather, there are only relatively small differences in emphasis and approach that are difficult to grasp initially and even harder to retain. The fact that time and space allotted to the analysis of most issues is brief adds to the confusion. Time and space constraints are most severe for television, where the time for discussing major issues usually is counted in one- to three-minute segments. Even during the presidential debates, which were designed to clarify the issues, the format called for three-minute replies to questions with two-minute follow-ups. Obviously, major issues cannot be adequately discussed in such a brief period. Nonetheless, the candidates, knowing the brief attention span of audiences, for the most part did not even use the allotted time in full.

Neither image nor issue learning seems to be affected by the audience's prior appraisal of the candidates. We had asked core panelists to use a seven-point scale to indicate various degrees of agreement or disagreement with statements about the candidates' trustworthiness, temperamental suitability for the presidential office, and ability to improve government efficiency and reduce unemployment. Those who viewed one or both candidates favorably learned at the same rates as those who viewed one or both unfavorably. Actual learning rates also were unaffected by partisanship. Carter supporters learned at comparable rates about both Ford and Carter and vice versa. Nonetheless, self-estimates told a different story. Respondents thought they had learned more about their favorite. Since this self-assessment was not born out by the data on actual learning, we concluded that actual learning was not influenced by partisan attitudes.

IMPACT OF AGE, SEX, EDUCATION, AND LIFESTYLE

We have already observed from Tables 3–1 and 3–2 that certain demographic factors, such as sex and age, appear to have some bearing on learning from the media and hence, potentially, an influence on the agenda-setting process. We shall now take a closer look at these factors. Tables 3–3 and 3–4 show the yearly agendas of personally most important issues, the issues respondents talked most about, and the issues deemed to be of greatest importance to people in the community. When one compares the answers of men and women, the patterns are quite similar. Economic issues, such as inflation, taxes, and unemployment, were at the top of personal, talk, and public agendas of both sexes. Next came a variety of social problems, such as welfare programs, care of the elderly, health care, and crime, followed by foreign affairs and defense problems. The data in Table 3–4 show that, compared with sex differences, age differences accounted for greater variations in personal, public, and talk agendas.[4]

If one considers a five percentage point differential as substantial, men's and women's personal agendas differed substantially (9 percentage points) in rating government credibility as a major issue, with women less inclined to think credibility important than men. Correspondingly, women talked less about credibility as an issue (8 percentage points). Women talked more than men about social problems and crime (7 percentage points), apparently because this is an area of greater personal insecurity and concern for them. Women also referred slightly more often to economic issues, especially inflation, and talked less about foreign affairs and energy conservation than men. While the differences were slight, they conform to the stereotypical views of distinctions between men and women.

TABLE 3-3

Personal, Talk, and Public Issue Agendas by Voters' Sex (in percentages)

Issue	Personal Agenda		Talk Agenda		Public Agenda	
	Women	Men	Women	Men	Women	Men
Foreign affairs, defense	12	9	6	8	1	1
Government credibility	1	10[a]	1	9[a]	1	1
Social problems, crime	16	12	18	11[b]	10	10
General economy, taxes, inflation, jobs	59	55	47	46	72	70
Environment and energy	3	6	2	5	1	2
Lifestyles, race, busing	5	5	5	4	6	4
Current political events	2	1	5	5	4	5
Miscellaneous, don't know, no answer	2	2	16	12	6	7

Notes: Personal agendas indicate issues respondents rated as personally most important to them; *talk agendas* indicate issues respondents discussed most often; *public agendas* indicate issues respondents considered to be most salient to the general public in their area.

N = 2,342 replies. The N's for personal agenda were 505 for women, 523 for men; the N's for talk agenda were 478 for women and 472 for men; the N's for public agenda were 180 for women and 184 for men.

[a]p < 0.001
[b]p < 0.01

Source: Compiled by authors.

TABLE 3–4

Personal, Talk, and Public Issue Agendas by Voters' Age (in percentages)

Issue	Personal Agenda		Talk Agenda		Public Agenda	
	Older	*Younger*	*Older*	*Younger*	*Older*	*Younger*
Foreign affairs, defense	16	5[a]	9	6	1	1
Government credibility	3	8[b]	3	7[c]	1	1
Social problems, crime	15	13	16	14	11	10
General economy, taxes, inflation, jobs	55	60	42	50[b]	69	72
Environment and energy	3	6	2	4	2	2
Lifestyles, race, busing	4	6	2	6[b]	4	6
Current political events	2	1	6	4	6	4
Miscellaneous, don't know, no answer	3	1	20	9[a]	7	5

Notes: Personal agendas indicate issues respondents rated as personally most important to them; *talk agendas* indicate issues respondents discussed most often; *public agendas* indicate issues respondents considered to be most salient to the general public in their area.

N = 2,342 replies. The N's for personal agenda were 502 for older and 526 for younger respondents; the N's for talk agenda were 444 for older and 506 for younger respondents; the N's for public agenda were 171 for older and 193 for younger respondents.

Older respondents were over 40 years of age; younger respondents were 40 and younger.

[a]p < 0.001
[b]p < 0.01
[c]p < 0.05

Source: Compiled by authors.

Compared with three areas of substantial difference between men and women, there were five areas of substantial difference between age groups. (See Table 3–4.) Older people were more concerned (11 percentage points) in their personal agendas about foreign affairs and defense matters than their younger counterparts, but they were less concerned (5 percentage points) about such economic issues as taxes, jobs, and inflation. Considering the typical demands and experiences of various life cycle stages, these are plausible differences. Older people may well be more concerned about foreign affairs because they have experienced more arms races and wars. They often are less concerned about the economy because their financial status is better established and, aside from health care, major family expenses are reduced. Likewise, their concern over government credibility is greater, in line with earlier historical trends, than that of the younger generation, who exhibit less faith (5 percentage points). With greater concern about the economy, younger people talk more (8 percentage points) about economic problems with others than do older people. Again, as befits people with broader experiences, older people have a much broader agenda of miscellaneous topics for conversation (11 percentage points) than do younger people.

A comparison of the types of diary stories selected by men and women of all ages again shows that male and female interests are only marginally different. Men and women paid about the same amount of attention to so-called "men's" and "women's" issues, such as gun control and abortion.[5] However, women expressed more interest than men in human interest stories, in crime and accident tales, and in features covering home and garden information. They showed somewhat less interest in international politics and in general national, state, and local political affairs.

As noted earlier, women did not recall as much as men, and women were less specific in their comments and descriptions. When the panelists were questioned in successive interviews about the content of specific stories, men as a group recalled more facts than did women. Thirty-two percent of their recalls presented three or more facts compared with 13 percent of the women's recalls. An average of 25 percent of the story reports by males and 37 percent of those by females were devoid of any facts beyond acknowledgment that the story was familiar. Age distinctions presented a more mixed picture. Twenty-four percent of the story reports of the younger group, compared with 21 percent of those of the older contingent, contained three or more facts per story. However, more responses from the younger group (34 percent) than from the older group (27 percent) indicated total lack of factual knowledge.

Poorer recall performance may be related to the fact that women are less aware of needing information for specific purposes and have fewer opportunities to discuss public policies. Motivation for acquiring and remembering political information is therefore reduced.[6] However, when women were asked why they failed to remember stories, they did not say that they had little need for them. Rather, their reasons were quite similar to those given by men.

Women did report slightly different patterns in reasons for remembering than men, though. Women mentioned human interest as a motive twice as often (25 percent versus 12 percent). They also mentioned personal importance twice as frequently as men (8 percent versus 4 percent). They cited skepticism about the accuracy of stories less frequently than men as a reason for forgetting about them (26 percent versus 35 percent). And they hardly ever talked about remembering stories for job-related reasons whereas men gave this reason 3 percent of the time.

Analysis of background data on core panel members shows that men's greater alertness to politics goes back to childhood.[7] Fifty percent of the men, compared with 40 percent of the women, reported substantial interest in politics during their pre-adult years. Men recalled more than twice as many specific political incidents from their early years than did women, and these incidents covered a much wider spectrum of issues. Wars and elections were remembered by both sexes. Beyond these topics, women tended to stick to general economic concerns and local issues, while men remembered a broad spectrum of national and international issues. Men recalled using media more during their growing years. Both sexes remembered that their mothers had used media less for political information than had their fathers and that their mothers had been less knowledgeable about politics. Thus the panelists' role models conformed to the stereotype that depicts women as having little interest in politics, taking minor roles in political discussion, and paying only fleeting attention to political news.

To summarize our findings about the impact of age and sex: There are differences in the learning processes of men and women and in the saliences they assign to certain topics, but they are comparatively minor and just as readily explained by lifestyle differences as by inherent differences between the sexes. The same holds true for the considerably more marked differences apparent among people going through different stages of the life cycle. However, even though most of the differences would disappear if lifestyles of men and women of all ages became identical, sex and age distinctions must be considered as factors in agenda-setting as long as lifestyles remain distinct.

Education is another important variable that confounds the findings about sex and age differences. Many of the age and sex distinctions in political learning disappear when one controls for education.[8] To measure the effects of education on learning, we correlated data on learning from the presidential debates with the resondents' educational status. Pearson correlations between the number of issues learned from the debates and the number of candidate qualities learned were 0.47 and 0.59, significant at the 0.05 and 0.01 levels respectively. In fact, respondents with more formal education displayed greater knowledge throughout the election year and learned more than those with less formal education.

Once learning has taken place, spurred by formal education or other incentives, it becomes an independent factor to spur further learning. This happens because existing knowledge provides a framework into which new information can be fitted more easily than where no framework exists. Moreover, prior knowledge whets the appetite for additional information to round out what is already known.

EFFECTS OF PRIOR KNOWLEDGE, INTEREST, AND EXPOSURE

We tested the effects of prior knowledge by comparing the respondents' specific knowledge of candidate qualifications and campaign issues with prior knowledge scores. Prior knowledge was measured by the extent of recall of election stories in each of the interviews, starting in February 1976. We found that those who recalled election stories best learned most. The correlation between the degree of prior knowledge and the number of issues learned during the presidential debates, for instance, was 0.56, significant at the 0.05 level. The correlation between prior knowledge and the number of image qualities learned was 0.67, significant at the 0.001 level.

One might have assumed that the comparatively uninformed would have learned most from the debates because they realized that they needed additional information and the debates were their last chance to catch up. Similarly, one might have assumed that the comparatively well-informed would learn little because they would ignore additional election information, believing that they had already learned all there was to know and all they needed to know. Contrary to such expectations, the present study indicates that learning trends are stable and cumulative throughout the election year and that high achievers excel throughout. Accordingly, learning about issues and candidates was highly correlated. Those who learned most about issues learned most about candidates as well. When both variables were measured by learning of specific information during the presidential debates, the correlation coefficient was 0.75, significant at the 0.001 level.

We also examined the effect of the panelists' interest in the election on exposure to news and on the level of learning from news. Rather than

FIGURE 3–1

Trends in Interest in the Election

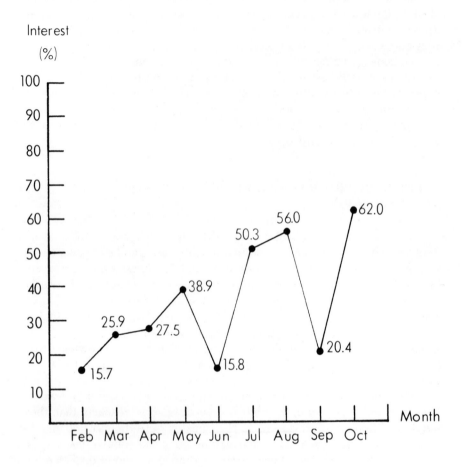

Note: The interest level represents the proportion of election-related stories recorded in the respondent's diaries during each month.

Source: Compiled by authors.

relying solely on self-appraisals, which often differ from results based on behavioral data, we judged the level of interest in the election by the frequency of election stories in each respondent's diaries. Presumably, inclusion of election stories in diaries indicates that the writer was actively pursuing election information, rather than merely voicing an interest.

Figure 3–1 plots the percentage of election-related stories out of the total number of news stories recorded by the respondents in their diaries each month. It shows that the overall level of interest measured by diary entries fluctuated corresponding to the major campaign events. Exposure to election stories fluctuated likewise. It increased throughout the primaries, then dropped to the original level. It rose again during the Republican and Democratic conventions, only to plummet once more after the conventions. It reached its highest peak with the debates and the election climax. A monthly plotting of the number of newspaper and television election stories shows a similar configuration, although the percentage for election stories, compared with other stories, was lower in the media than in the diaries.

Political learning and recall of election stories increased in a pattern parallel to the interest and exposure curves. It peaked during the primaries, the conventions, and the debates. For example, during the presidential debates, those who had displayed greater interest prior to the debates learned more than less interested panelists. This was especially true for highly interested people who had had little previous opportunity for becoming well-informed. The debates presented them with a chance to catch up rapidly. These people learned an average of 4.6 issues, compared with 0.7 issues for a comparable group whose interest was low. On image learning, the gap between low- and high-interest voters was somewhat smaller, possibly testimony that image characteristics are intrinsically more interesting. Highly interested panelists learned an average of five image qualities—one third more than panelists who scored low on election interest. The correlation between prior interest and learning about images was significant ($r = 0.37$, $p < 0.01$). This was not true for the correlation between prior interest and learning about issues ($r = 0.21$).

Length of exposure to news and the medium chosen for exposure also made a difference. In debate learning, for instance, those who watched the event on television learned more than those who followed it on radio, in newspapers, or in news magazines. Relative length of exposure and overall learning about candidates and issues were also positively and significantly related. The correlation coefficient between length of television exposure and issue learning was 0.41 ($p < 0.05$) when measured by specific issues mentioned by respondents and 0.45 ($p < 0.05$) when measured by specific image qualities reported by the respondents.

IMPACT OF MESSAGE CONTENT

Thus far we have talked largely about various audience attributes and attitudes that appear to affect learning. We have focused on the role that message attributes play in the learning process, although we have noted that people ignore or forget messages that appear boring and uninteresting.

What audiences are able to learn from the media obviously hinges on the type of information presented in stories. Our content analyses show that a vast amount of information was indeed available. In fact, attentive audience members should have been able to learn a good deal about most public policy issues involved in the campaign and about the personalities, past experiences, and job qualifications of the major candidates. If one assumes careful attention to media offerings throughout the election year, the information supply was certainly adequate, even when one applies the traditionally strict criteria of democratic theory that call for high levels of political knowledge by average voters.

The appraisal becomes less favorable when one uses democratic ideals to assess the balance between issue and image information and between attention to campaign activities and public policy issues. While featuring public policy issues more heavily than reflected in audience learning, the media gave primary emphasis to candidate qualities and the hoopla of the election campaign. On an average, 27 percent of the coverage was devoted to issues, compared with 60 percent for various image qualities and 13 percent for campaign events. For Carter, Ford, and Reagan, issue coverage averaged 34 percent, leaving 55 percent for image qualities and 11 percent for campaigning. The audience picked up most heavily on the preponderant image data. However, it would be unfair to cast the full blame on the media for the audience's penchant for that type of personality-oriented information that democratic purists decry. Our study provides ample evidence that audiences are quite capable of using discretion in what they learn and do not learn.

When one considers that retention tests showed a sharp decline in recall after a six-week span, one must also question the adequacy of story repetition to cope with forgetting and early inattention. Many important stories that had appeared at the start of the campaign year were not repeated, partly because media try to avoid repetition and partly because there were newer stories clamoring for attention. Typical panelists, who skipped stories during the primaries to wait for the finalists to emerge, then found it difficult to fill a number of knowledge gaps. Some people were aware that they had passed up valuable information that had appeared in the media earlier in the year; others accused the media of never presenting it.

Even when one discounts information from the primaries entirely, a massive amount of mass media information remained available to average voters.[9] Our study indicates that the nature and presentation of this information account in part for the comparatively low rate of learning.

However, it must be emphasized that busy lifestyles and the low priority people generally put on politics also contribute significantly to making political learning a small slice of the average individual's thoughts and concerns. Even if media stories were consistently informative and fascinating, it is unlikely that audience attention and use patterns would shift radically.

What are content-related deterrents to learning? We shall again use the presidential debates as an example. When the debates were staged in 1976, in the last weeks before election, it was hoped that they would supply the voters with additional information about candidates and issues. At the very least, they would provide a way to pull together the various bits of candidate and issue knowledge that had become available throughout the campaign year. It was also expected that the debates would provide excellent opportunities for comparing the candidates within similar settings. Since the entire event—rather than a media-selected portion—was broadcast, it was anticipated that listeners would make their own judgments with a minimum of media influence. The reality turned out to be quite different from the expectations.

Although people were interested in the campaign and had looked forward to the debates as a good "show," most failed to sit through the 90-minute spectacle. Only half of those who watched a particular debate stayed for the entire broadcast. One-third of the panelists were complete dropouts in each debate, mostly because of admittedly trivial competing activities. Half skipped the vice-presidential debates entirely. The deterrents to watching were manifold. Most people felt that the presentations were not really new, that they were rehearsed and phony, that they were boring, overly complex, and studded with dull statistics. Many complained about the format, calling it an extended news conference rather than a debate. Others felt that most issues of genuine concern to the public had been ignored.

The complaint about the general dullness of election news reflects a perennial problem in campaign coverage. With the campaign strung out over so many months, there needs and is bound to be a lot of repetition of the same information. As one respondent put it, "The more you see, the more you tend to get a sense of déjà vu." Media audiences quickly assume that there is nothing new and fail to pay attention except for noting who won or lost a primary, a caucus vote, or a debate. By the time the presidential debates took place, little new information could be expected. At best, the debates might reinforce prior knowledge or retrieve fading knowledge from limbo; they could produce little substantive novelty to generate excitement. When the first debate confirmed that it was all "old stuff," it depressed the desire to look for new information in subsequent debates.

Problems of credibility also plague campaign learning. Much campaign oratory is dismissed as "rhetoric" not worthy of serious attention. This disdain for campaign pledges is a serious deterrent to learning.[10] In fact, many respondents take the dishonesty of campaign rhetoric so much for granted that they do not discredit individual politicians for it. Hence expressions of doubt about the credibility of politician's talk exist side by side with fairly high trustworthiness ratings of individual politicians.

As a result of the many deterrents to learning, attention to the debates and learning from them were quite modest despite the fact that between 80 million and 90 million Americans watched the presidential contenders and 70 million tuned in for at least portions of the 60-minute vice-presidential spectacle. Even the hope that people would make independent evaluations was partially frustrated. After listening to postdebate news commentary, many people abandoned their own evaluations for the media's appraisals of who had won or lost and the reasons for winning or losing.[11]

Probably the most difficult learning situation of the entire campaign occurs during the primary elections when a dozen or more potentially serious presidential contenders must be evaluated. The media must present adequate information about all these candidates without overwhelming the audience with too much detail. On the whole, they do not perform this task well. Indeed, it is questionable whether it can be successfully handled, given the constraints of space and time.

The media cope with the problem by concentrating on a handful of the contenders who, in their judgment, are the frontrunners. Hence, during the primaries, when people needed information about all the candidates for agenda formation and voting choices, three out of every four comments about candidates were devoted to Ford, Carter, and

TABLE 3–5

Candidate Coverage Patterns During the Primaries

Rank	Carter	Ford	Reagan	Wallace
1	Issue stands	Issue stands	Issue stands	Style/image
2	Style/image	Personality	Personality	Personality
3	Personality	Style/image	Job competence	Issue stands
4	Campaign events	Job competence	Style/image	Campaign events
5	Job competence	Campaign events	Campaign events	Philosophy
6	Philosophy	Philosophy	Philosophy	Job competence

°Humphrey rankings are included because the media and the public discussed him as a potential candidate, even though he never entered the race formally.

Note: Rank order of frequency of mention in Chicago *Tribune*. N = 1213 mentions.

Source: Compiled by authors.

Reagan. When presidential qualities were discussed in a positive vein, two-thirds of the remarks referred to Carter, Ford, and Reagan. This left little room for airing the virtues of Wallace, Brown, Humphrey, Udall, Jackson, and Church in a comparable manner.

The image dimensions covered for each candidate differed as well, making comparisons and agenda formation difficult. For example, during the primaries, the Chicago *Tribune* gave top coverage to issue stands for only five of the nine major candidates, as Table 3–5 shows. Coverage ranged from a high of 40 percent for Reagan to a low of 16 percent for Brown. The table also illustrates the heavy media emphasis on style and personality, averaging 42 percent of total coverage, and the relative slight of job competence and the political philosophy of the candidates, averaging 18 percent. Mentions of job competence ranked in fourth place or lower for eight of the nine candidates.

For the respondents, these differences in coverage meant that some raw materials for image construction were scarce for certain candidates. For instance, if one wanted to incorporate style and image characteristics into one's candidate images, one would find this far more difficult for Jackson, for whom 14 percent of the coverage dealt with these qualities, than for Wallace, for whom they constituted 30 percent of coverage. If one wanted information on issue stands for these two candidates, it would be less available for Wallace (20 percent of coverage) than for Jackson (32 percent of coverage).

Learning is also very difficult because there is a crossfire of claims and counterclaims by candidates and their supporters. The media, for the most part, merely report these conflicting claims but do little to check out the facts or guide the audience in other respects. This leaves the audience confused or encourages it to tune out to avoid confusion.

Overall, campaign information appears to be pitched at too high a level of complexity for the average person who is unwilliing to spend even

Brown	Humphrey°	Udall	Jackson	Church
Style/image	Issue stands	Style/image	Issue stands	Personality
Personality	Personality	Personality	Campaign events	Style/image
Issue stands	Campaign events	Issue stands	Personality	Issue stands
Campaign events	Job competence	Job competence	Job competence	Job competence
Job competence	Style/image	Campaign events	Style/image	Campaign events
Philosophy	Philosophy	Philosophy	—	—

moderate amounts of time mastering the political news.[12] Our findings show clearly that the bulk of the panelists, including many college-educated respondents, consider much political information difficult to comprehend. They also show that people with higher educational achievements do, indeed, learn more political information and complain less frequently about its complexity. This raises the hope that the problem of excessive complexity may diminish as educational levels continue to rise.

SUMMING UP

We have approached our examination of political learning during the 1976 campaign more or less within the typical framework of democratic optimism about the political knowledge of the average voter. Not unexpectedly, this has doomed us to disappointment. Actual learning levels do not generally come close to the democratic vision of voters who fully understand the issues, know the positions of the candidates, and are able to evaluate them and judge the capabilites of the candidates to perform as promised. The perennial finding that actual learning is much more modest should be no cause for despair. Rather, it should be a reminder that empirical studies, such as ours, form the basis for developing new theories about political learning and voter knowledge levels to replace those that have been found wanting. The major findings, summed below, indicate the kind of political learning that can currently be expected during presidential election campaigns and that forms the backdrop for agenda-setting.

Most importantly, we found that learning scores are meager. Despite large amounts of available information, most people learn very few dimensions of the candidates' images and even fewer aspects of issues. Most learning is confined to "awareness"—the ability to confirm cognizance of information about issues and images without the ability to recall relevant facts spontaneously. Only a few respondents are able to define the positions taken by both candidates on any particular issue. Large numbers of stories go completely unnoticed or are rapidly forgotten. In light of the ignorance about important aspects of issues and images, one must conclude that many judgments about salience probably lack a solid independent knowledge base. Instead, they appear to be founded on more or less rote learning from the media. However, there is also some evidence that knowledge bases underlying the judgments may at times be forgotten while the judgment is remembered.

To be remembered, stories must be interesting above all. Their general significance or importance for the respondents' work or social life is secondary. However, the significance or relevance of stories may enhance their interest. Stories that strain the audience's credulity or intellectual powers or fail to hold its attention are apt to be forgotten.

Respondents find it easier to learn about images than about issues, enhancing the chances for image agenda-setting. Among image attributes, those pertaining to personality traits and style factors are better remembered than those pertaining to job qualifications and ideology. Candidates and media, catering to the audience's preferences for personal information, structure their presentations to highlight these aspects.

The substance, quality, and quantity of learning vary according to sex, age, education, and lifestyle. Education and lifestyle appear to be the key factors, with most age and sex distinctions disappearing when one controls for years in school and life settings.

Prior knowledge, high interest, and high exposure are all linked positively to learning. The knowledge-rich thus learn at accelerated rates, leaving the knowledge-poor further behind. Although additional opportunities for agenda-setting are produced by increased exposure, greater knowledge permits greater freedom to form independent judgments. Hence agenda-setting may actually be reduced for the most well-informed.

The media presented ample information of all types during the 1976 campaign but emphasized personal qualities of the candidates and campaigning activities. Audiences ignored much of what was presented, especially information on public policy issues, because they found it confusing, dull, repetitive, and often contradictory. Since political information gathering does not enjoy a high priority in the life of the average voter, it seems doubtful that greater attractiveness in content and presentation could overcome the appeal of conflicting demands on the respondents' time.

In sum, learning is slim and spotty for a variety of reasons that are unlikely to change drastically in the foreseeable future. This makes agenda-setting, when it does occur, largely an act of faith in media judgments. It is often not a considered choice that has been based on the wealth of data that the media have made available.

NOTES

[1]Walter Weiss, "Effects of the Mass Media of Communication,"in *The Handbook of Social Psychology*, 2nd ed., vol. 5, eds. Gardner Lindzey and Elliot Aronson (Reading, Mass.: Addison Wesley, 1969), pp. 77–195.

[2]However, a greater number of the older respondents reported not using newspapers at all.

[3]The import of emphasis on personal qualities is discussed more fully in Doris A. Graber, "Personal Qualities in Presidential Images: The Contribution of the Presss," *Midwest Journal of Political Science* 16 (1972): 46–76; Doris A. Graber, "Press Coverage and Voter Reaction,"

Political Science Quarterly 89 (1974): 68–100; and Thomas E. Patterson, *The Mass Media Election: How Americans Choose Their President* (New York: Praeger, 1980), chap. 12.

[4]Sex and generational differences in political cognitions and attitudes are discussed in John W. Soule and Wilma E. McGrath, "A Comparative Study of Male-Female Political Attitudes at Citizen and Elite Levels," in *A Portrait of Marginality: The Political Behavior of the American Woman*, eds. Marianne Githens and Jewel Prestage (New York: David McKay, 1977), pp. 178–95. Gerald Pomper, *Voters' Choice: Varieties of American Electoral Behavior* (New York: Dodd, Mead, 1975) pp. 90–118; and Doris A. Graber, "Agenda-Setting: Are There Women's Perspectives?," in *Women and the News*, ed. Laurily Keir Epstein (New York: Hastings House, 1978), pp. 15–37.

[5]For an identification of "women's" issues, see Soule and McGrath, "A Comparative Study of Male-Female Political Attitudes."

[6]The importance of goal-oriented information seeking is discussed in Charles Atkin, "Instrumental Utilities and Information Seeking," in *New Models of Mass Communication Research*, ed. Peter Clarke (Beverly Hills: Sage, 1973), pp. 205–42.

[7]The literature on the effects of early sex role socialization is large and controversial. See, for example, Anthony M. Orun, Roberta S. Cohen, Sherri Grasmuck, and Amy W. Orun, "Sex Socialization and Politics," *American Sociological Review* 39 (1974): 197–209 and sources cited there. See also Kirsten Amundsen, *The Silenced Majority* (Englewood Cliffs: Prentice Hall, 1971) and Virginia Sapiro, "Socialization to Political Gender Roles Among Women," Midwest Political Science Association paper, Chicago, 1977.

[8]Statistical data on the impact of education, exposure, and interest on learning levels during the 1976 campaign are presented in John Kessel, *Presidential Campaign Politics: Coalition Strategies and Citizen Response* (Homewood, Ill.: Dorsey Press, 1980), pp. 192–96.

[9]Early in the campaign, becoming familiar with the candidates is a purely academic exercise for most voters. Most of the pack who are running in the primaries obviously have little or no chance of making it and will soon be forgotten. This makes many voters feel it is not worthwhile to bother to learn about them. Instead, it makes sense to merely watch the returns to find out who has survived the latest race and to keep score on the few frontrunners. Patterson *The Mass Media Election*, chaps. 13 and 14, comments on the implications of minimal learning during the primaries.

[10]Kenneth Andersen and Theodore Clevenger, Jr., "A Summary of Experimental Research on Ethos," *Speech Monographs* 30 (1963): 59–78; Carl I. Hovland and Walter Weiss, "The Influence of Source Credibility on Communication Effectiveness," *Public Opinion Quarterly* 16 (1961): 635–50.

[11]Frederick T. Steeper, "Public Response to Gerald Ford's Statements on Eastern Europe in the Second Debate," *The Presidential Debates: Media, Electoral, and Policy Perspectives*, eds. George F. Bishop, Robert G. Meadow, and Marilyn Jackson-Beeck (New York: Praeger, 1978), pp. 81–101.

[12]Even image formation is difficult, as discussed in Dan Nimmo and Robert L. Savage, *Candidates and Their Images* (Pacific Palisades: Goodyear, 1976), pp. 81–108. A recent study seems to indicate that simple forms of news presentation, such as those prevailing in ordinary television newscasts, can serve as "knowledge levelers" between people of various educational levels. See W. Russell Neuman, "Patterns of Recall among Television News Viewers," *Public Opinion Quarterly* 40 (1976): 115–23.

four

DIFFERENT ROLES OF NEWSPAPER AND TELEVISION IN AGENDA-SETTING

As Chapters 1 and 2 point out, agenda-setting research has sought to investigate the relationship between issues and subjects prominently emphasized in the mass media (media agenda) and the salience of such topics in the minds of the public (public agendas). Because newspapers and television have been regarded as the most important and pervasive news outlets, they have most often constituted the media component in such studies.[1]

CONFLICTING RESEARCH FINDINGS

McCombs and Shaw's seminal agenda-setting study did not show any significant differences between the two media.[2] Many subsequent researchers assumed no such differences and proceeded to use aggregate media agendas.[3] In such studies, inferences were drawn from the aggregate media measures following the assumption that the mass media constitute a homogeneous entity exerting influence on the public.

Other researchers have found that newspapers seem to be more effective than television at setting the public agenda of issues. The array of issues emphasized by newspapers is a better match for the public's agenda than is true of television.[4] However, there are limitations. Palmgreen and Clarke discovered that the stronger agenda-setting effect of newspapers is limited to certain types of issues.[5] On local issues newspapers appear to exert a strong influence while—as would logically be expected—national

45

television news has no impact on these issues at all. On the other hand and contrary to previous research, the national TV network news programs were found to be superior to newspapers in shaping the public's agendas of national issues. These findings may be influenced by the fact that, unlike earlier research, the Palmgreen and Clarke study was not conducted during a national political campaign when news consumption patterns are apt to differ from more ordinary times. Other studies, analyzing television content only, also have found significant agenda-setting effects produced by television, but such results have not been uniformly attained.[6]

In the face of conflicting findings, the viewpoint that the two media perform different agenda-setting roles appears to dominate. But in spite of a strong pattern of support for the "differential effects" proposition, inconsistency in measurement and problem formulation hinders conclusive inferences about the comparative agenda-setting functions of newspapers and television news. A large part of the problem is methodological: It is difficult, if not impossible, to cite two studies employing the same methodology. Operational definitions, contingent conditions, and critical variables differ from one study to the next to the extent that true replication and verification are hard to find.

Time frame in the agenda-setting research is probably the most elusive concept. It refers to the total time-lapse during which the assumed agenda-setting effects take place. Decisions on appropriate time formulations are difficult to make. The theoretical conceptualization of the agenda-setting phenomenon does not stipulate the nature of time frame. Not surprisingly, most time frame choices appear to be motivated by intuition rather than substantiated theory. While McCombs and Shaw's and Palmgreen and Clarke's time frames are somewhat similar, Tipton, Haney, and Baseheart's is nearly doubled in duration.[7] Since different time frames may result in different conclusions about the effects of newspapers and television, it is conceivable that Tipton and his colleagues measured an agenda-setting process that is somewhat different from those measured in the two other studies. As was shown by Eyal, different temporal configurations and combinations within a given time result in accordingly varied findings.[8]

Within the time frame period, three major components have been identified by Eyal, Winter, and DeGeorge: *time lag* refers to the elapsed time between the independent variable (the media agenda) and the dependent variable (the public agenda); *duration of the media agenda* is the total interval during which the media measure is collected; and *duration of the public agenda* refers to the overall time span during which the public agenda measure is gathered.[9]

The *number and nature of issues under study* can also be seen as

variables in the agenda-setting process that may make intermedia comparisons difficult. McCombs and Shaw analyzed seven issues in their 1972 study. Tipton et al. studied seven respondent issues and nine media-covered issues, while Palmgreen and Clarke studied an agenda of 55 local and 33 national issues. More recent research provides evidence that the *type of issue* constitutes an independent variable affecting the agenda-setting process.[10] Issue obtrusiveness (that is, the amount of personal experience and contact with the issues by the respondents) appears to diminish the relationship between media and public agendas. Eyal found strong and significant media agenda-setting effects on unobtrusive topics but minimal media influence on the public agenda where more obtrusive (personally experienced) issues were concerned.[11]

Social context and local variables have been viewed as factors holding the potential to influence agenda-setting. Along with direct experiences, the social, economic, and political contexts combine to create an overall environmental, community-specific context capable of affecting the agenda-setting process.[12] Such differences in context have rarely been examined as factors that may explain seemingly inconsistent findings in agenda-setting.

Past studies also have varied in their definitions of what constitutes the public agenda. McCombs and Shaw examined the "intrapersonal" agenda or what their respondents considered to be the important issue for themselves *personally*. Tipton et al. and Palmgreen and Clarke, on the other hand, measured what Becker, McCombs, and McLeod termed the "perceived community agenda," soliciting responses to the question of what the respondents believed to be the major issues facing others. Other researchers have studied the public's "interpersonal" agenda, a measure of what individuals discussed with others.[13]

The *format of information* is another important variable to which insufficient attention has been given in the past. In their study of the 1972 presidential elections, Patterson and McClure compared the impact of campaign information presented in the form of television news and advertising. They concluded that television news had minimal impact on public awareness of issues and on the perceptions of candidates' images. Conversely, they suggested that televised political advertising accounted for a significant rise in audience awareness of the candidates' positions on issues.[14] This conclusion supports Shaw and Bowers' finding that political commercials on television perform a different agenda-setting role than other televised information. They found that the appearance of issues in commercials appears to raise the salience of those issues for the audience.[15]

Not only do political commercials vary in format from other news, but they also feature different issue arrays from those reported in general media stories. Comparing the agenda of issues reported in the local newspaper (the Charlotte *Observer*) with the candidates' advertising agenda, Bowers found no significant correlations. Correlations between the candidates' advertising agenda and the television news agenda were low.[16] By contrast, Carey found that "press coverage across media (TV, newspapers, and magazines) was remarkably consistent."[17] Carey had compared the media agendas of three national television networks, three national magazines, and three national newspapers.

EXPLANATIONS FOR IMPACT DIFFERENCES

Given the agenda-setting framework, one would expect that media agendas would have correspondingly similar effects on the audience agendas. To the extent that this is not the case—and many studies suggest that it is not—the differential influence of newspapers and television might be explained by factors other than content. This proposition suggests that the media, per se, do not create all the differences. Rather, various media may exert separate influences as a result of audience-related variables such as time-use and media-use habits, duration of exposure, political interest, and differential credibility attached to each news medium.

Although broad explanations in terms of audience-related variables have not has yet been systematically and consistently pursued, a number of specific explanations have been offered. Many scholars have theorized that the characteristics of television are ill-suited to teaching the relative salience of issues.[18] The television viewer is time-bound and is forced to follow a series of reports presented in rapid succession. The newspaper reader, on the other hand, may attend to the newspaper fare at his own time and at his individual pace and can reread and re-examine the information made available by the newspaper. In addition, newspaper formats permit more frequent repetition of items over time.

On the basis of such differences, according to McCombs:

Newspapers are the prime movers in organizing the public agenda. They largely set the stage of public concern. But television news is not wholly without influence. It has some short-term impact on the composition of the public agenda. Perhaps the best way to describe and contrast these influences is to label the role of the newspaper as agenda-setting and the role of television as spotlighting. The basic nature of the agenda seems often to be set by the newspapers, while television primarily reorders or rearranges the top items of the agenda.[19]

Based on data gathered in Charlotte, N.C., in 1972, McCombs found that as the election date drew nearer (October), the public agenda showed a better match with television than with newspapers. McCombs concluded that two distinct phases seemed to exist in the agenda-setting process:

> Early in the campaign newspapers are the initiators and prime movers of public opinion, and television plays a very minor agenda-setting role. The newspaper's characteristics permit coverage of public issues early in their development. But, as time goes on, and as the election date approaches, television becomes instrumental in making political issues salient for many voters, especially those not reached by newspapers.[20]

According to this view, then, the role of television varies over time and is not limited to merely reinforcing the newspaper agenda. Rather, McCombs argues, "Television news cuts into reality at a different angle. It is, for one, more visually oriented. Television news also has a very different style from news stories in the print media. TV news is not newspaper news with pictures."[21]

While these observations appear to be plausible and logical explanations for impact differences, other audience factors may also be significant. For instance, television audiences engage in different consumption patterns than do newspaper audiences. Such media-specific audience variables may offer an alternative explanation for the apparent agenda-setting superiority of newspapers. In the past, comparatively few efforts have been made to test the roles of the media in light of the nature and behavior of their audiences as well as in light of their content. The concept of "need for orientation" is one of the few audience-oriented variables that has been systematically applied in agenda-setting research. One of the major findings by Weaver is a positive correlation between need for orientation and the agenda-setting effect of both newspapers and television[22]

Scattered throughout the literature one can find other audience variables, used to better explain the agenda-setting phenomenon. Bowers examined high and low users of television for political news, and McClure and Patterson looked at light and heavy viewers and readers.[23] Others have examined various demographic attributes and such variables as political interest, group membership, and so on. However, most studies treat the public as homogeneous.

IMPACT OF AUDIENCE VARIABLES ON AGENDA-SETTING

To test the impact of audience variables on agenda-setting for intrapersonal and interpersonal agendas, we examined the effects of time frame, environmental context, level of education, issue obtrusiveness, and varied periods within the campaign year. This research was designed to appraise the different agenda-setting roles played by newspapers and television in the present study when one controls for these variables.

Media and voter data collected during the 1976 presidential election year were analyzed in two distinct time frame designs at each of two different periods. Each analysis consisted of a different combination of three elements: media agenda measuring period, time lag, and subsequent public agenda measuring period. The first, and shorter, period includes four weeks of media content measurement, four weeks of time lag, and two weeks of voter agenda measurement. The second, and longer, time frame design consists of four weeks of media agenda measurement, eight weeks of time lag, and two weeks of voter data collection. Thus, one design is 10 weeks long, and the other extends over 14 weeks. Figure 4-1 illustrates the two designs within each of two separate time periods.

Issue obtrusiveness was determined on the basis of a factor analytic procedure. This exploratory procedure resulted in two groups of issues in the February to May period, consisting of seven unobtrusive issues (crime, race relations, social problems, environment and energy, government credibility, government spending, and foreign affairs) and four obtrusive issues (general state of the economy, unemployment, inflation, and taxes). Initial analysis revealed that while only weak agenda-setting effects could be found with the entire array of issues, such effects emerged more strongly for the unobtrusive issues.

This distinction between obtrusive and unobtrusive issues was not found for the August to October period, suggesting that all 11 issues were perceived similarly later in the campaign. This finding may have been a consequence of voter learning during the earlier part of the campaign. Consequently, in attempting to focus on the context within which agenda-setting is most likely to occur, only the seven unobtrusive issues entered the February to May analysis, while all 11 issues were used in the later period.

Table 4-1 shows the correlations between the media and voter agendas in the February to May period for the two temporal designs. Within the shorter time frame, the overall picture shows similar levels of association for both media with the voter agendas in Illinois and a stronger association between the television and voter agendas in the other sites. Within the longer time frame, the results are also mixed but show a somewhat higher association between the newspaper and voter agendas than between the TV and voter agendas.

Examining these results by location, the match between the television and intrapersonal voter agendas in New Hampshire is strong within both time frames. However, the newspaper agenda is highly associated with the voter intrapersonal agenda only during the longer time frame. The pattern

FIGURE 4–1
The Study Design

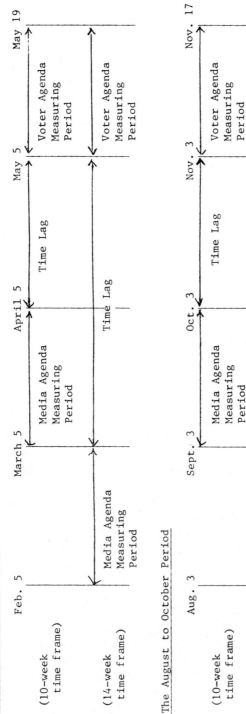

Source: Compiled by authors.

51

TABLE 4–1

Correlations (Spearman's Rhos) Between Media and Voter Unobtrusive Issue Agendas in the February to May Period of the 1976 Campaign

Location	Medium	Intrapersonal Voter Agenda	Interpersonal Voter Agenda
The 10-Week Time Frame			
New Hampshire	Newspaper	−0.21	0.50
	Television	0.74	0.43
Indiana	Newspaper	0.36	0.03
	Television	0.37	0.69
Illinois	Newspaper	0.86	0.96
	Television	0.77	0.93
The 14-Week Time Frame			
New Hampshire	Newspaper	0.64	0.73
	Television	0.70	0.58
Indiana	Newspaper	0.50	0.65
	Television	0.19	0.58
Illinois	Newspaper	0.87	0.97
	Television	0.62	0.85

Source: Compiled by authors.

is similar for the interpersonal agendas. Stronger associations between the newspaper and voter agendas are found in the 14-week time period than in the 10-week period. Thus, in the New Hampshire setting, we can find traces of the spotlighting versus agenda-setting distinction between the two media.

In Indiana, the correlations also point to the spotlighting versus agenda-setting distinction, as evidenced by the stronger correlations between the newspaper and voter agendas in the extended time frame. Thus the general pattern is that within the larger context of 14 weeks the agenda-setting impact of newspapers is greater than that of television. Within the shorter time period of 10 weeks, the reverse effect is evident. Television generally exerts greater influence than newspapers in both New Hampshire and Indiana.

In Illinois, by contrast, the associations between the voter and newspaper agendas are consistently stronger than the match between the television and public agendas. This pattern is not affected by the type of public agenda analyzed, but it is more pronounced in the 14-week period than in the 10-week period. One clue to the difference in the Illinois findings is provided by comparing the panels of voters from the three sites.

As Chapter 2 points out, the samples of voters from the three communities did not differ appreciably in age, sex, and income, but they did differ in education and occupation. The Illinois panel consisted of more white-collar workers (84 percent) than the Indiana panel (61 percent) or the New Hampshire (57.5 percent), and considerably more of the Illinois panel had graduated from college (65 percent) than had those in Indiana (28 percent) or New Hampshire (31 percent).

Perhaps, then, the higher levels of voter education and occupational status and the more cosmopolitan atmosphere of Evanston, Ill., contributed to a closer match between the media and voter issue agendas during the primary period of the campaign, at least for the seven more unobtrusive issues.

What were the patterns later in the campaign, closer to election time? Overall the results support the spotlighting versus agenda-setting distinction between the two media: newspapers appear to be the motivating agenda-setting factor in the longer run whereas television is more effective four weeks later, except in Illinois where television appears more influential than newspapers in both time frames (see Table 4–2).

TABLE 4–2
Correlations (Spearman's Rhos) Between Media and Voter Issue Agendas in the August to October Period of the 1976 Campaign

Location	Medium	Intrapersonal Voter Agenda	Interpersonal Voter Agenda
The 10-Week Time Frame			
New Hampshire	Newspaper	0.41	0.20
	Television	0.52	0.41
Indiana	Newspaper	0.10	0.30
	Television	0.52	0.48
Illinois	Newspaper	−0.28	−0.15
	Television	0.43	0.25
The 14-Week Time Frame			
New Hampshire	Newspaper	0.60	0.43
	Television	0.45	0.35
Indiana	Newspaper	0.73	0.76
	Television	0.33	0.29
Illinois	Newspaper	−0.11	−0.09
	Television	0.27	0.22

Source: Compiled by authors.

As in the earlier period of the campaign year, environmental context and locality appear to influence the nature of the agenda-setting process. While the results for Indiana and New Hampshire are similar, no agenda-setting impact of newspapers is found in Illinois. This result is diametrically opposed to those found in the February to May primary period. However, once again, the different demographic character of the Illinois site provides a plausible explanation. The more highly educated and urbane voters of the Evanston panel appear to have decided on their own agendas of issues by the fall period of the campaign, agendas that were quite different from the newspaper ranking of issues and only minimally similar to the television agenda. It should be remembered, too, that the August to October results are based on all eleven issues, which reduces the chance for demonstrating agenda-setting, whereas the February to May results are based on only the seven unobtrusive issues, making the appearance of an agenda-setting effect more likely.

Tables 4–3 and 4–4 summarize these results in relation to the spotlighting versus agenda-setting role of television and newspapers. As can be seen, this pattern holds partly for the February to May period and more strongly for the August to October period. It is interesting that the higher educational and occupational levels of the voters in Evanston seem to work against agenda-setting roles for newspapers and television, perhaps because these higher-status voters rely more on other sources of information, including interpersonal discussion, for establishing their issue agendas than do less educated and lower-status voters.

TABLE 4–3

Pattern of Results Supporting the Agenda-Setting Role of Newspapers and the Spotlighting Role of Television in the February to May Period of the 1976 Campaign

Location	Intrapersonal Voter Agenda	Interpersonal Voter Agenda
New Hampshire	No	No
Indiana	Yes	Yes
Illinois	No	No

Source: Compiled by authors.

TABLE 4–4

Pattern of Results Supporting the Agenda-Setting Role of Newspapers and the Spotlighting Role of Television in the August to October Period of the 1976 Campaign

Location	Intrapersonal Voter Agenda	Interpersonal Voter Agenda
New Hampshire	Yes	Yes
Indiana	Yes	Yes
Illinois	No	No

Source: Compiled by authors.

SUMMING UP

Several variables were examined in an attempt to explore the differential nature of the agenda-setting process initiated by newspapers and television. The factor of environmental context or location, represented by the three sites and the differences in education and occupation of the voters, appeared to affect the roles of television and newspapers in setting the agenda of issues in the presidential campaign. For highly educated individuals who are likely to have white-collar jobs (Illinois), both media seem to exert agenda-setting influence early in the campaign year. However, as time goes on, the agenda-setting effect of both media diminishes. Where the population is of a lower educational level and more likely to have blue-collar jobs, the impact of the two media is mixed in the early period of the election year, but fairly clear agenda-setting effects of newspapers appear to give way four weeks later to television's spotlighting impact.

Another major factor considered in this research is that of time frame. Differences are apparent between the 10- and 14-week periods, especially as the election year draws to an end. Newspapers dominate the longer time frame and television catches up a month later as the prime agenda-setter. Clearly, the agenda-setting process is not static and constant. Its effects vary as time goes on and as proximity to election day becomes a factor.

Finally, issue obtrusiveness appears to be an important variable in agenda-setting. Without the distinction of obtrusiveness, little association between the media and public agendas could be traced in the February to May period. But when public issues are sorted out on the basis of personal involvement, we begin to see more distinct media effects. Apparently, when individuals are experiencing the real-life impact of major issues, they hold little need to be told by the mass media that such matters are important, nor do they require newspapers and television to initiate interpersonal discussion of such issues.

In later chapters on issue agenda-setting, when the agendas from all three sites are combined into aggregate voter and media agendas, many of these same patterns identified in the three individual communities also hold. Newspapers appear to be providing the primary, or baseline, agenda of issues for the campaign, especially in the early months, and television news appears to be taking its cues on issue importance from the more stable newspaper agenda. Thus the distinctions between newspaper and television agenda-setting, at least as far as issues are concerned, seem to transcend some of the differences in community setting and voter characteristics.

NOTES

[1]Some researchers have used magazines for the media agenda. See G. Ray Funkhouser, "The Issues of the Sixties: An Exploratory Study in the Dynamics of Public Opinion," *Public Opinion Quarterly* 37 (Spring 1973): 62–75; Gerald Stone, "Cumulative Effects of the Media," Paper presented at the Conference on Agenda-Setting Research, Syracuse (New York) University, Fall 1974; and Carolyn Stroman, "Race, Public Opinion and Print Media Coverage," Ph.D. dissertation, Syracuse (New York) University, 1978. Other researchers have used radio for the media agenda. See Wenmouth Williams and David C. Larsen, "Agenda-Setting in an Off-Election Year," *Journalism Quarterly* 54 (Winter 1977): 744–49. But, in general, the use of newspapers and television in media agenda-setting studies is the rule rather than the exception.

[2]Maxwell E. McCombs and Donald L. Shaw, "The Agenda-Setting Function of Mass Media," *Public Opinion Quarterly* 36 (Summer 1972): 176–87.

[3]See, for example, John Carey, "Setting the Political Agenda: How Media Shape Campaigns," *Journal of Communication* 26 (Spring 1976): 50–57; Anne K. Hilker, "Agenda-Setting Influence in an Off-Year Election," American Newspaper Publishers Association *News Research Bulletin* 4 (November 1976): pp. 7–10; and Kisun Hong and Sara Shemer, "Influence of Media and Interpersonal Agendas on Personal Agendas," Paper presented at the annual convention of the Association for Education in Journalism, Madison, Wisconsin, August 1977.

[4]See Leonard P. Tipton, Roger D. Haney, and John R. Baseheart, "Media Agenda-Setting in City and State Election Campaigns," *Journalism Quarterly* 52 (Spring 1975): 15–22; Marc Benton and P. Jean Frazier, "The Agenda-Setting Function of Mass Media at Three Levels of 'Information Holding'," *Communication Research* 3 (July 1976): 261–74; Robert D.

McClure and Thomas E. Patterson, "Setting the Political Agenda: Print vs. Network News," *Journal of Communication* 26 (Spring 1976): 23–28; Maxwell E. McCombs, "Newspapers Versus Television: Mass Communication Effects Across Time," pp. 89–105, in *The Emergence of American Political Issues: The Agenda Setting Function of the Press*, eds. Donald L. Shaw and Maxwell E. McCombs (St. Paul: West, 1977); David H. Weaver, "Political Issues and Voter Need for Orientation," in Shaw and McCombs, *The Emergence of American Political Issues*; and L. Edward Mullins, "Agenda-Setting and the Young Voter," pp. 133–48, in Shaw and McCombs, *The Emergence of American Political Issues*.

[5]Philip Palmgreen and Peter Clarke, "Agenda-Setting with Local and National Issues," *Communication Research* 4 (October 1977): 435–52.

[6]R. S. Frank, *Message Dimensions of Televised News* (Lexington, Ma.: Lexington Books, 1973); Donald L. Shaw and Thomas A. Bowers, "Learning from Commercials: The Influence of TV Advertising on the Voter Political 'Agenda'," Paper presented at the annual convention of the Association for Education in Journalism, Fort Collins, Colorado, 1973; and Harold G. Zucker, "The Variable Nature of News Media Influence," pp. 225–40, in *Communication Yearbook II*, ed. Brent D. Ruben (New Brunswick, N.J.: Transaction Books, 1978).

[7]McCombs and Shaw, "The Agenda-Setting Function of Mass Media"; Palmgreen and Clarke, "Agenda-Setting with Local and National Issues"; and Tipton, Haney, and Baseheart, "Media Agenda-Setting in City and State Election Campaigns."

[8]Chaim H. Eyal, "Time Frame in Agenda-Setting Research: A Study of Conceptual and Methodological Factors Affecting the Time Frame Context of the Agenda-Setting Process," Ph.D. dissertation, Syracuse (New York) University, 1979.

[9]Chaim H. Eyal, James P. Winter, and William F. DeGeorge, "Time Frame for Agenda-Setting," Paper presented at the annual convention of the American Association for Public Opinion Research, Buck Hill Falls, Pennsylvania, May 1979.

[10]McCombs and Shaw, "The Agenda-Setting Function of Mass Media"; Tipton, Haney, and Baseheart, "Media Agenda-Setting"; Palmgreen and Clarke, "Agenda-Setting with Local and National Issues"; Zucker, "The Variable Nature of News Media Influence"; and Eyal, "Time Frame in Agenda-Setting Research."

[11]Eyal, "Time Frame in Agenda-Setting Research."

[12]Rodney Forth and Laurily Epstein, "Agenda-Setting Research: The Effects of Social Context on Individual and Group Behavior," Paper presented at the annual convention of the Midwest Association for Public Opinion Research, Chicago, November 1979.

[13]McCombs and Shaw, "The Agenda-Setting Function of Mass Media"; Tipton, Haney, and Baseheart, "Media Agenda-Setting"; Palmgreen and Clarke, "Agenda-Setting with Local and National Issues"; and Lee B. Becker, Maxwell E. McCombs, and Jack M. McLeod, "The Development of Political Cognitions," in *Political Communication: Issues and Strategies for Research*, ed. Steven H. Chaffee (Beverly Hills: Sage, 1975).

[14]Thomas E. Patterson and Robert D. McClure, *The Unseeing Eye: The Myth of Television Power in National Elections* (New York: G.P. Putnam, 1976).

[15]Shaw and Bowers, "Learning from Commercials."

[16]Thomas A. Bowers, "Candidate Advertising: The Agenda is the Message," pp. 53–67, in Shaw and McCombs, *The Emergence of American Political Issues*.

[17]Carey, "Setting the Political Agenda, " p. 57.

[18]McCombs and Shaw, "The Agenda-Setting Function of Mass Media"; William Glavin, "Political Influence of the Press," American Newspaper Publishers Association *News Research Bulletin* 4 (November 1976), pp. 1–6; McClure and Patterson, "Setting the Political

Agenda"; Maxwell E. McCombs, "The Agenda-Setting Function of the Press," Paper presented at a conference on Women and the News, Washington University, St. Louis, September 1977; Maxwell E. McCombs, "Expanding the Domain of Agenda-Setting Research: Strategies and Theoretical Development," Paper presented at the annual convention of the Speech Communication Association, Washington, D.C., December 1977; McCombs, "Newspapers Versus Television"; and Maxwell E. McCombs and David Weaver, "Voters and the Mass Media: Information-Seeking, Political Interest, and Issue Agendas," Paper presented at the annual conference of the American Association for Public Opinion Research, Buck Hill Falls, Pennsylvania, May 1977.

[19]Maxwell E. McCombs, "Elaborating the Agenda-Setting Influence of Mass Communication," Paper prepared for the bulletin of the Institute for Communication Research, Keio University, Tokyo, Japan, Fall 1976, p. 6.

[20]McCombs, "Newspapers Versus Television," p. 97.

[21]McCombs, "Newspapers Versus Television," p. 98.

[22]Maxwell E. McCombs and David Weaver, "Voters' Need for Orientation and Use of Mass Media," Paper presented at the annual convention of the International Communication Association, Montreal, Canada, April 1973; Weaver, "Political Issues and Voter Need for Orientation"; and David H. Weaver and Maxwell E. McCombs, "Voters' Need for Orientation and Choice of Candidate: Mass Media and Electoral Decision Making," Paper presented at the annual conference of the American Association for Public Opinion Research, Roanoke, Virginia, June 1978.

[23]Bowers, "Candidate Advertising: The Agenda is the Message," and McClure and Patterson, "Setting the Political Agenda."

II

INTEREST, ISSUE, AND IMAGE AGENDA-SETTING

five

MASS COMMUNICATION AND INTEREST IN THE PRESIDENTIAL CAMPAIGN

INTEREST AND MEDIA USE CYCLES

Interest in politics is a cyclical phenomenon among American voters, regularly rising and ebbing every four years with the coming and going of the presidential election. This quadrennial peaking of interest is clearly illustrated in Table 5–1.

Roughly 40 percent of our panel respondents expressed high interest in presidential politics prior to the New Hampshire primary. Even this figure, obtained in the early February interview, may represent a rising level of interest from previous months. Also remember that our panels consisted of only registered voters. However, political interest continued to build during the primary season, so that by July 60 percent of the voters expressed high interest in the presidential campaign. In short, while only two out of five voters expressed high interest in presidential politics at the beginning of the year, three out of five voters expressed high interest by midsummer.

From July on—through the conventions, the televised debates, and all the other events of the campaign—the proportion of voters in our panel expressing high interest in the presidential campaign stabilized at about 60 percent. This turned out to be just slightly above the 54 percent actual voting rate of the 1976 election.

The point of stabilization in campaign interest roughly coincides with the traditional pattern of decision making by voters.[1] Once the leading candidates are known for each party, a majority of American voters usually

TABLE 5–1

Proportion of Voters "Very Interested" in the Presidential Campaign Over Time (in percentages)

February	March	May	July	August	September	October	November Turnout
39.4	50.7	53.7	60.6	57.1	57.8	60.3	96.9
(n = 137)	(n = 136)	(n = 136)	(n = 127)	(n = 133)	(n = 128)	(n = 126)	(n = 130)

Note: The question to measure campaign interest: "At this time how interested are you in the presidential campaign?" The responses: "very interested," "somewhat interested," and "not at all interested." (Note that this measure of interest differs from the behaviorally defined concept of interest used in Chapter 3.)

Source: Compiled by authors.

have selected the candidate they vote for in November. Surveys conducted by the Center for Political Studies at the University of Michigan show that this held true for 54 percent of the voters in 1976. In the aggregate, both general interest in the presidential campaign and vote decisions seem to stabilize in mid- to late summer, with people who have made their choices generally exhibiting greater interest than those who have not yet done so. The explanation seems to be that early vote choice is a by-product of steady interest, rather than its culmination. The pattern of early vote choice by substantial numbers of voters has important implications for campaigning, forcing candidates to put major effort into the early part of the campaign. The pattern also spells trouble for candidates who decide to enter the campaign at midsummer.

However, the situation is not quite as rigid as aggregate figures suggest. In 1976, for instance, the proportion of people who were sure about their choices declined markedly between July and September. It rose again in October, after the bulk of campaigning, including the presidential debates, had been concluded.

Turning to the aggregate trends in the use of newspapers and television for news about politics, Table 5–2 shows the use of these mass media by voters across 1976. Use of both newspapers and television to follow politics began at a low point in December and rose quickly to its peak in March. This is the heart of the primary season and a time when presidential politics quadrennially burst anew on the scene with a profusion of newspaper features and television specials. Thereafter, media use settles down to a stable level for the remainder of the political year. The only deviation from this long period of stability from the late primaries to the general election is the drop in newspaper use during August. The slump is probably accounted for by the vacations and increased outdoor activities in late summer that disrupt normal indoor activity patterns.

Overall, newspapers and television show highly similar use patterns across 1976. When the proportion of voters reporting heavy use are rank-ordered across the six points in time separately for each medium and then compared, the resulting correlation is +0.83 (Spearman's Rho). However, these two trends in Table 5–2 are highly dissimilar from the trend in political campaign interest in Table 5–1. Both trends of media use yield correlations of approximately zero with the aggregate trend of interest in the presidential campaign.

The explanation for the discrepancy is simple. The voters in our sample needed information to make vote choices for the primary election only in early spring. The New Hampshire primary fell in late February, the Illinois primary in mid-March, and the Indiana primary in early May. Thereafter, interest continued high, but the usefulness of exposure to news was diminished. Moreover, much of the news coverage after the

TABLE 5–2

Proportion of Voters Using Newspaper/Television "A Great Deal" to Follow Politics (in percentages)

Medium	December	March	May	July	August	October
Newspaper	28.2	43.8	37.8	34.4	26.5	38.4
	(n = 142)	(n = 137)	(n = 127)	(n = 128)	(n = 128)	(n = 125)
Television	30.5	48.2	39.3	37.5	38.6	41.3
	(n = 141)	(n = 137)	(n = 127)	(n = 128)	(n = 132)	(n = 126)

Note: The specific measures of media use: "During the past month how much did you use the newspaper for news about political issues and events? not at all, very little, some, a great deal" (newspaper political information seeking), and "During the past month how much did you use television for news about political issues and events? not at all, very little, some, a great deal" (television political information seeking). Only those answering "a great deal" to each question were considered "heavy" political information seekers from newspaper or television.

Source: Compiled by authors.

initial primaries was a repeat of already familiar themes. Since exposure requires effort and competes with other activities, it decreased. With the onset of summer and the lure of outdoor interests, contervailing demands on the respondents' time cut even more deeply into media use.

Finally, it should be noted that at all six points across 1976 the proportion of our panel reporting extensive use of TV to follow politics exceeds the proportion reporting extensive use of newspapers to do so. This same pattern of media use in following politics during presidential campaigns has been observed in numerous national surveys over the past 25 years.[2] Television is more frequently used to follow presidential politics than are newspapers, whether the comparison is in terms of the preferred mass medium for keeping up with politics or in terms of the absolute amount of time spent with each mass medium's political messages. Watching candidates in the flesh, in a variety of interesting settings, is judged by the audience to be far more entertaining than reading about political positions or the complex problems facing the nation. While television news satisfies the quest for easy, painless enlightenment, its messages are meager and bland compared with the information available to newspaper audiences.

POLITICAL INTEREST EFFECTS ON MASS MEDIA USE

While the aggregate trends for interest in the presidential campaign and use of the mass media to follow politics show no correlation with each other because the effect peaks only when information is crucial for political action, numerous studies of individual voters show different results. A substantial linkage between political interest and use of the mass media has been demonstrated, particularly in studies undertaken close to Election Day. The benchmark 1940 Erie County survey found that the more interested people are in an election, the more they expose themselves to political communications.[3] The follow-up 1948 Elmira study used panel data to underscore the direction of effect, demonstrating that the greater the amount of exposure to political messages in the mass media the greater the increase in political interest from late summer to midfall.[4] However, the presence of a spiral effect also was recognized, so that the interest stimulated by exposure to mass media in turn stimulated further exposure to mass communication.[5]

More recent research by Atkin, Galloway, and Nayman[6] sums up well the state of our knowledge about the interplay between exposure to the mass media for political information and an individual's level of political interest. Secondary analysis of a national sample interviewed soon after Election Day in 1972 showed modest, but significant, correlations between political interest and four separate measures of exposure to news-papers, television, magazines, and radio, even with controls for educational level and social class. While this supports the hypothesis that a functional relationship exists between political interest and the use of mass communication, it does not specify the sequence of effects.

Evidence on this point is supplied by Atkin, Galloway, and Nayman from two panel studies of college students. All the respondents were eligible voters for the first time in a major election. In both panels the effects from early October to the day before the election clearly were reciprocal for interest in the campaign and exposure to national news content on the presidential campaign. (However, this analysis is limited to the final five weeks of the 1972 campaign, and none of the correlations measuring the relationships of these variables across time exceed the simple correlations for a fixed point in time.)

This reciprocal, spiral effect of mass media exposure and political interest on each other also has been observed outside the election campaign setting. Across the four undergraduate college years, exposure to the general news content of the mass media stimulated a rising interest in politics among students. This heightened interest in turn stimulated specific forms of information-seeking in the mass media, such as subscribing to a weekly news magazine.[7]

The general concept of an agenda-setting function of mass communication also suggests the impact of exposure to the news media on an individual's level of interest in politics. Just as the press exerts some influence on the perceived salience of various public issues and political candidates, perhaps it also exerts influence on the level of interest in politics taken as a broad, all-encompassing category of concern. This application of the concept of agenda-setting to political behavior is much broader than traditional considerations of the agenda-setting influence of the press on the salience of public issues or political candidates in the public mind. In this view the various elements of politics considered elsewhere in this book—the issues of the election, the contending candidates, and the various attributes of each—are lumped together in a single agenda item: the presidential campaign. This item is simply one of many considerations among each citizen's array of concerns.

Viewed at this broad level, what can we say about the agenda-setting role of television and newspapers? To what extent can the news media influence the position of the presidential campaign on the larger agenda of individual concerns during an election year? Is the dominant direction of effect from the media to individual levels of interest? How much of a spiral do we find in the relationship between media exposure and interest in the campaign across the election year?

Beyond testing this basic question about the direction of effect between use of the mass media to follow politics and interest in politics, there are two follow-up questions:

Do television and newspapers play the same political communication role here? Other evidence from agenda-setting reseach and other aspects of political communication have suggested differing roles for the two news media.

Over what interval of time do we find the strongest correlation between these two variables? What is the time lag, say, between use of the mass media and increases in political interest? Or vice versa? How does the audience's need for information affect the time lag?

A statistical technique called crosslagged correlation analysis was used to analyze the relationship across time between interest in the presidential campaign and use of mass media. Usually, correlations are used to examine the relationship between two variables measured at the same time. Such an analysis summarizes the extent to which the two variables are similar or dissimilar at that point. But in crosslagged correlation analysis the statistics summarize the extent to which one variable at time one is similar or dissimilar to another variable at a later time, time two.

The logic of this kind of analysis is quite simple. If X is the cause of Y or influences the value of Y, the correlation of X at time one with Y at time two should be stronger than Y at time one with X at time two. In other words, a cause at time one should correlate with its subsequent effect more strongly than an effect at time one with its cause at time two.

If an explicit hypothesis on the direction of effect can be framed, crosslagged correlation analysis pits the research hypothesis against its antithesis. When the direction of effect is ambiguous and no single research hypothesis can be stated, crosslagged correlation analysis has the advantage of pitting two opposing hypotheses against each other. That essentially is the case here.

In Table 5–3 are the crosslagged correlations between interest in the presidential campaign and the use of television to follow politics across the entire 1976 election year. Using the precampaign period before the opening primary in New Hampshire as the starting point, the dominant influence is from interest in the campaign to use of mass communication to follow politics. In four of the five comparisons the effect of February political interest on subsequent use of TV is much stronger than the subsequent effects of early media use.

But the picture changes as we move into the height of the primary season—reflected in the March and May interviews with our panels. Now the dominant influence reflected in the crosslagged correlations is from

TABLE 5–3
Correlations (Gamma Coefficients) Between Use of Television and Interest in the Campaign

			February	March	May	July	August	October
December media use	→	campaign interest	0.31	0.03	0.09	0.14	0.12	0.16
February campaign interest	→	media use		0.33	0.45	0.24	0.35	0.31
March media use	→	campaign interest		0.30	0.26	0.52	0.30	0.45
March campaign interest	→	media use			0.26	0.09	0.21	0.39
May media use	→	campaign interest			0.46	0.53	0.47	0.45
May campaign interest	→	media use				0.19	0.26	0.51
July media use	→	campaign interest				0.40	0.48	0.39
July campaign interest	→	media use					0.51	0.55
August media use	→	campaign interest					0.60	0.51
August campaign interest	→	media use						0.56

Notes: The question to measure campaign interest: "At this time how interested are you in the presidential campaign?" The responses: "very interested," "somewhat interested," and "not at all interested." (Note that this measure of interest differs from the behaviorally defined concept of interest used in Chapter 3.)

The specific measures of media use: "During the past month how much did you use the newspaper for news about political issues and events? not at all, very little, some, a great deal" (newspaper political information seeking), and "During the past month how much did you use television for news about political issues and events? not at all, very little, some, a great deal" (television political information seeking). Only those answering "a great deal" to each question were considered "heavy" political information seekers from newspaper or television.

The underlined entries are those correlations whose value exceeds the Rozelle-Campbell baseline. Essentially a significance test, this baseline is the value expected in the crosslagged correlations simply on the strength of the synchronous (same-time) correlations and the correlations of each variable with itself across time. For details on the calculation of this statistic, see Leonard Tipton, Roger Haney, and John Baseheart, "Media Agenda-Setting in City and State Election Campaigns," *Journalism Quarterly* 52 (Spring 1975): 15–22.

Source: Compiled by authors.

media use to subsequent interest in the campaign. It was, of course, during this very time period that use of the mass media to follow politics peaked among the voters in our panel. The data in Table 5–3 document the subsequent summer and fall effects of this extensive media use. Heavy use of mass communications in the spring for orientation to the presidential election seems to generate extensive interest in the election during subsequent months.

Significantly, the absolute values of the correlations peak during July. That is, the cumulative effects of heavy TV use in March and May peak during the summer, suggesting a time lag of from two to four months in the influence of mass communication coverage on subsequent voter interest in the presidential election. A simpler explanation for the July peak may be the fact that during this time the Democratic convention introduced an enigmatic new political figure to the presidential scene. Mass media use whets interest, but there must be significant political happenings to fan it to top levels.

Past this peak period of information-seeking, the relationship between use of mass communication to follow politics and interest in the presidential election is largely reciprocal. One also should recall that during these latter months of the election year interest in the campaign had reached a plateau among the members of our voter panel.

Turning to Table 5–4, we can examine the relationship between use of newspapers and interest in the presidential campaign. While there is some evidence there that campaign interest is the prime mover early in the year, the evidence is less clear because of the reciprocal effects of early newspaper use and political interest when we examine the results for July and August. Interest in the campaign and use of newspapers through March have about the same impact on each other as during July and August. For the spring months there again is some evidence of the impact of newspaper use on subsequent levels of interest in the presidential campaign, but the pattern is not as distinct as it was for the television data in the previous table. The data for May, when the pattern of newspaper use affecting subsequent interest in the campaign is sharpest, again show a lag of two months or more.

Although three distinct time periods can be traced to some extent in both the television and newspaper data, the patterns are more prominent for television. There are many more distinct differences in the TV data between the competing crosslag hypotheses. It also should be noted that the absolute values of the TV/campaign interest crosslagged correlations exceed the newspaper/campaign interest correlations in 22 of 30 comparisons possible between Tables 5–3 and 5–4. All five synchronous (same-time) correlations are stronger for the television/campaign interest relationship. This dominance of television as both an agenda-setter and as

TABLE 5-4
Correlations (Gamma Coefficients) Between Use of Newspapers and Interest in the Campaign

		February	March	May	July	August	October
December media use	↑ campaign interest	0.28	0.15	0.12	0.24	0.25	0.05
February campaign interest	↑ media use		0.18	0.41	0.23	0.27	0.24
March media use	↑ campaign interest		0.29	0.08	0.23	0.31	0.08
March campaign interest	↑ media use			0.36	0.26	0.23	0.36
May media use	↑ campaign interest			0.38	0.31	0.38	0.01
May campaign interest	↑ media use				0.17	0.15	0.15
July media use	↑ campaign interest				0.30	0.28	0.06
July campaign interest	↑ media use					0.11	0.19
August media use	↑ campaign interest					0.31	0.03
August campaign interest	↑ media use						0.31

Notes: The question to measure campaign interest: "At this time how interested are you in the presidential campaign?" The responses: "very interested," "somewhat interested," and "not at all interested." (Note that this measure of interest differs from the behaviorally defined concept of interest used in Chapter 3.)

The specific measures of media use: "During the past month how much did you use the newspaper for news about political issues and events? not at all, very little, some, a great deal" (newspaper political information seeking), and "During the past month how much did you use television for news about political issues and events? not at all, very little, some, a great deal" (television political information seeking). Only those answering "a great deal" to each question were considered "heavy" political information seekers from newspapers or television.

The underlined entries are those correlations whose value exceeds the Rozelle-Campbell baseline. Essentially a significance test, this baseline is the value expected in the crosslagged correlations simply on the strength of the synchronous (same-time) correlations and the correlations of each variable with itself across time. For details on the calculation of this statistic, see Leonard Tipton, Roger Haney, and John Baseheart, "Media Agenda-Setting in City and State Election Campaigns," *Journalism Quarterly* 52 (Spring 1975): 15–22.

Source: Compiled by authors.

an object of influence replicates one of the findings of a study of the famous Kennedy-Nixon television debates.[8] There the dramatic nature of part of the 1960 telecast political communication may have accounted for TV use showing a stronger correlation than newspaper use with prior interest in the campaign. But here we find the same pattern well before the televised debates of 1976.

The general nature of television buffs, compared with people who rely on newspapers, may provide the explanation. People with a steady interest in politics are more likely to satisfy it on a regular basis through the use of newspapers. Television buffs have a more volatile interest in the news, seeking it out only when it seems entertaining or useful. Scanning television news to aid in voting decisions for the primaries whets these viewers' appetite for campaign news, especially when there are "specials" such as nominating conventions or presidential debates.

FURTHER TESTS OF THE RELATIONSHIP

In an attempt to further explore the relationship between media use and political interest across these three time periods, a number of three-variable models were analyzed. Each model was an attempt to elaborate a sequence of effects among our voters across the election year. A typical model: February campaign interest → May use of TV → July campaign interest. Altogether, five different models were elaborated.[9] None of them, however, successfully survived all the three-way tests. In some cases, holding constant the value of the intervening variable did not eliminate the relationship between independent and dependent variables at all levels of the control variable as it should have. In other cases, holding constant the value of the independent variable eliminated the relationship between the intervening and dependent variables as it should not have.

In short, while the crosslagged correlations in Tables 5-3 and 5-4 suggest a spiral pattern of effects across three different segments of the election year, this same pattern of effects is not reproduced in the behavior of even most individual voters. This appears to be another instance of social trends that are not simple summations of the sequence of events in individual lives.

Both the newspaper and television analyses reported here also were replicated using a broader measure of media use. In the replication, measures of the specific use of mass communication for political information were replaced by measures of the overall frequency of exposure to newspapers or to television news. Neither of these general news exposure measures showed any significant impact on subsequent interest in the presidential campaign. Both analyses again suggested that interest in the presidential campaign at the beginning of the year stimulated subsequent exposure to the news media. But the data for other periods of the year showed a reciprocal relationship between exposure to the news media and interest in the presidential campaign. This suggests that the individual's attentiveness to political fare, tapped by such measures as use of the media to follow politics and by such psychological variables as need for orientation, is an important contingent condition for the appearance of agenda-setting effects.

Sex and age are other important factors. In the aggregate, women showed lower interest levels than men of comparable age, and older voters showed lower interest levels than younger voters. Nonetheless, women over the age of 40 showed the highest levels of media use for political information, although they spent less time daily reading newspapers than did men and they read them less systematically.

Another analysis examined the interplay between the frequency of personal conversations about politics and level of campaign interest. Like the pattern for television exposure in Table 5–3, this analysis found that initial campaign interest in February stimulated subsequent conversations about politics. However, for all the later periods the evidence was mixed, suggesting reciprocal effects of interest and interpersonal communication. Again, women reported less discussion of politics than men and, unlike men, they did not rate any of their discussions as serious.

Finally, it is important to note that the variable under discussion in this chapter is interest in the presidential campaign, not a more global measure of general political interest. The latter variable probably is best regarded as a stable background characteristic. As such, general political interest is conceptually and empirically distinct from interest in the presidential campaign. This latter point, that the two are empirically distinct, is documented in Table 5–5. A detailed repeat of Table 5–1, this new table examines the proportion of voters expressing high interest in the presidential campaign separately for those with low and high general political interest. At each point across 1976, a higher proportion of registered voters with high political interest also have a high interest in the presidential campaign. But the gap between the two groups steadily diminishes as the election nears, showing a striking convergence from February to March and again from August to September.

This convergence across the election year results from two quite disparate trends among the two groups. For our voters with low political interest, there is a steady, near monotonic increase in the proportion expressing high interest in the campaign. From February until October, there is a 150 percent increase in the number of voters with low political interest who express high interest in the campaign. But among voters with high political interest, the pattern is curvilinear across the year, beginning

TABLE 5–5

Proportion of Voters "Very Interested" in the Presidential Campaign Over Time According to General Political Interest (in percentages)

| General Political Interest | February | March | High Interest in Campaign | | | | | | October | November Turnout |
			May	July	August	September				
Low	22.6	39.0	42.7	50.0	46.8	51.3			55.3	96.2
High	66.7	67.3	71.2	75.5	71.2	66.0			66.7	98.0
Difference	44.1	28.3	28.5	25.5	24.4	14.7			11.4	1.8

Source: Compiled by authors.

73

and ending with two-thirds of this group expressing high interest in the campaign. The highwater mark for this group is July, the period of the national conventions and the point in the year when many ballot decisions become final. Perhaps the passing of the major campaign media events and the indecision of how to cast one's ballot ends the most significant season of the political year. Recall that from that point on the effects of media exposure and campaign interest are largely stable and reciprocal.

SUMMING UP

Paralleling several of the earlier studies, there is evidence here of a spiral effect in the patterns of mass media exposure and interest in the campaign. At the beginning of the election year the key variable is how interested each individual is in the coming presidential election. This initial level of interest is significantly related to the levels of media use, especially use of television to follow politics, throughout most of the remainder of the year. However, in line with the prediction from agenda-setting theory, there is evidence that television exposure during the spring presidential primaries plays a significant role in stimulating subsequent voter interest in the campaign. But for the remainder of the election period, there is a strong reciprocal relationship between use of the mass media to follow politics and interest in the campaign.

Perhaps the stronger agenda-setting effects of the mass media occur during the spring because that is when the primaries and their coverage in the news begin to define the political situation. Perhaps other agenda-setting effects also are stronger during this period of initial orientation and definition. In any event, this look at mass communication and campaign interest suggests that the political setting—whether the period under examination is preprimary, presidential primaries, conventions, or the traditional fall election campaign—is critical in specifying both the political role and use of mass communication.

NOTES

[1]Angus Campbell, Philip Converse, Warren Miller, and Donald Stokes, *The American Voter* (New York: John Wiley, 1964). Also see Norman H. Nie, Sidney Verba, and John P. Petrocik, *The Changing American Voter* (Cambridge, Mass.: Harvard University Press, 1976), and Warren E. Miller and Teresa E. Levitin, *Leadership and Change: The New Politics and the American Electorate* (Cambridge, Mass.: Winthrop, 1976).

[2]George Comstock, Steven Chaffee, Natan Katzman, Maxwell McCombs, and Donald Roberts, *Television and Human Behavior* (New York: Columbia University Press, 1978).

[3]Paul Lazarsfeld, Bernard Berelson, and Hazel Gaudet, *The People's Choice* (New York: Columbia University Press, 1944), p. 42.

[4]Bernard Berlson, Paul Lazarsfeld, and William McPhee, *Voting* (Chicago: University of Chicago Press, 1954), p. 247.

[5]Ibid., p. 248.

[6]Charles K. Atkin, John Galloway, and Oguz B. Nayman, "News Media Exposure, Political Knowledge and Campaign Interest," *Journalism Quarterly* 53 (Summer 1976): 231–37.

[7]Maxwell McCombs and L. Edward Mullins, "Consequences of Education: Media Exposure, Political Interest and Information-Seeking Orientation," *Mass Comm Review* 1 (August 1973): 27–31. Also see Thomas E. Patterson, *The Mass Media Election: How Americans Choose Their President* (New York: Praeger, 1980).

[8]Reuben Mehling, Sidney Kraus, and Richard D. Yoakam, "Pre-Debate Campaign Interest and Media Use," in *The Great Debates*, ed. Sidney Kraus (Bloomington: Indiana University Press, 1962), p. 230.

[9]For a discussion of the logic and testing procedures of elaboration analysis, see Morris Rosenberg, *The Logic of Survey Analysis* (New York: Basic Books, 1968).

six

MASS COMMUNICATION AND ISSUES IN THE PRIMARIES

Although many political scientists in the United States are still not in agreement as to the importance of issues in national and local elections, there does seem to be a trend among political researchers to ascribe greater importance to issues in recent U.S. elections.[1] At the same time, there seems to be a growing awareness among communication researchers that the mass media (especially newspapers and television) are important forces in shaping public concern (or lack of concern) over certain issues.[2] Much of the agenda-setting research has documented the correlation between media emphasis of issues and public concern over the same issues, especially during election campaigns.[3]

But there are still many unanswered questions regarding the role of newspapers and television in structuring the issues of an election campaign, especially in the early stages. Adequate media information and analysis of the implications of this information are particularly important for the primaries because the primaries involve a highly complex situation. Voters need to evaluate large numbers of candidates. Even if we exclude candidates who kept their hats in the ring for very brief periods only in 1976, who entered very few primaries, and who received little media coverage, the slate of actual candidates to be covered in 1976 numbered 13. In addition, two noncandidates, Hubert Humphrey and Edward Kennedy, were widely discussed and considered potential late entries into the presidential contest.

Guidance from the media is also more essential in the primaries than at other times because party labels are not available to help the voter in making choices. Once one has decided to vote in either the Democratic or Republican primary, one has few party cues about which of the various contenders running for these parties should be nominated.

This chapter describes the issues emphasized by newspapers and television during the 1976 U.S. presidential election primary period (defined by us as January 1 through June 15), voters' concerns with various issues during this time, and the relationships between media emphasis on issues and voter concern over such issues.

THE CAMPAIGN SETTING

The 1976 U.S. presidential campaign began well before the first state primary election in New Hampshire on February 24, and it featured at least eleven Democratic candidates and two Republican contenders. The new federal finance laws adopted in the wake of Watergate and the surge in the number of presidential primaries made it easier for dark horse candidates to enter the race. Changes in party rules for the selection of convention delegates made it feasible to win by small increments without the need to capture whole states. These considerations pointed to a far earlier start of campaigning than had been customary. In fact, Jimmy Carter, the ultimate winner of the contest, had started his campaign in earnest as early as 1972.[4]

During the long primary season (from February 24 in New Hampshire to June 8 in Ohio), Jimmy Carter won primaries in New Hampshire, Vermont, Florida, Illinois, North Carolina, Wisconsin, Pennsylvania, Texas, Indiana, Georgia, the District of Columbia, Connecticut, Kentucky, Tennessee, Arkansas, South Dakota, and Ohio.[5] At least three Democratic hopefuls withdrew during this primary period: Senator Birch Bayh of Indiana (March 4), former North Carolina Governor Terry Sanford (January 23), and former Oklahoma Senator Fred Harris (April 8).

In addition to Carter, other winners of Democratic primaries included Idaho Senator Frank Church (four), Senator Henry Jackson of Washington (two), California Governor Jerry Brown (two), and Alabama Governor George Wallace (one).

On the Republican side, the only seriously considered candidates were the incumbent President Gerald R. Ford and former California Governor Ronald Reagan. Although Ford won primaries in 10 states and had, unofficially, delegates from two other states in his camp, Reagan posed a serious challenge to Ford by winning primaries in 11 states and by picking up delegates in 9 other states that held state conventions. Ford won delegates from six other states in state coventions.[6]

Thus the 1976 presidential primary period included a large number of Democratic candidates, the strongest of them being a relatively unknown former Georgia governor and peanut farmer, and only two viable Republican candidates, both of nearly equal strength even though one was president at the time he was running. These conditions made for exciting—and unpredictable—primary elections in which issues, as well as candidate images and political ideologies, played an important part.

The media we studied treated the election as a major topic, devoting on an average from 10 to 15 percent of their news stories to it. Coverage levels ebbed and flowed, with major primaries stimulating increased coverage. Many of these stories dealt with several issues, along with information about the personal and professional qualifications of the candidates. While not exceptionally prominent, election stories fared well, judged by placement in the early sections of papers and broadcasts, inclusion of pictures, and time and space devoted to them. Thus the issues featured in these stories had a good chance of coming to the attention of the media audience.

Prominence of a story, however, had little to do with its status on personal agendas. High prominence ratings did not assure that a story was rated important, and low prominence did not guarantee that it would be deemed unimportant. Frequency of mention appeared to be a better predictor of personal salience of stories. Interestingly, frequency and prominence were not significantly correlated. Furthermore, television and newspaper agendas were more similar when judged by the frequency with which certain issues were featured rather than by the prominence assigned to them.

That prominence factors have less impact on personal agenda formation than frequency of mention is also apparent from data we collected on reading patterns. We asked core panelists to mark all stories in a newspaper that had come to their attention while they were reading or leafing through the paper. We found that back pages, brief stories, and stories with minuscule headlines often received much greater attention than stories displayed more prominently. The key to attention to stories with low prominence ratings lay in the respondent's interests and priorities.

MEDIA EMPHASIS ON ISSUES

What were the major issues presented to the voters by the three commercial television networks and by the newspapers we studied in Indianapolis, Evanston, and Lebanon? Table 6–1 indicates that foreign affairs and defense, government credibility, and crime were the issues most emphasized by the three newspapers we studied during the 1976 primaries. This reflected concern over the political situation in Africa, where the Soviet Union, supported by Cuba, was playing midwife in the birth of Moscow-oriented regimes. Unrest in the Middle East and Soviet military buildups in central Europe further heightened concern about the adequacy of U.S. defense. The credibility issue was a legacy from the Watergate period that had been followed by attempts to restore government credibility. Crime, of course, is a perennial problem that received nationwide emphasis in 1976 through various incidents involving such terrorist groups as the Symbionese Liberation Army and through a series of airline highjackings.

Although the three television networks also stressed foreign affairs and national defense most heavily during the primaries, government credibility was not given much emphasis in television news until the end of the primary season. Instead, the TV networks emphasized economic problems and environmental/energy issues early in the primary season and put somewhat more emphasis on crime near the end of the season (see Table 6–1). The emphasis on economic, environmental, and energy problems did not seem to match the fever charts of real world problems. Economically, the primary season was a period of steady, if unspectacular, recovery from the 1973–75 recession. Likewise, while environmental protection and dependence on Mideastern oil continued to be matters of public concern, there were no unusual events requiring attention to these issues.

These patterns may suggest that the television networks followed the lead of the newspapers in emphasizing government credibility and crime, but the newspapers did not follow television's early emphasis on general economic problems and environmental/energy issues. To some extent, then, the newspapers we studied appeared to be setting the agenda for the television network news programs during the primaries. Given the fact that broadcast media personnel do watch newspapers closely for stories and story emphases they may have missed, this pattern seems quite reasonable. The lagged correlations in Figure 6–1 confirm that the newspaper issue agenda remained quite stable from January to June, whereas the television issue agenda changed more over time. The newspaper agenda appeared to have its greatest influence on the television agenda during the period between February and May, according to the cross-lagged correlations in Figure 6–1, and the television issue agenda became noticeably more similar to the newspaper agenda from February to May, according to the same-time correlations (0.69 in February and 0.90 in May).

Taken together, newspapers and television placed most emphasis on foreign affairs and defense, government credibility, and general economic issues during the 1976 primaries. Crime was also emphasized,

TABLE 6–1

Issues Emphasized by Selected Newspapers and the Three Commercial Television Networks During the 1976 Primary Season

| Issues | January 1–February 5 | | | | February 6–March 16 | | | | March 17–May 5 | | | | May 6–June 15 | | | |
| | Newspapers | | Television | | Newspapers | | Television | | Newspapers | | Television | | Newspapers | | Television | |
	Per-cent	Rank	Per-cent	Rank	Per-cent	Rank	Per-cent	Rank	Per-cent	Rank	Per-cent	Rank	Per-cent	Rank	Per-cent	Rank
Foreign affairs, defense	14.5	1	39.7	1	13.0	1	34.6	1	12.3	1	25.3	1	13.4	2	22.0	1
Government credibility	13.2	2	3.4	6	6.8	4	1.5	7	11.0	3	2.5	5	14.1	1	11.2	2
Crime	12.2	3	6.9	4	10.9	2	2.6	5	11.2	2	5.9	3	11.8	3	5.7	3
Social problems	7.5	4	4.3	5	9.1	3	3.9	4	9.4	4	4.6	4	7.6	4	2.2	7
General economy	4.3	5	9.6	2	3.4	5	8.3	2	4.7	5	11.3	2	3.6	5	5.5	4
Environment and energy	2.3	6	7.2	3	3.3	6	4.5	3	2.1	6	1.9	6	2.4	6	4.1	5

Government spending and size	1.9	7	0.8	8	1.7	7	1.7	6	1.5	7	0.8	7	1.2	7	0.5	8.5
Race relations and busing	1.0	8	1.3	7	1.0	8	0.9	8	0.7	9.5	0.2	10.5	1.1	8	2.7	6
Taxes	0.7	9	0.5	9.5	0.4	10	0.4	9	0.8	8	0.6	9	1.0	9	0.0	11
Unemployment	0.4	10	0.5	9.5	0.7	9	0.2	11	0.7	9.5	0.2	10.5	0.6	10	0.4	10
Inflation	0.3	11	0.3	11	0.3	11	0.3	10	0.3	11	0.7	8	0.4	11	0.5	8.5
(N)	(3,623)		(624)		(3,742)		(2,535)		(3,823)		(2,744)		(4,199)		(2,368)	

Note: The rankings of issues by the three newspapers included in this study (Indianapolis *Star*, Lebanon [N.H.] *Valley News*, and Chicago *Tribune*) were combined into one newspaper ranking because they were highly correlated (Spearman's Rhos = 0.70 to 0.94 for the four time periods used in this table).

The rankings of issues by the three TV network evening news broadcasts (ABC, CBS, and NBC) were combined into one television ranking because they were highly correlated (Spearman's Rhos = 0.77 to 0.97 for the four time periods used in this table).

Each newspaper article three column inches or longer and each television network evening news story was coded into one issue. More than one category was used for a story only if it equally emphasized more than one issue. The 31 most common issue categories were compressed into the 11 general issue categories used here. Stories referring to the other 34 issue categories generally comprised less than 10 percent of all stories coded and of all issues mentioned by our panel members in response to open-ended survey questions.

Source: Compiled by authors.

FIGURE 6–1

Crosslagged Correlational Analysis (Spearman's Rhos) Between Newspaper and Television Agendas During the 1976 Primary Season

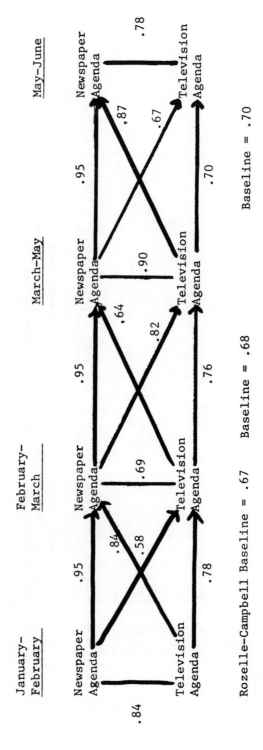

Source: Compiled by authors.

especially by the newspapers. There was considerably more agreement between newspapers and television about the top three issues by the end of the primary season than at the beginning of the year, with television falling in line with newspapers rather than vice versa.

Whether these issues were emphasized by newspapers and television because they were being emphasized by the candidates is not entirely clear, inasmuch as our study did not include a direct analysis of the candidates' speeches, writings, and news conferences. We do know, however, that one of Carter's main issues in the early Florida primary and throughout the other primaries was government credibility—the need to restore honesty in government and trust between the people and their leadership.[7] As shown in Table 6–1, the newspapers we studied emphasized government credibility as a campaign issue (especially at the beginning of the year and at the end of the primary period), whereas the TV networks did not allot much coverage to this issue until May 1976.

Another issue, emphasized by a leading Republican candidate, was U.S. foreign policy and national defense. Beginning before the March 9 Florida primary, Reagan criticized U.S. foreign policy as "timid" and "vacillating," and he focused on what he contended was the nation's fall to military inferiority behind the Soviet·Union. As Table 6–1 indicates, the foreign affairs and defense issue was consistently the most heavily stressed during the entire primary season, except near the end when it narrowly fell to second place behind government credibility in newspaper coverage.

For both issues (foreign affairs and government credibility), it is not clear from our study whether newspaper emphasis preceded or followed candidate emphasis . Both Reagan and Carter were stressing these issues before the 1976 primary season, and our content analysis began in January 1976. Reagan also emphasized economic problems and sought to link increased government spending with inflation in a nationally televised address on March 31, 1976.[8] This was matched by considerable emphasis by the TV networks on news dealing with the economy—especially in the first three time periods. The newspapers in our study stressed economic problems far less than did the TV networks until the end of the primary period when the relative amount of coverage became more equal (see Table 6–1). Government spending and size, stressed by Democratic candidate George Wallace, were not given much emphasis by either newspapers or television during the entire primary season.

Editors and news directors obviously used discretion about which issues to emphasize and which candidates to cover. While the most promising Democratic and Republican candidates could count on attention to themselves and at least some of their issues, third party candidates and issues were likely to be ignored. Without more systematic analysis of how much emphasis was given to various issues by the candidates both before and during the primary elections, it is not possible to speculate further on whether the candidates were important agenda-setters of issues for the media or vice versa, whether the process was reciprocal or whether some other sources (e.g., public opinion poll reports or pressure group activities) were setting the agenda for both candidates and the news media.

Another feature of issue coverage, which deserves mention because it affects the significance that media audiences assign to stories, is the linkage between issues and specific candidates. During the 1976 primaries, when amount of coverage of the issue stands of the ten most heavily covered candidates was examined, 29 percent referred to Ford, 28 percent to Carter, and 21 percent to Reagan. The remaining 22 percent of issue coverage was split among Wallace, Jackson, Brown, Udall, Shriver, Church, and Harris.

A look at the types of issue stands explored for each candidate during the primaries also showed a great deal of diversity. For instance, issues related to the conduct of government were most often linked to the Ford campaign. Social problems, particularly racial issues, were stressed most in connection with the Carter campaign. Emphases on foreign affairs and economic problems referred most often to Reagan.

Overall, no single policy issue received very much coverage during the primary season as compared with the coverage given to the progress of the campaign and the candidates' daily schedules. Analytical pieces, exploring particular issues and policy options in depth, were rare. In general, quantities of stories were more than ample, when measured by the public's willingness and ability to absorb and retain election news. Nonetheless, one must wonder whether the uneven distribution of coverage among the various candidates hurt them as well as the voters. The candidates who received little coverage were unable to get their stories to potential followers. In turn, the voters were unable to consider these candidates and their issue stands or compare them with the issue stands of more fully covered contenders.

The media made it difficult to compare the issue stands of even those candidates about whom they provided a good deal of information. This happened mainly for two reasons. One was incomplete coverage. For example, comparison in any one area, such as foreign policy, environmental protection, or race relations, may be difficult because the stand of one candidate may be explained while information on other candidates' stands on the matter is lacking. The second reason springs from the practice of presenting conflicting appraisals of the merits of these issue stands. When some stories call a line of policy stands sound while others condemn it as unsound and possibly foolish, readers are hard-put to resolve the contradictions. Their response may be either to ignore the conflicting media stories entirely or to assign lesser importance to them than might be true otherwise. They may also be more tempted to rely on nonmedia sources for guidance about issue appraisal.

VOTER CONCERN WITH ISSUES

In studying the relationship between media emphasis on issues and voter concern over issues, much previous research has been concerned with *intrapersonal salience*—the extent to which a person feels an issue is personally important to him or her.[9] But there is also evidence to suggest that media coverage of issues influences the extent to which an issue is discussed with other people (*interpersonal salience*) and the extent to which an issue is perceived to be important to others in the community (*perceived community salience*).[10]

In this study, all three kinds of issue agendas were measured—the intra- and interpersonal issues in all eight interviews during 1976 and the perceived community issues in four of these eight interviews (Febuary, July, August, and October).[11] Which of these ways of measuring issue concerns will be the most useful in predicting outcomes such as voting and political activity is an empirical question.[12] It might seem plausible that the issues that a person claims are of most personal concern would be the ones most important in influencing his or her choice of candidates in an election. However, the community agenda may be even more important. We know that willingness to expose one's views publicly—to openly declare one's personal priorities—varies according to a person's assessment of the trends of opinion in his or her social environment.[13] Most people will express only those views that are likely to be socially shared and acceptable.

If so, this willingness to conform to the perceived community agenda (the issues that a person thinks are most important to other voters in the community) could indicate that it may be more important in the longer run than the issues that are initially of most personal concern. The desire to adapt to the perceived community agenda could play a major role ultimately in shaping the intrapersonal agenda. Public opinion researcher Noelle-Neumann has argued that measures showing how a person assesses the community's climate of opinion and its future development "prove to be more sensitive to change than questions about the respondent's own opinions."[14]

In our study the intrapersonal issue agendas (Table 6–2) and the interpersonal agendas (Table 6–3) for all our panel members, considered as a group, were quite similar. These voters were personally concerned

TABLE 6-2
Intrapersonal Salience During the 1976 Primary Season

Issues	February Percent	February Rank	March Percent	March Rank	May Percent	May Rank
Foreign affairs, defense	3.8	8.5	14.7	4	20.9	1
Government credibility	4.6	7	3.9	7.5	5.2	6
Crime	6.9	6	0.0	11	5.2	6
Social problems	14.5	3	5.4	5	5.2	6
General economy	16.8	2	20.2	1.5	18.7	2
Environment and energy	11.5	4	4.7	6	3.7	8.5
Government spending and size	1.5	11	2.3	9	3.7	8.5
Race relations and busing	3.8	8.5	1.6	10	3.0	10
Taxes	2.3	10	3.9	7.5	1.5	11
Unemployment	9.9	5	15.5	3	10.4	4
Inflation	17.6	1	20.2	1.5	14.9	3
(N)	(131)		(129)		(134)	

Source: Compiled by authors.

TABLE 6–3
Interpersonal Salience During the 1976 Primary Season

Issues	February		March		May	
	Percent	Rank	Percent	Rank	Percent	Rank
Foreign affairs, defense	4.2	9	11.3	3.5	16.2	2
Government credibility	5.1	7.5	2.8	8.5	5.4	7
Crime	5.9	6	5.7	6	9.9	6
Social problems	13.6	3	11.3	3.5	10.8	4.5
General economy	16.1	2	20.8	1.5	18.0	1
Environment and energy	9.3	4.5	4.7	7	2.7	9
Government spending and size	5.1	7.5	2.8	8.5	1.8	11
Race relations and busing	2.5	10	1.9	10.5	2.7	9
Taxes	1.6	11	1.9	10.5	2.7	9
Unemployment	9.3	4.5	10.4	5	12.6	3
Inflation	17.8	1	20.8	1.5	10.8	4.5
(N)	(118)		(106)		(111)	

Source: Compiled by authors.

about the same issues that they discussed most often during the primaries. (Spearman's Rhos between the two kinds of issue agendas were 0.93 in February, 0.80 in March, and 0.88 in May.)[15] These issues were inflation, general economic problems, and social problems at the beginning of the year. Near the end of the primaries, in May, this changed in the face of media reports about increasing unrest and fighting in Middle Eastern countries and a NATO warning about Soviet military buildup in central Europe. Voters then became considerably more concerned about (and talked more about) foreign affairs and defense issues in addition to economic problems. During the entire primary period, our panel members as a group seemed least concerned about (and talked least often about) taxes, race relations, and government spending. (See Tables 6–2 and 6–3.)

But when asked in February what issues they thought were most important to the voters in their communities, the voters in our study chose taxes rather than inflation as most important, followed by general economic problems, and social problems (health, education, and welfare issues). (See Table 6–4.) Race relations, environmental issues, and foreign affairs were chosen by our panel members as least important to others, in spite of the fairly high ranking the environment had received as an issue of personal concern and as an issue discussed most often with others. (See Tables 6–2 and 6–3.)

In other words, although the rankings of issues of most personal interest and issues discussed most often with others were quite similar for

TABLE 6–4

Perceived Community Salience During the 1976 Primary Season

	February	
Issues	Percent	Rank
Foreign affairs, defense	0.8	11
Government credibility	5.3	7.5
Crime	9.2	4.5
Social problems	10.8	3
General economy	13.8	2
Environment and energy	3.8	9.5
Government spending and size	5.3	7.5
Race relations and busing	3.8	9.5
Taxes	18.3	1
Unemployment	8.4	6
Inflation	9.2	4.5
(N)	(131)	

Source: Compiled by authors.

the voters in our study as a group (Spearman's Rho = 0.93 in February), the ranking of issues perceived to be important to other voters in the community deviated considerably (Spearman's Rho = 0.30 for the interpersonal agenda and 0.41 for the intrapersonal agenda). This finding supports Noelle-Neumann's argument that measures of how people assess the general climate of opinion will yield different results from measures of the person's own opinions.[16] However, it does not support the concept of a "spiral of silence" in which personal preferences that deviate from perceived community norms are not openly expressed.

FIGURE 6–2

Crosslagged Correlational Analysis (Spearman's Rhos) Between Newspaper Issue Agendas and Voter Issue Agendas During the 1976 Primary Season

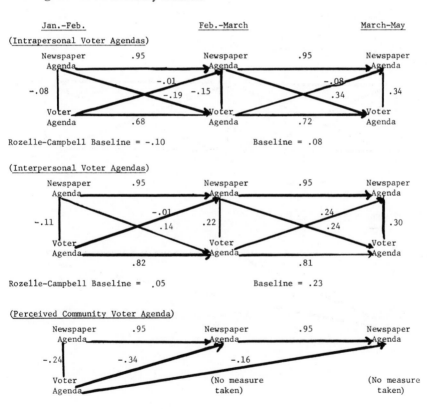

Source: Compiled by authors.

FIGURE 6–3

Crosslagged Correlational Analysis (Spearman's Rhos)
Between Television Issue Agendas and Voter Issue Agendas
During the 1976 Primary Season

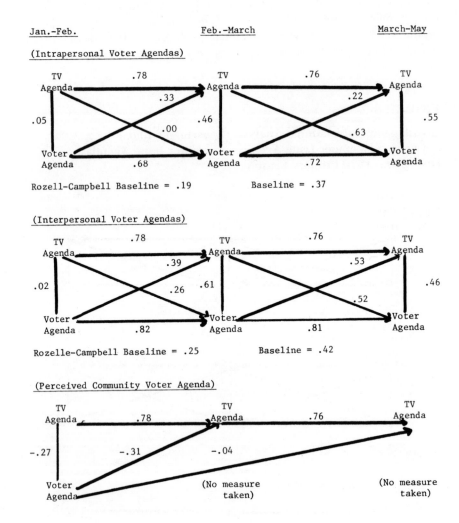

Source: Compiled by authors.

MEDIA EMPHASIS ON ISSUES AND VOTER CONCERN WITH ISSUES

All Voters

At the beginning of the primary period, there were some sharp discrepancies between the relative emphasis given certain issues by the media and the relative concern over those same issues by all the voters in our study. Figure 6–3 reveals that all of the correlations between the combined newspaper issue agenda in February and the various voter agendas in February are negative, and Figure 6–4 indicates that the two positive correlations between the combined TV agenda and the voter agendas in February are negligible in strength (see Figures 6–2 and 6–3).

A quick glance at Tables 6–1, 6–2, 6–3, and 6–4 indicates why these correlations are so low. Foreign affairs, government credibility, and crime were emphasized by the newspapers in our study in January and February, but these issues were near the bottom of the combined voter agenda in February. The voters in our study were more concerned about, and were discussing more often, the economy and various social problems.

But near the end of the primary season, in May, after a steady stream of news about fighting in the Middle East and Africa and Communist block intervention in these areas, the voters had become dramatically more concerned about foreign affairs and national defense. Accordingly, the combined voter agenda became considerably more similar to the combined TV network and combined newspaper agendas (see Table 6–1 and Figure 6–3). With both newspapers and television emphasizing foreign affairs more heavily than all other issues during most of the primary period, the voters apparently could not resist the influence of such consistently heavy media coverage.

Although the TV networks seemed to be following the lead of the newspapers in putting more emphasis on government credibility and crime as the primaries unfolded, in the face of no really new developments in these areas, the voters maintained about the same level of concern over and discussion of these issues throughout the primary period. And, in spite of television's abandonment of an early emphasis on general economic problems and environmental/energy issues, the voters maintained the same high level of concern over and discussion of the economic problems throughout the primaries. However, they reduced their concern over environmental/energy problems (see Tables 6–1 and 6–4).

In short, when looking at the issues individually, the only clear evidence of media agenda-setting during the primaries is the dramatic increase in voter salience of the foreign affairs and defense issue following the combined stress on that issue by newspapers and television. This is not surprising, considering that foreign affairs is a relatively "unobtrusive" issue—one with which people are likely to have little direct experience and, therefore, one about which they are more likely to rely on the news media for information.[17]

One of the principal effects of both newspaper and television news coverage during the 1976 primaries, therefore, seems to have been to increase the salience of foreign affairs and national defense among voters. Since these were key issues in the Reagan campaign, heavy coverage may have given him added strength in the primaries. Another possible effect of consistently low newspaper emphasis on environmental and energy problems may have been a decrease in emphasis on these issues by the TV networks and a decrease in overall voter concern about them during the primaries. However, we must be cautious in interpreting relative decline in prominence as an actual decline in concern. If concern levels are measured on a hypothetical scale of 1 to 10, concern about environmental and energy issues could remain stationary at point 7 while dropping from first place as other concerns surpassed that level.

The correlations in Figure 6–2 also suggest that combined voter issue agendas became more similar to the combined newspaper issue agenda during the primary period, rather than vice versa. The newspaper agenda is more strongly correlated with the voter agendas in May than in February, and the voter agendas clearly change more over time than does the newspaper agenda. This conclusion is also supported by the newspaper issue rankings in Table 6–1, which are nearly constant over the entire primary period.

Figure 6–3 indicates that the television issue agenda changed considerably more over time than did the newspaper agenda. This made it more difficult to tell whether the voter agendas were responding to the TV agenda or vice versa. It is clear, however, that the television agenda and the intrapersonal and interpersonal voter agendas were more closely matched at all three points in time than were the newspaper and voter agendas. For the intrapersonal voter agendas, the crosslagged correlations in Figure 6–3 suggest that the voter agenda had more influence on the TV agenda from January to March, but that the TV agenda had more influence on the voter agenda from March to May.

One explanation for these findings is that the early primary polling on the issues done by at least one of the network news shows (CBS) may have resulted in more emphasis of the issues of most personal concern to the voters. This increased emphasis may have contributed later in the primary season to even more similarity of issue emphasis between the TV news shows and the voters. This does not seem to be the case for the issues discussed with others, however. Both TV and voter discussion agendas seemed to be influencing each other during the primaries.

In short, the correlations between the combined TV agenda and the voter agendas in March and May were noticeably higher than similar correlations for the combined newspaper agenda. But it was not clear whether the TV issue agenda was changing over time in response to voter concerns, or whether the voter concerns were changing in response to the TV emphasis on issues. Both appeared to be happening, and TV issue emphasis also seemed to be influenced by newspaper emphasis on issues. The newspaper agenda did not change much at all during the entire primary season, ruling out any major influence on it by either television coverage or voter concerns during this time period.

The finding that the television network news issue agenda was more similar to the overall combined voter agenda than was the combined newspaper agenda during the primaries runs counter to several earlier agenda-setting studies.[18] It is, however, consistent with a 1977 study by Palmgreen and Clarke,[19] in which they found that national network news agendas were more closely correlated with public agendas than were newspaper agendas. Unlike earlier research, Palmgreen and Clarke's study was *not* conducted during a national political campaign. Because the findings reported here come from the early stages of a national political campaign, before interest in politics reached its quadrennial peak, they perhaps are more similar to Palmgreen and Clarke's findings than to the findings of other studies conducted later in such campaigns.

The finding that newspapers seemed to be setting the issue agenda for the TV network news shows is not surprising. Epstein's study of television news making showed that such outside sources as the *New York Times*, the Associated Press, and United Press International establish a basic agenda of possible stories for the networks. As Epstein puts it, "Network news is reactive to the other media in the sense that it depends almost wholly on them (especially the *New York Times* and AP and UPI wire services) for its basic intelligence input about the news of the day."[20]

But Epstein is quick to note that the TV networks can still pick and choose from this basic intelligence input. This would explain why, in the short run, TV and newspaper agendas may differ, even though there is a long-range trend toward television conformance to newspaper agendas. As evidence of selectivity by television decision-makers, Epstein points out that in one six-week period, the three commercial networks' evening news programs carried a total of 431 film stories, but only 57 of these stories appeared on all three networks.[21] A similar ability to select is also reflected in our analysis of the issue content of the TV news programs during the 1976 primaries, in which we found high (0.77 to 0.97), but not perfect, correlations between the issue agendas of the three networks. But the overall conclusion from our analysis of TV news issue emphasis during the primaries is that the individual network issue agendas were much more similar than disssimilar.

McCombs, in analyzing data gathered in Charlotte, N.C., during the 1972 presidential campaign, concluded that early in the campaign newspapers are the initiators and prime movers of public opinion, and television plays a very minor agenda-setting role.[22] The data from the 1976 primary period do not entirely support the assertion that television plays a very minor agenda-setting role early in the campaign (the correlations between the TV agenda and the public agenda are stronger than those between the newspaper agenda and the public agenda); however, the 1976 data do indicate that the changes that occurred in the TV agenda during the primary period were in the direction of the newspaper agenda and that the newspaper agenda remained nearly constant throughout the primaries.

These findings suggest that even though the television agenda more closely matched the voter agenda than did the newspaper agenda, both TV and voter agendas were changing during the primary period in response to the newspaper agenda (and perhaps in response to other factors such as voters' direct experiences with, and conversations about, various issues). It appears, then, that newspapers were the initiators and prime movers of television emphasis on various issues early in the 1976 presidential campaign, and this television emphasis then resulted in increased voter concern about these issues.

Newspaper Readers and Television Viewers

But even though the previous conclusions appear plausible in light of data gathered during the 1972 and 1976 election campaigns, the findings reported here, thus far, are based on the rankings of concern over issues by *all* voters, regardless of media exposure habits. If newspapers and television affect voter's issue priorities in a presidential election campaign, we would expect to find greatest similarity between newspaper and voter issue agendas for voters who use newspapers most. The same should hold true for television.

In this study, the voters in the three communities were divided into three groups—high newspaper/low television, low newspaper/high television, and high newspaper/high television—on the basis of their answers to questions about how much they used newspapers and television for news of political issues and events. Those who said, "a great deal" to both questions were classified as high newspaper/high television types. And those voters who answered "not at all," "very little," or "some" to both questions were classified as low newspaper/low television types and were eliminated from the study. Only those who answered "a great deal" to either question about newspaper or television use for political information were retained in the study because we were interested in studying the direct impact of newspaper and television coverage on voters.[23]

When the issue agendas of the three media user groups are compared with the issues agendas for all voters in the study, similarities are evident. For the intrapersonal agendas, the Spearman's Rhos range from 0.68 to 0.92 during the primary season interviews (February, March, and May). For the interpersonal agendas, the Rhos range from 0.68 to 0.94, and for the perceived community agendas, the Rhos range from 0.73 to 0.92. These strong correlations suggest that the overall voter issues agendas displayed in Tables 6–2, 6–3, and 6–4 are fairly accurate summaries of the issue agendas of the three media use groups (high newspaper/low television, low newspaper/high television, and high newspaper/high television users).

Comparisons of the issue agendas of the three media user groups with the newspaper and television agendas during the primary elections show the same patterns displayed in Figures 6–2 and 6–3. The correlations with the television agenda are stronger than with the combined newspaper agenda, especially for the high television/low newspaper users, and the correlations between voter and media agendas are stronger later in the primary season.

The strongest correlations (Rhos of 0.70 and 0.74) occurred between the TV issue agenda in February/March and the high TV/low newspaper voter group agendas in May, about a two-month time lag. This finding is consistent with the overall voter agenda correlations in Figure 6–3. This suggests that concern over issues and frequency of discussion of issues develop over time in response to television emphasis of such issues. The same seems to hold true for newspapers in the 1976 primaries, but to a lesser degree.

The agenda correlations are generally stronger for interpersonal agendas than for intrapersonal agendas. Apparently, both newspapers and television had greater influence on the issues voters talked about than on the issues they viewed with greatest personal concern. This held especially true for those voters relying mainly on newspapers for political information. This is not surprising, of course, since media stories furnish a shared basis for discussion.

As in the agenda correlations for all voters displayed in Figures 6–2 and 6–3, there is evidence that between March and May newspapers and television were setting the agenda for voters (especially those voters who relied more heavily on television than on newspapers) rather than vice versa. The correlations between the low newspaper/high television voter agendas in March and the television agenda in May were 0.16 and 0.14, but the correlations between the TV agenda in March and the voter agendas in May were 0.70 and 0.74. This indicates that the voter agendas in March had little impact on the TV agenda in May, but that the TV agenda in March had considerable impact on the voter agenda in May. The same holds true, to a lesser extent, for newspapers and those voters who relied heavily on newspapers (Rhos of -0.27 and -0.19, versus those of 0.25 and 0.42).

Thus, we conclude that differences in newspaper and television use for political information led to differences in issue priorities during the primary elections of 1976. Television news fans tended to be concerned about, and to discuss, the same issues emphasized by television. Voters who relied mainly on newpapers or on both newspapers and TV for political information had more-independent agendas.

Voters' Need for Orientation

In addition to patterns of media use, audience interests and motives lead to differential media effects. From recent studies of the uses made of, and gratifications obtained from, mass media, we have learned that a person's *motives* for using mass media may be just as important, if not more so, than his or her levels of media exposure in predicting and explaining media effects.[24]

One motive that has proved fairly useful in past studies for predicting differing media agenda-setting effects is need for orientation. This concept, based mainly on Tolman's theory of "cognitive mapping," is a combination of level of interest in a subject, such as politics, and level of uncertainty about that subject.[25]

Tolman, a psychologist, argued in 1932 that each person strives to "map" his world, to become familiar with his surroundings (both physical and mental), and to fill in enough detail to orient himself. From Tolman's theory of cognitive mapping and from various studies of information seeking, McCombs and Weaver have developed the following definition of political need for orientation.

		Uncertainty	
		Low	High
Relevance	Low	Low Need for Orientation	Moderate Need for Orientation
	High	Moderate Need for Orientation	High Need for Orientation

In this definition, a high level of interest in the subject of a message (for example, political campaign information) coupled with a high level of uncertainty regarding this subject (for example, not knowing which candidate to support) produces a high need for orientation. Either high interest and low uncertainty or low interest and high uncertainty results in a moderate need for orientation. Finally, low interest combined with a low level of uncertainty produces a low level of need for orientation.[26] Previous studies support the hypothesis that voters with a higher need for orientation are more susceptible to media agenda-setting than are those with a lower need for orientation.[27]

In the present study, political interest was measured throughout the election year by asking each voter, at various times, how interested he or she was in the presidential campaign. Those voters who said they were "very interested" were considered to have a "high" level of political interest, and those who said they were "somewhat" or "not at all interested" were considered to have a "low" level of political interest.

Political uncertainty was measured by asking each voter how he or she felt at that time about voting for president in November. Those voters who said they would "definitely" vote for a particular candidate were considered to have a "low" level of political uncertainty. Those who had made a tentative decision to vote for a particular candidate and those who didn't know which candidate for whom they would vote were considered to have a "high" level of uncertainty.[28]

Using these measures, the sample of voters was divided into three groups—those with a low level of political need for orientation, those with a moderate level, and those with a high level of political need for orientation. When the issue agendas of these three need-for-orientation groups were compared with the overall voter issue agendas in Tables 6–2, 6–3, and 6–4, fairly strong similarities were found among the intrapersonal agendas in February, March, and May (Spearman's Rhos ranged from 0.65 to 0.92). Among the interpersonal agendas, the level of similarity was not as great (Rhos ranged from 0.37 to 0.94). Perceived community agendas were the most similar of all (Rhos ranged from 0.81 to 0.91), suggesting that Table 6–4 is a good summary of the three different need-for-orientation group agendas.

When the various need-for-orientation voter issue agendas were compared with the newspaper and television agendas during February, March, and May, some of the same general patterns found for all voters—illustrated in Figures 6–2 and 6–3—were evident. The weakest agenda correlations occurred in February, followed by stronger ones in March and the strongest associations in May. Somewhat stronger correlations were found for the interpersonal agendas than for the others in March and May, especially for those voters with a high need for orientation about politics.

For the intrapersonal agendas, there was no clear pattern by level of need for orientation.

As in Figures 6–2 and 6–3, the correlations between the combined television issue agendas and the various voter agendas were generally stronger than the correlations between the combined newspaper agendas and the voter agendas, especially for those voters with a moderate or high level of need for orientation. And the highest correlations were between the combined television issue agenda in February/March and the voter issue agendas in May for those voters with a moderate level of need for orientation (intrapersonal Rho = 0.64) and for those with a high level of need for orientation (interpersonal Rho = 0.57).

In short, then, a voter's level of need for orientation did have some impact on which issues he or she felt were important and which issues he or she discussed with others during the primary elections. Voters with a high level of need for orientation tended to discuss the same issues emphasized by television and, to a lesser extent, newspapers during the last half of the primary period. Voters with a moderate level of need for orientation were somewhat more inclined to be personally concerned about these issues.

Obtrusive and Unobtrusive Issues

Although mentioned as an important consideration as early as 1975,[29] little attention has been given in past agenda-setting research to such stimulus attributes as the nature of the issue under study.

Typically, agenda-setting studies have treated the issues in aggregate form, comparing a rank-ordered list of media-emphasized issues to another rank-ordered list of public issue saliences.[30] Most often, these lists of topics and issue areas are derived from prior measures of the most frequently mentioned issues in public opinion surveys. Once such a list is constructed, content analysis methods are used on mass media messages to determine the level of emphasis placed on these topics by the media and, subsequently, to assess the degree of relationship between the media and public measures.

Such procedures have, at least implicitly, been based on the assumption that the news media's impact is the same for all types of issues and topics. This assumption, however, should not be accepted blindly. As Zucker points out, it is likely that the mass media hold greater potential to influence public opinion about some issues than about other issues.[31] In other words, it may be presumptuous to expect that the entire list of issues be transferred to the public agenda, much less in the same order.

Intuitively, Zucker distinguished between "obtrusive" and "unobtrusive" issues on the basis of the estimated amount of direct public contact with the topics, independent of media emphasis.[32] He found that this dichotomy, along with a measure of duration of exposure in the mass media, explains major portions of the degree of media influence on subsequent audience agendas.

Our 1976 election data provide empirical support for Zucker's intuitive notion of differing media agenda-setting influence on the public salience of different types of issues. A comparison of the degree of media emphasis on all 11 issues of the official agenda in May of 1976 with the subsequent level of their public salience, within a variety of time frames, resulted in generally low correlations, indicating a lack of close correspondence between the media issue agendas and public agendas. Could one, on the basis of such results, conclude that the mass media had no agenda-setting effect on subsequent public conceptions of what was important? As will be shown later, the answer is no.

In modern Western society, "reality" consists of a duality of perceptions, a distinction that may not be entirely clear to most individuals in their daily lives. One is the "real world" of actual experience, encompassing events and conditions that directly affect the lives of individuals and their acquaintances. The other is the "media reality," which is a picture of the world filtered through the mass media. This is the world beyond our personal experience. For example, our view of the reality of inflation may be formed by our own observation of continuously increasing prices at the neighborhood supermarket, whereas our perception of corruption in government draws almost entirely on mass media reports. It is thus plausible that the mass media are highly effective in transferring to the public domain the salience of issues that are primarily a part of media reality. By contrast, they may be less effective, or ineffective, in transferring the salience of "real world" issues with which the voter is personally acquainted.[33]

Since all events do not occur simultaneously, the rise and fall in prominence and display of mass mediated issues takes place within different periods of time. Thus, even if one accepts the questionable assumption of uniform media impact on the salience of all issues, such impact may be exerted within time periods of varying duration, as well as within different periods in time, for different issues. If this is indeed the case, an aggregate of many political, social, and economic issues, analyzed in the traditional agenda-setting fashion, may produce confounded results. Indeed, the results obtained in the initial analysis of the 11 issues in our 1976 data set constituted such confounded findings. The actual agenda-setting effect was concealed in generally low "average" measures of agenda-setting influence.

When the 11 issues were factor-analyzed to examine the pattern of public responses and media mentions and to determine which issues shared common denominators, two distinct groups emerged. The first or main group consisted of seven issues: crime, race relations and busing, social problems, the environment and energy, government credibility, government spending and size, and foreign affairs. The second group contained the remaining four issue areas: unemployment, taxes, inflation, and the general state of the economy.

Three major characteristics are clearly apparent as the common denominators in the two issue groupings. First, the smaller group of issues consists of economic topics, whereas the larger one contains general political and social issues. Second, the economic group contains issues of almost daily concern and corresponds to the *obtrusive* category in Zucker's dichotomy of topics, while the other issues appear to be more *unobtrusive*. Third, the unobtrusive issues are generally renewed issues that have faded from the limelight until they were reintroduced to the campaign by the candidates and by the mass media. The obtrusive issues, on the other hand, had been subjects of continuous and constant concern to both the media and the public for a substantial time even before the start of the campaign year.

The four economic issues are obtrusive in that each directly affects the lives of a substantial number, if not all, of the panel members. The subject areas subsumed under the unobtrusive category, on the other hand, appear to be more remote from the personal realm of direct and regular experience. Individuals, in general, are not continuously and regularly aware of the impact of government spending, foreign affairs, and similar unobtrusive issues. In all probability, it is unlikely that a significant number of respondents have had personal encounters with issues such as crime, race relations, and environmental protection.

It is logical to assume that firsthand experience has a greater impact on an individual's concerns than do mass media reports. When both salience sources are present, the former is likely to override the latter. Under this assumption, the less direct experience with the issues, the more likely one is to acquire salience from the mass media. More than 50 years ago, Walter Lippmann observed that in light of the limited amount of experience in real life, it is the press that provides the major opportunities of contact with the unseen environment, bridging the gap between "the world outside and the pictures in our heads."[34] This means that the agenda-setting influence of mass media will be stronger when unobtrusive issues are highlighted through frequent mention and prominent display, especially during the period in which such issues emerge in the mass media.

To examine this proposition empirically, the agenda-setting hypothesis was retested with the 1976 election data, controlling for the two types of issues. The overall level of association between the media's issue agendas and the public agendas during the primaries had been generally low, suggesting a very modest agenda-setting impact by newspapers and television. Tables 6–5 and 6–6 show that, even when controlling for individual communities, the correlations between media agendas and voter agendas were generally weak.

But when we ascertained the level of association between the media and public agendas separately for obtrusive and unobtrusive groupings, we found an array of high and positive correlations with the unobtrusive issues and low and most often negative correlations with the obtrusive ones by the end of the primary season.

Tables 6–7 and 6–8 display a sample of obtained correlations for the three issue groupings: the unobtrusive issues, the obtrusive issues, and the aggregate of the two.[35] For comparative purposes, the time periods with the highest obtained unobtrusive issue correlations were selected for display; in the tables, these correlations were juxtaposed with the meas-

TABLE 6–5

Highest Obtained Correlations (Spearman's Rhos) Between the Media and Intrapersonal Voter Issue Agendas in May 1976

Media	New Hampshire	Indiana	Illinois
Newspapers	0.18	0.29	0.29
Television	0.25	0.30	0.18

Note: These are the highest obtained correlations among a multitude of tests using various time frames.
Source: Compiled by the authors.

TABLE 6–6

Highest Obtained Correlations (Spearman's Rhos) Between the Media and Interpersonal Voter Issue Agendas in May 1976

Media	New Hampshire	Indiana	Illinois
Newspapers	0.33	0.34	0.48
Television	0.05	0.53	0.32

Source: Compiled by authors.

TABLE 6–7

A Sample of Obtained Correlations Between the Media and Intrapersonal Voter Issue Agendas, Controlling for Issue Obtrusiveness

Media	New Hampshire			Indiana			Illinois		
	All Issues	Unobtrusive	Obtrusive	All Issues	Unobtrusive	Obtrusive	All Issues	Unobtrusive	Obtrusive
Newspapers	0.10	0.67	0.32	0.09	0.60	0.06	0.12	0.95	0.20
Television	0.08	0.74	0.33	0.02	0.59	0.06	−0.13	0.95	0.32

Source: Compiled by authors.

TABLE 6–8

A Sample of Obtained Correlations Between the Media and Interpersonal Voter Issue Agendas, Controlling for Issue Obtrusiveness

Media	New Hampshire			Indiana			Illinois		
	All Issues	Unobtrusive	Obtrusive	All Issues	Unobtrusive	Obtrusive	All Issues	Unobtrusive	Obtrusive
Newspapers	0.01	0.85	−0.32	0.22	0.65	−0.26	0.30	0.97	0.50
Television	0.05	0.58	0.60	0.42	0.82	0.11	0.05	0.96	0.32

Source: Compiled by authors.

103

ures of association found under the obtrusive and aggregate conditions in the same time periods. The results clearly reveal the importance of distinguishing between issue types in agenda-setting research. Of the twelve unobtrusive correlations across the three sites and the two media, all are moderately strong or strong. By comparison, the highest correlation obtained with the aggregate of 11 issues is 0.42, while the highest found with the obtrusive issues is 0.60.

These patterns show that during the primary season of the election year, newspapers and television were instrumental in bringing before their audiences those issues and problems with which voters had minimal direct experience. In other words, the mass media seemed to introduce new areas of concern to the public agenda of issues. But media coverage of the obtrusive economic issues, which had been of public concern for some time and which had already reached their "ceiling" of maximum salience, simply highlighted or, at best, reinforced their existing prominence and importance. Thus it is with the unobtrusive issues that the mass media performed their most noticeable agenda-setting role.

In general, with the unobtrusive issues only, there was a higher correspondence between the voters' interpersonal agenda than intra- personal agenda and the previous agendas of newspapers and television (expressed in median correlations of 0.84 for the former and 0.71 for the latter). These results make clear that the agenda-setting influence of newspapers and television on the public salience of unobtrusive issues manifests itself especially in what people choose to discuss with others. No noticeable difference between television's and newspapers' general influ- ence on the public salience of unobtrusive issues was found (median correlation of 0.76 for newspapers compared with 0.78 for television).

The differences between obtrusive and unobtrusive issues are also demonstrated by the diaries that 18 members of the Evanston core panel completed. Three out of five issues most frequently covered by the *Chicago Tribune*, the local newspaper for the panel, were also the leading issues in the diaries. The other two accounted for comparatively much less diary mention. Conversely, several issues that received little coverage in the paper received a lot of coverage in the diaries. The same held true for television. In each case, those issues that figured most prominently in the diaries, despite their lack of attention by the media, met the criteria of obtrusive issues.

The diary data thus support our findings that issues that receive comparatively little coverage by the media may soar to the top in public attention. Once a threshhold of awareness is reached for an issue, either through personal experience or through media coverage, the audience

may elevate it to high status on its personal agenda and even on its interpersonal agenda.

The primary season results strongly support the proposition of variable media agenda-setting impact on the salience of different issues in all
three communities. The picture is less clear in the summer and fall
periods. When temporarily unobtrusive issues become obtrusive again as a
consequence of ample media coverage, the distinction between obtrusive
and unobtrusive issues becomes less clear. To put it in other words, over
time media experience may become just as "real" as personal experience.
Repeated exposure to those issues experienced primarily via mass communication may transform them into the functional equivalent of obtrusive issues that directly impinge on the individual. In short, over time,
distinctions between direct and mediated experiences may blur.

Issue obtrusiveness apparently is not a constant and universal attri-
bute of specific issues, nor is it a stable and determined characteristic of
any given topic. Such factors as social context and local conditions during
particular time periods may be as important as the degree of direct
experience. Thus, issue obtrusiveness is a continuous variable that may be
present in varying degrees or absent altogether. Extensive personal
experience appears to be the strongest factor that provides a counter-
vailing force to the pull of media agenda-setting. But vicarious experiences, through media exposure, may also be internalized so that they
become quasipersonal experiences that resist subsequent media agenda-
shaping forces.

The impact of local conditions on issue obtrusiveness can be illustrated by an example. The issue of taxation may be a pressing obtrusive
concern in a particular region of the country. At the same time, it may
constitute an unobtrusive topic in another area, where tax rates are low
and taxation is neither perceived nor experienced as a problem. Similarly,
crime may become a painfully real experience for many individuals in a
particular location at a given time period although it may previously have
been totally remote and unobtrusive. Thus, local and temporal settings
appear to be crucial components of the measure of issue obtrusiveness.

It is probably a sign of the times that the issues perceived as obtrusive
in Lebanon, Indianapolis, and Evanston during the 1976 campaign year
were economic in nature. It was a period of near recession, considerable
unemployment, constant public concern with high taxes, and anxiety
about inflation. These are issues and conditions that affect the daily lives of
people to a degree that makes them obtrusive and resistant to counter-
vailing media pressures. People who are victims of unemployment, inflation, and high taxes, and those who struggle daily through other economic

hardships, hold no need to be told by the media that these matters are important.

SUMMING UP

These are the major conclusions from this analysis of mass communication and issues in the 1976 primaries.

Both newspapers and television appeared to play important roles in focusing voter attention on certain issues, especially on unobtrusive issues, during the presidential primaries. Whereas the newspaper ranking of issues remained quite constant throughout the January through June period and thus served as a baseline for both television and voters, the television issue agenda changed over time to become more similar to the newspaper agenda. The voter agendas also changed over time to become more similar to the earlier television agendas.

The issues emphasized most heavily by both newspaper and television by the end of the primaries (foreign affairs/defense and government credibility) were also stressed by the two front-running candidates (Ronald Reagan and Jimmy Carter). But not all of the issues emphasized by these candidates were also emphasized by the media, indicating that the television networks and the newspapers in our study did have some discretion about which issues to stress. However, this discretion seemed to be limited to choosing among those issues emphasized by the leading candidates in the primaries.

The similarities of the intrapersonal and interpersonal issue agendas of the voters in our study indicated that these voters generally were personally concerned about the same issues that they discussed with others during the primaries. But the ranking of issues perceived to be important to other voters in the community deviated considerably from the rankings of issues considered personally most important and discussed with others. This supports Noelle-Neumann's argument that measures of how people assess the general climate of opinion are different from measures of people's own opinions. In addition, the perceived community agenda deviated considerably from the newspaper and television agendas, suggesting that it was an independent measure of public concern over issues.

When looking at the issues individually during the primaries, the clearest evidence of media agenda-setting is the dramatic increase in voter concern over the foreign affairs and national defense issue following the combined stress on that issue by both newspapers and television and the decrease in voter concern and TV stress on environmental and energy problems following consistently low emphasis by the newspapers during the primaries. This increased voter concern over foreign affairs and national defense, spurred by reports of serious foreign policy problems, may have helped Ronald Reagan in the primaries, because it was one of the issues he repeatedly stressed during this time.

Whereas newspaper emphasis on issues clearly seemed to lead voter concern with and discussion about such issues during the primaries, this was not so true for television, especially early in the primary season. Even though the correlations between the TV agendas and the voter agendas were noticeably higher than similar correlations for newspapers, it was less clear whether the TV issue agenda was changing over time in response to voter concerns or whether the voter concerns were changing in response to the TV emphasis on issues. After March, it appeared that the TV agenda was leading the voter intrapersonal agenda, rather than vice versa.

The results of correlational analyses with all voters combined and controlling for type of media use for political information and need for orientation suggested that concern over issues among voters—and discussion of these issues with others—develops over a two-month time period or so in response to television and, to a lesser extent, newspaper emphasis on these issues. In addition, those voters who relied mainly on television for political information tended to be concerned about and to discuss the same issues emphasized by television, whereas those voters who relied mainly on newspapers for political information or on both newspapers and television had issue agendas that were generally more independent of the media agendas.

A voter's level of political need for orientation (interest in the campaign and uncertainty about for whom to vote) did have an effect on which issues he or she believed to be important and which issues were discussed with others during the primaries. Those voters with a high level of need for orientation (high interest and high uncertainty) tended to discuss the same issues emphasized by the television networks and, to a lesser extent, by the newspapers included in our study. Those voters with a moderate level of need for orientation (high on interest or uncertainty and low on interest or uncertainty) were somewhat more inclined to be personally concerned about the same issues emphasized in the media (especially television) than were those voters with a low or high level of need for orientation.

In addition to patterns of media use for political information and levels of need for orientation, the nature of the issues under study also affected the agenda-setting process. Our data suggest that during the 1976 primary period, newspapers and television were important agenda-setters of unobtrusive issues—those problems with which voters had minimal direct experience. But media coverage of the more obtrusive economic issues, which had been of public concern for some time before the campaign, had little impact on the relative salience of these issues.

Taken together, these results indicate that the front-running candidates in the primary elections (Reagan and Carter) probably had some impact on which issues were emphasized by newspapers and television during the 1976 primaries, but that newspapers continued to emphasize pretty much the same issues throughout this period. Both television and voter issue emphasis changed to resemble more closely newspaper emphasis on issues, especially for those voters who relied primarily on television for political information. The issue agendas of voters who relied primarily on newspapers were more independent of both newspaper and television issue agendas. The explanation may be that newspaper readers generally have higher socioeconomic status, which may give them access to more sources of political information and a chance to develop more independent views about campaign issues.

Whereas media use patterns and motives to follow the campaign affected both voters' personal issue priorities and their priorities for discussion, the overall patterns for all voters were not changed drastically during the primaries by media use habits or motivation to attend to the campaign. This is probably due to the rather homogeneous nature of the sample of voters studied here and the relative constancy of media emphasis on various issues during the primary period. Whatever the case, there is evidence here that newspapers and television helped to set the agenda of issues during the primaries, especially for the more unobtrusive issues, in spite of varying voter media exposure habits and levels of motivation to follow the campaign.

NOTES

[1]See, for example, C. Anthony Broh, *Toward a Theory of Issue Voting* (Sage Professional Papers in American Politics, vol. 1, series no. 04-011, Beverly Hills: Sage Publications, 1973), pp. 6–10; Samuel A. Kirkpatrick, William Lyons, and Michael R. Fitzgerald, "Candidates, Parties, and Issues in the American Electorate," *American Politics Quarterly* 3 (July 1975): 35–71; Gerald M. Pomper, " From Confusion to Clarity: Issues and American Voters, 1956–68," *American Political Science Review* 66 (1972): 415–28; and David E. Repass, "Issue Salience and Party Choice," *American Political Science Review* 65 (1971): 389–400.

[2]See, for example, Donald L. Shaw and Maxwell E. McCombs, *The Emergence of American Political Issues: The Agenda-Setting Function of the Press* (St. Paul: West, 1977); Maxwell E. McCombs and Donald L. Shaw, "The Agenda-Setting Function of Mass Media," *Public Opinion Quarterly* 36 (Summer 1972): 176–87; Lee B. Becker, Maxwell E. McCombs, and Jack M. McLeod, "The Development of Political Cognitions," in *Political Communication: Issues and Strategies for Research*, ed. Steven H. Chaffee (Beverly Hills: Sage, 1975);

and Maxwell E. McCombs, "Agenda-Setting Research: A Bibliographic Essay," *Political Communication Review* 1 (1976): 1–7.

[3]Ibid.

[4]F. Christopher Arterton, "The Media Politics of Presidential Campaigns: A Study of the Carter Nomination Drive," in *Race for the Presidency*, ed. James David Barber (Englewood Cliffs, N.J.: Prentice Hall, 1978), pp. 26–54.

[5]See Mary E. Clifford, Raymond Hill, and Stephen Orlofsky, *1976 News Dictionary* (New York: Facts on File, 1977), pp. 257–58.

[6]Ibid.

[7]Ibid., p. 258.

[8]Ibid., pp. 259–60.

[9]See McCombs, "Agenda-Setting Research: A Bibliographic Essay"; McCombs and Shaw, "The Agenda-Setting Function of Mass Media"; and Chapter 2 in this volume.

[10]See Becker, McCombs, and McLeod, "The Development of Political Cognitions," and Shaw and McCombs, *The Emergence of American Political Issues*.

[11]The wording for the general introduction to all issue measures was, "In the previous interviews we have asked about the problems and issues now facing the United States. Your concerns may be the same from interview to interview, or they may change over time. It doesn't matter. We are interested in your opinion *today*."

The wording for the *intrapersonal* issue measure was, "Of the various problems and issues now facing the United States, which is the most important to you personally?" (open-ended response)

The wording for the *interpersonal* issue measure was, "Which of these problems and issues have you talked about most often with others since the last interview?" (open-ended response)

The wording for the *perceived community* issue measure was, "Now let's shift from the issues important to you to the issues most important to the entire community. They may or may not be most concerned with the same issues you are. Which issues do you think are most important to the voters around here?" (open-ended response)

The distinctions between these different kinds of issue saliences were first suggested in Jack M. McLeod, Lee. B. Becker, and James E. Byrnes, "Another Look at the Agenda-Setting Function of the Press," *Communication Research* 1 (April 1974): 131–66. They suggested that researchers should differentiate between an individual's personal concerns, the concerns discussed with others, and the concerns of the community at large as perceived by an individual, regardless of which of these concerns proved most useful in predicting various outcomes such as voting and campaign activity.

[12]Ibid.

[13]Elisabeth Noelle-Neumann, "The Spiral of Silence: A Theory of Public Opinion," *Journal of Communication* 24 (Spring 1974): 43–51. See also Elisabeth Noelle-Neumann, "Turbulences in the Climate of Opinion: Methodological Applications of the Spiral of Silence Theory," *Public Opinion Quarterly* 41 (Summer 1977): 143–58.

[14]Noelle-Neumann, "Turbulences in the Climate of Opinion," p. 157.

[15]A Spearman's Rho of +1.0 indicates a perfect correlation between two sets of rankings. A Rho of 0.0 indicates no correlation, and a Rho of −1.0 indicates that one ranking is just the opposite of the other (a perfect inverse correlation).

[16]Noelle-Neumann, "Turbulences in the Climate of Opinion," p. 157.

[17]See Harold G. Zucker, "The Variable Nature of News Media Influence," in *Communication Yearbook II*, ed. Brent D. Ruben (New Brunswick, N.J.: Transaction Books, 1978), pp. 225–40, for a discussion of different television agenda-setting effects with regard to obtrusive and unobtrusive issues. Zucker's study found some support for greater television agenda-setting with regard to unobtrusive issues than obtrusive ones from 1968 through 1976.

[18]See McCombs, "Agenda-Setting Research: A Bibliographic Essay," and Shaw and McCombs, *The Emergence of American Political Issues*, for examples of such studies.

[19]Philip Palmgreen and Peter Clarke, "Agenda-Setting with Local and National Issues," *Communication Research* 4 (October 1977): 435–52.

[20]Edward Jay Epstein, *News from Nowhere: Television and the News* (New York: Vintage Books, 1974), p. 37.

[21]Ibid., p. 38. However, dissimilar stories may still fall into the same subject categories, yielding much higher correlations than one would anticipate from Epstein's analysis.

[22]Maxwell E. McCombs, "Newspapers Versus Television: Mass Communication Effects Across Time," in Shaw and McCombs, *The Emergence of American Political Issues*, pp. 89–105.

[23]The actual wording of the questions was, "During the past month how much did you use the newspaper for news about political issues and events? not at all, very little, some, a great deal." The same question was asked for television, substituting the word "television" for "newspaper."

[24]See, for example, Jack M. McLeod and Lee B. Becker, "Testing the Validity of Gratification Measures Through Political Effects Analysis," in *The Uses of Mass Commmunications: Current Perspectives on Gratifications Research*, eds. Jay G. Blumler and Elihu Katz (Beverly Hills: Sage, 1974), pp. 137–64, and Jay G. Blumler, "The Role of Theory in Uses and Gratifications Studies," *Communication Research* 6 (January 1979): 9–36.

[25]E. C. Tolman, *Purposive Behavior in Animals and Man* (New York: Appleton-Century, 1932).

[26]For a more detailed rationale for using the concepts of relevance and uncertainty and combining them in this manner see David H. Weaver, "Political Issues and Voter Need for Orientation," in Shaw and McCombs, *The Emergence of American Political Issues*. Although levels of relevance and uncertainty could certainly be considered individual predictors of mass media effects, it is easier to deal with one predictor rather than with two, especially when dividing a group of voters into different subgroups. Also, by combining uncertainty (the perceived existence of a problem) with relevance (the perceived importance of the problem), one is tapping the major components of many of the psychological utilitarian theories of motivation in a single fairly abstract concept that may be applied to a wide variety of settings.

[27]See Weaver, "Political Issues and Voter Need for Orientation," and David H. Weaver, Maxwell E. McCombs, and Charles Spellman, "Watergate and the Media: A Case Study of Agenda-Setting," *American Politics Quarterly* 3 (October 1975): 458–72.

[28]The wording of the political relevance measure throughout the study was, "At this time, how interested are you in the presidential campaign?" and the response categories were "very interested, somewhat interested, and not at all interested." Respondents were considered to have a "high" level of political relevance if they answered "very interested" and a "low" level of political relevance if they answered "somewhat interested" or "not at all interested."

The wording of the political uncertainty measure was "Which *one* of these statements *best describes* how you feel right now about voting for president in November? 1) I definitely will vote for the Democratic candidate for president. 2) I probably will vote for the Democratic candidate for president. 3) I probably will vote for the Republican candidate for president. 4) I definitely will vote for the Republican candidate for president. 5) I don't know which party I will vote for. 6) I probably will not vote for president.

Respondents were considered to have a "high" level of uncertainty about politics if they agreed to statements 2, 3, or 5, and a "low" level of uncertainty about politics if they agreed to statements 1 or 4. Those few respondents saying they probably would not vote were not included in the analysis.

[29]Becker, McCombs, and McLeod, "The Development of Political Cognitions."

[30]See, for example, Shaw and McCombs, *The Emergence of American Political Issues*; McCombs, "Agenda-Setting Research: A Bibliographic Essay"; and Palmgreen and Clarke, "Agenda-Setting with Local and National Issues."

[31]Zucker, "The Variable Nature of News Media Influence."

[32]Ibid.

[33]Lutz Erbring, Edie N. Goldenberg, and Arthur Miller, "Front-Page News and Real-World Cues: A Look at Agenda-Setting by the Media," *American Journal of Political Science* 24 (February 1980): 16–49.

[34]Walter Lippman, *Public Opinion* (New York: The Free Press, 1922), pp. 18 and 203.

[35]The overall results from which these displayed findings were selected consist of correlations from repeated tests of the agenda-setting hypothesis within 12 distinct time frames. In these tests, the voter agendas were compared with previous media agendas of different lengths, ranging from two to eight weeks. In addition, the time lag between the media and voter agendas was systematically varied from zero to eight weeks. This procedure was designed to avoid arbitrary selection of time periods and to control for the effect of time.

seven

MASS COMMUNICATION AND ISSUES IN THE SUMMER CAMPAIGN

During the primary season of the 1976 presidential campaign (January 1 through June 15), our data suggest that both newspapers and television played important roles in focusing voter attention on certain issues, especially unobtrusive issues with which voters were likely to have little, if any, direct experience. The relative emphasis on issues by the newspapers remained fairly constant, and the relative emphasis on issues by television and the voters changed over time to become generally more similar to the newspaper ranking of issues. We also found that some, but not all, issues stressed most heavily by newspapers and television during the primary period were also being stressed by the two front-running candidates (Ronald Reagan and Jimmy Carter).

Turning to the summer period (June 16 through August 21), which issues did newspapers and television stress? Which issues were of concern to the voters in our study as they speculated on who would be nominated in New York City as the Democratic candidate and in Kansas City as the Republican candidate? And, finally, what were the relationships between media rankings of issues and voter rankings of these same issues?

THE SUMMER CAMPAIGN SETTING

After a long series of primary elections that ended in Ohio on June 8, Jimmy Carter, whose early victories had earned him the coveted front-runner label from the media, emerged the favorite of the Democrats.

Ronald Reagan and Gerald Ford were nearly evenly matched for the Republican presidential nomination, even though Ford as the incumbent president would normally be expected to be in the lead. In fact, Reagan won primaries in 11 states, compared with Ford's wins in 10 states. Because of Reagan's strong challenge to Ford, there was speculation throughout the summer about whether Ford would be nominated as his party's candidate during the Republican national convention in Kansas City from August 16 to 19. There was also much speculation about a split in the Republican party between the supporters of Ford and Reagan, which could hurt the Republican candidate's chances in the November election.

About one month after the last primary in Ohio, the Democratic Party met July 12–15 in New York City at its 37th quadrennial convention. In contrast to the 1972 convention there was more of a spirit of unity, and Jimmy Carter led Morris Udall and Jerry Brown by an overwhelming margin on the first ballot count to win the Democratic presidential nomination.[1] On July 15, Carter named Senator Walter Mondale of Minnesota as his choice for vice presidential candidate from among six U.S. senators on his final list. The choice of Mondale, made on the last day of the convention, provided the only major surprise during the four-day meeting.

The Democratic platform emphasized more employment, reform of the welfare system, tax reform, pardons for Vietnam war resisters, cooperation with the Soviet Union, and progress toward arms control. It also advocated busing as a last-resort tool of desegregation, legislation to prohibit oil companies from holding interests in competing forms of energy, national health insurance, and opposition to a Constitutional amendment to prohibit abortion.[2]

A month later, on August 16th, the Republican Party met in Kansas City at its 31st quadrennial convention. In contrast to the Democratic convention's mood of harmony, the skirmishing between Ford and Reagan forces was evident, having begun during the August 8–13 preconvention meetings of the party's Rules and Platform Committees.[3] Ford's supporters won most of the initial fights in these meetings, and Reagan forces lost an important decision when the convention delegates narrowly defeated the Reagan-supported rule change to force President Ford to name his vice-presidential choice at least 10 hours before balloting began on the presidential nomination.

Ford won the presidential nomination on August 19 on the first ballot by a slim margin (1,187 votes to Reagan's 1,070, with 1,130 needed for nomination).[4] He later surprised most delegates and political observers at an afternoon press conference the same day by announcing his choice of conservative Senator Robert Dole of Kansas as his running mate.

The Republican platform called for an end to deficit spending, tax reductions for individuals and small businesses, a lessening of export controls on farmers, federal aid for local law enforcement, a superior national defense capability, and an overhaul of the welfare system. The platform opposed further gun controls, the divestiture of oil companies, compulsory national health insurance, and wage and price controls. It supported ratification of the Equal Rights Amendment and a Constitutional amendment to prohibit abortions.[5]

In light of the emphasis of the Democratic and Republican party platforms on the issues of employment, taxes, foreign affairs/national defense, busing/race relations, energy, and such social problems as gun control, welfare, and health costs, what were the issues presented to the voters by the three commercial television networks and by the newspapers we studied in Indianapolis, Evanston, and Lebanon?

MEDIA EMPHASIS ON ISSUES

Table 7–1 indicates that foreign affairs/defense, social problems, crime, and government credibility were the issues most emphasized by the newspapers we studied during the 1976 summer campaign, essentially the same issues as had been stressed by the newspapers during the primaries. The three television networks also emphasized these issues in their coverage of the summer presidential campaign, but they gave more emphasis relatively to general economic problems than to social problems in the first part of the summer (see Table 7–1).

There were few changes in the newspaper ranking of issues from early to late summer, continuing the pattern of relative constancy found in the primary period. The most pronounced changes in ranking were for the crime and social problems issues, with social problems decreasing in relative coverage to a level more consistent with their relative coverage during the primaries. Crime, on the other hand, was covered more heavily by the newspapers in the second half of the summer than was any other issue, for the first time during the election year (see Table 7–1).

There were generally more changes in the network television ranking of issues from early to late summer than in the newspaper ranking, as illustrated by across-time correlations in Figure 7–1. And, as had been the case in the primary season, many of the major changes in the TV ranking were in the direction of the newspaper ranking. The ranking of the social problems issue shifted from "6" in the first part of the summer to "2" in the second part, making it more similar in relative coverage to the newspaper issue agenda. And the general economy issue received less relative TV emphasis in later summer (a ranking of "5") than in early summer (a ranking of "2"), another change that brought the TV issue agenda closer to the newspaper agenda. Another notable change in the TV ranking of issues was a change in the ranking of the race relations issue from "5" in early summer to "10.5" in later summer. This de-emphasis in coverage of race relations was consistent with the relatively lower newspaper coverage of this issue throughout the primaries and the summer campaign period (see Table 7–1). A look at real world events does not provide an explanation for these shifts in television priorities.

The same-time correlations in Figure 7–1 also confirm that the newspaper and television issue agendas became more similar from June to August (0.71 in June/July as compared with 0.85 in July/August). Although both crosslagged correlations (0.86 and 0.80) exceed the baseline of 0.67, which suggests that the newspaper agenda had an influence on the television agenda and vice versa, it is clear from the across-time correla-

FIGURE 7–1

Crosslagged Correlational Analysis (Spearman's Rhos) Between Newspaper and Television Issue Agendas During the 1976 Summer Campaign

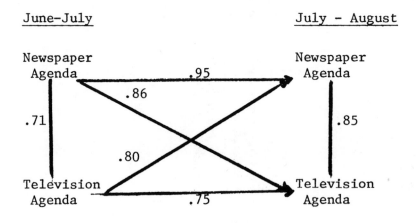

Rozelle–Campbell Baseline = .67

Source: Compiled by authors.

TABLE 7-1

Issues Emphasized by Selected Newspapers and the Three Commercial Television Networks During the 1976 Summer Campaign

Issues	June 16–July 11				July 12–August 21			
	Newspapers		Television		Newspapers		Television	
	Percent	Rank	Percent	Rank	Percent	Rank	Percent	Rank
Foreign affairs, defense	14.1	1	15.5	1	11.4	2	18.6	1
Government credibility	8.8	4	6.9	4	11.1	3	6.7	3.5
Crime	10.0	3	12.6	3	12.8	1	6.7	3.5
Social problems	12.0	2	1.6	6	6.1	4	7.7	2
General economy	4.0	5	13.2	2	4.8	5	6.5	5
Environment and energy	2.6	6	0.8	7	2.9	6	2.8	6

Government spending and size	2.5	7	0.5	9	1.7	7	0.5	8
Race relations and busing	1.5	8	4.6	5	1.3	8	0.2	10.5
Taxes	1.4	9	0.2	10	0.6	9	0.2	10.5
Unemployment	0.3	10.5	0.0	11	0.5	10.5	0.5	8
Inflation	0.3	10.5	0.6	8	0.5	10.5	0.5	8
(N)	(1,839)		(634)		(3,185)		(1,259)	

Notes: The rankings of issues by the three newspapers included in this study (Indianapolis *Star*, Lebanon [N.H.] *Valley News*, and Chicago *Tribune*) were combined into one newspaper ranking because they were positively correlated (Spearman's Rhos = 0.84 to 0.90 for the Chicago *Tribune* and the Indianapolis *Star* and 0.43 to 0.93 for the *Valley News* and the other two newspapers in this study, for the two time periods used in this table).

The rankings of issues by the three TV network evening news broadcasts (ABC, CBS, and NBC) were combined into one television ranking because they were positively correlated (Spearman's Rhos = 0.94 to 0.97 for the two time periods used in this table).

Each newspaper article three column inches or longer and each television network evening news story was coded into one, two, or three of 65 issue categories. More than one category was used for a news story only if it equally emphasized more than one issue. The 31 most common issue categories were condensed into the 11 general issue categories used here. Stories referring to the other 34 issue categories generally comprised less than 10 percent of all stories coded and of all issues mentioned by our panel members in response to open-ended survey questions.

Source: Compiled by authors.

tions that the television agenda did more of the changing across time (0.75) than did the newspaper agenda (0.95).[6] That is, the television issue agenda changed to become more similar to the newspaper agenda, while the newspaper issue agenda remained almost constant. Although these findings do not prove that the newspaper ranking of issues set the issue agenda for the television networks, they do suggest it.

The stability in the newspaper ranking of issues throughout the primaries and the summer period suggests that newspaper editors were not influenced to any great degree by the pronouncements of the candidates or party platforms during the national conventions or by the issues stressed by politicians, pressure groups, pollsters, and political analysts. The editors kept assigning about the same news priority to various issues from January through August of 1976.

Apparently they were following what Richard Hofstetter has called an "incentive model," rather than a "campaign politics" model, of news coverage.[7] In the incentive model, news is what news editors find most advantageous to present, given the constraints of their jobs and audiences. By contrast, the campaign politics model involves reporting that parallels compaign activity levels in substance and in amount of attention to various types of election news. Use of the incentive model suggests that newspaper editors may indeed have a considerable amount of discretion in deciding how much emphasis to give to various issues. The beat system, whereby reporters cover a limited array of social institutions and public figures and agencies on a regular basis, may also explain the constancy of news flow. Reporters assigned to these beats during the 1976 election year were remarkably consistent in the amount of their emphasis on various issues during the first eight months of the campaign.

Given the same set of campaign actors and events and basically the same news sources, it is interesting that the television issue agenda would fluctuate more than the newspaper agenda. Whether this fluctuation was due more to the time and visual constraints of television or more to the increased responsiveness (and dependence) of television reporters to "media events" is not clear from the data we have gathered in this study. But a recent study of television and newspaper coverage of the 1977 annual meeting of the American Association for the Advancement of Science (AAAS) suggests that television reporters are more dependent upon news sources (in this case, the officials of the AAAS) to tell them what is newsworthy than are newspaper reporters, primarily because of time and equipment constraints and lack of specialized knowledge.[8] The same is probably true in covering a political campaign. Among the many sources on whom television news editors might rely, newspapers are the most readily accessible, steady, and reliable suppliers of relevant information.

As was true for the leading candidates in the primaries, not all the issues emphasized in the Democratic and Republican party platforms were also emphasized by newspapers and television, but some were. The Democratic platform, for example, stressed the problems of unemployment and tax reform, but both newspapers and television gave these issues relatively little coverage (see Table 7–1). Similarly, the Republican platform emphasized less government spending, especially deficit spending, but newspapers and television ranked government spending and size fairly low in comparison with other issues.

Overall, though, media priorities were more in tune with the Republican platform than with the Democratic platform. Two of the four issues ranked highest during the summer campaign by newspapers and television (foreign affairs and crime) paralleled the Republican party issues. The Democratic platform concentrated more on various social problems and programs, environmental and energy matters, and race relations—issues that were consistently ranked lower than foreign affairs and crime by the newspapers and television network news shows we studied. The sole exception was the combined social problems issue. It was ranked higher than crime by the newspapers in the early summer and by the TV networks in the late summer (see Table 7–1).

Although both party platforms emphasized economic issues, such as tax reform, export controls, unemployment, and government spending, which were matters of considerable concern to the public, these issues were generally not ranked among the top four by the media we studied. However, general economic problems were ranked second by the television networks in the early summer. It is difficult to argue, therefore, that the media in our study were very responsive to the issue concerns of the two major political parties or to the concerns of the voters during the first eight months of the campaign.

VOTER CONCERN WITH ISSUES

This becomes even more apparent when the issue concerns of the voters in Tables 7–2, 7–3, and 7–4 are examined. As in the primary period, the economic issues (except for taxes) are at, or near, the top of the list of the issues of most concern to the voters in our study. As was true during the primaries, the ranking of the issues considered personally most important (intrapersonal) and the ranking of the issues discussed most often with others (interpersonal) are very similar (Spearman's Rho equalled 0.90 in July and 0.89 in August). Obviously, the voters in our study expressed greatest personal concern about the same issues that they discussed most often with other people during the summer campaign, just as they had done during the primary season.

TABLE 7–2

Intrapersonal Salience During the 1976 Summer Campaign

	July		August	
Issues	*Percent*	*Rank*	*Percent*	*Rank*
Foreign affairs, defense	7.2	5.5	8.5	4.5
Government credibility	7.2	5.5	5.4	7
Crime	8.0	4	8.5	4.5
Social problems	6.5	7.5	7.0	6
General economy	22.6	1	25.5	1
Environment and energy	6.5	7.5	3.9	9
Government spending and size	2.4	9.5	2.3	10
Race relations and busing	2.4	9.5	1.6	11
Taxes	1.0	11	4.7	8
Unemployment	12.0	3	10.9	3
Inflation	19.4	2	16.3	2
(N)	(124)		(129)	

Source: Compiled by authors.

TABLE 7–3

Interpersonal Salience During the 1976 Summer Campaign

	July		August	
Issues	*Percent*	*Rank*	*Percent*	*Rank*
Foreign affairs, defense	7.8	6	11.0	2.5
Government credibility	6.9	7	1.8	9.5
Crime	9.6	4.5	6.4	6
Social problems	9.6	4.5	8.3	5
General economy	10.4	3	21.1	1
Environment and energy	3.5	9	1.8	9.5
Government spending and size	5.2	8	3.7	7
Race relations and busing	2.6	10	0.9	11
Taxes	0.9	11	2.7	8
Unemployment	12.2	2	10.1	4
Inflation	17.4	1	11.0	2.5
(N)	(115)		(109)	

Source: Compiled by authors.

The story was different for appraisals of the community agenda. When asked in the July interview what issues they thought were most important to the other voters in their communities, our panelists ranked taxes considerably higher and the state of the general economy considerably lower than was true for their personal and interpersonal agendas (see Table 7–4). Specific economic issues such as taxes, unemployment, and inflation more clearly dominated the community agenda than the personal or interpersonal agendas. Foreign affairs and defense were also ranked lower for "the voters around here" than for the voters themselves.

As had been true in February, the ranking of issues perceived to be important to other voters in the community in July deviated considerably from the ranking of issues of most personal interest (Spearman's Rho = 0.09) and the ranking of issues discussed most often (Rho = 0.30). But in August, the perceived community voter agenda became more similar to the other two issue agendas (Rho = 0.63 with the intrapersonal agenda and 0.50 with the interpersonal). The most pronounced shift in the perceived community agenda was for the general economy issue, which rose from a ranking of "10" in July to a ranking of "3" in August, making it more similar in relative ranking to its ranking in the intrapersonal and interpersonal issue agendas.

TABLE 7–4

Perceived Community Salience During the 1976 Summer Campaign

Issues	July Percent	Rank	August Percent	Rank
Foreign affairs, defense	0.0	10	2.1	11
Government credibility	3.4	6	7.3	6.5
Crime	4.2	5	6.5	8
Social problems	5.8	4	11.4	2
General economy	0.0	10	9.8	3
Environment and energy	1.7	7.5	4.1	9
Government spending and size	0.0	10	2.4	10
Race relations and busing	1.7	7.5	7.3	6.5
Taxes	26.9	2	8.9	4
Unemployment	13.4	3	8.1	5
Inflation	39.5	1	26.0	1
(N)	(119)		(123)	

Source: Compiled by authors.

A visual inspection of the rankings of Tables 7–2, 7–3, 7–4 and the correlations in Figure 7–2 suggest that the perceived community issue agenda shifted to become more similar to the intra- and interpersonal issue agendas, rather than vice versa, providing no support for the hypothesis that the perceived community agenda played a major role in shaping the intrapersonal and interpersonal agendas. Explanations for this shift are not readily apparent. One plausible interpretation, for which the core panel data lend some support, is the fact that political discussions increased as the campaign progressed. This made it easier to develop a communitywide consensus about issue priorities.

But regardless of the kind of voter agenda being considered, the issue rankings in Tables 7–1, 7–2, 7–3, and 7–4 clearly indicate that the voters in our study were relatively less concerned about foreign affairs and defense than were newspapers and television during the summer campaign and relatively more concerned about the economic issues than were newspapers and television. And this mismatch of emphasis on issues by the media and the voters is reflected in the generally low, and even negative, correlations in Figures 7–2 and 7–3 between the media agendas and the voter agendas.

MEDIA EMPHASIS ON ISSUES AND VOTER CONCERN WITH ISSUES

All Voters

As has been mentioned the rankings of issues in Tables 7–1, 7–2, 7–3, and 7–4 indicate that the media in our study placed considerably more emphasis on foreign affairs and defense than did the voters. Panelists were most concerned about the economic issues, especially the general economy, inflation, and unemployment. As Figures 7–2 and 7–3 show, the combined TV network issue agenda was more similar to the intra- and interpersonal voter issue agendas in both July and August than was the combined newspaper agenda. Neither media agenda was at all similar to the perceived community agenda.

Media agendas and voter agendas tended to become slightly more similar to each other from July to August. The newspaper agenda changed least, followed by the TV agenda. The perceived community agenda changed most over time. Two of the three sets of crosslagged correlations in Figure 7–2 indicate a stronger association over time between the newspaper agenda and the voter agendas than vice versa, supporting the hypothesis that the newspaper agenda has more influence on the inter-

FIGURE 7–2

**Crosslagged Correlational Analysis (Spearman's Rhos)
Between Newspaper Issue Agendas and Voter Issue Agendas
During the 1976 Summer Campaign**

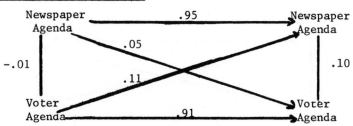

June – July   July – August

(Intrapersonal Voter Agendas)

Rozelle-Campbell Baseline = .04

(Interpersonal Voter Agendas)

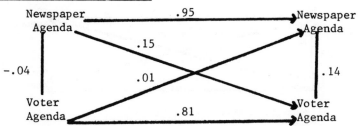

Rozelle-Campbell Baseline = .04

(Perceived Community Voter Agendas)

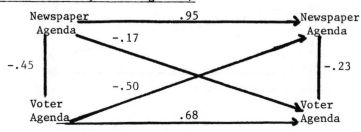

Rozelle-Campbell Baseline = −.28

Source: Compiled by authors.

FIGURE 7–3

**Crosslagged Correlational Analysis (Spearman's Rhos)
Between Television Issue Agendas and Voter Issue Agendas
During the 1976 Summer Campaign**

June - July   July - August

(Intrapersonal Voter Agendas)

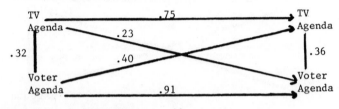

Rozelle–Campbell Baseline = .28

(Interpersonal Voter Agendas)

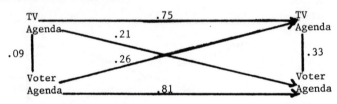

Rozelle–Campbell Baseline = .16

(Perceived Community Voter Agendas)

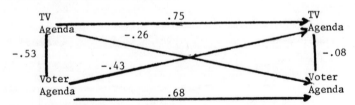

Rozelle–Campbell Baseline = −.22

Source: Compiled by authors.

personal and perceived community voter agendas than the other way round.

For television, the case is reversed. Two of the three sets of cross-lagged correlations in Figure 7–3 indicate a stronger association over time between the voter agendas and the television agenda, rather than vice versa. This lends some support to the hypothesis that the television networks were more influenced by voter concern over issues than vice versa during this time period. This hypothesis is also supported by the fact that the TV issue agenda changed more from July to August than did intra- and interpersonal voter agendas.

A plausible explanation is the fact that television producers are very conscious of audience size, thanks to periodic ratings, and carefully cater to the public to keep people tuned in. Further, the New York *Times* and CBS joined forces for a series of national polls, and NBC joined with a consortium of newspapers in conducting polls on issues and candidate images. These poll results may have had more impact on TV's limited coverage of issues than on the newspapers' more detailed treatment of issues. Undoubtedly, there are influences on voters' issue agendas other than mass media (such as personal values, experiences, acquaintances, and so on), and there are other influences on media agendas besides voter concerns (such as the values of reporters and editors, organizational constraints, the issues being emphasized by various news sources, and so on). But regardless of all these other influences, our data suggest that during the primary elections and the summer campaign the reciprocal influences of media on voters and voters on media were strong but varied for newspapers and television.

During the primaries, it was not clear whether the television agenda might be having more influence on the voter agenda or vice versa, but during the summer campaign it appeared that intrapersonal and interpersonal voter agendas might be having more influence on the television agenda than vice versa. Nevertheless, the TV networks continued to de-emphasize the economic issues of unemployment and inflation throughout the summer, even though the voters in our study ranked them quite high on their combined agenda. Technical constraints of the medium provide an explanation. Inflation and unemployment do not make for pictorially exciting stories with fresh daily footage. They are difficult to capsulize into one- and two-minute episodes.

In both the primary and summer campaigns, the overall voter and media agendas generally became more similar from the beginning of each campaign until the end, with both television and voter agendas moving generally in the direction of the more stable newspaper agenda. These findings suggest that even though the TV agenda more closely matched overall intrapersonal and interpersonal voter agendas than did the newspaper agenda, the newspaper agenda may have provided the baseline of issues for both television and the voters in our study.

Newspaper Readers and Television Viewers

The findings reported so far regarding issues in the summer campaign are, of course, based on all voters in our study, regardless of their media exposure habits. But if newspapers and television are having a substantial impact on voters' thinking in a presidential campaign, we would expect to find that more-regular users of newspapers would reflect the newspapers' agendas more closely than less regular users. The same should hold true for television.

As mentioned in Chapter 6, the voters in this study were divided into three groups—high newspaper/low television, low newspaper/high television, and high newspaper/high television— on the basis of their answers to questions about how much they used newspapers and television for news of political issues and events.[9] When the issue agendas of these three media use groups were compared with the issue agendas for all voters combined, the correlations (Spearman's Rhos) ranged from 0.71 to 0.88 for the intrapersonal agendas in July and August, from 0.69 to 0.94 for the interpersonal agendas, and from 0.62 to 0.95 for the perceived community agendas. These strong correlations indicate that the overall voter issue agendas displayed in Tables 7–2, 7–3, and 7–4 are fairly accurate summaries of the issue agendas of the three media use groups. Different patterns of media exposure did not substantially alter which issues were perceived as important by the voters in our study.

When the issue agendas of the three media use groups are compared with the newspaper and television agendas during the summer campaign period, some of the same patterns illustrated in Figures 7–2 and 7–3 for all voters are evident. The voter issue agendas are generally more similar to the television agendas than to the newspaper agendas, except for the perceived community voter agenda, which is equally dissimilar to both media agendas, and the correlation between voter and media agendas are generally stonger in the latter part of the summer than in the earlier part. This probably reflects greater exposure because of the heating up of the campaign.

The stongest correlations (Rhos of 0.45 and 0.55) occurred between the TV issue agenda in July/August and the high TV/low newspaper voter group intrapersonal and interpersonal agendas in August. As we learned from the core panel, this was a period of ample television watching because of the Democratic convention in mid-July and the Republican convention in mid-August. As we would expect to find, the high TV/low newspaper voters' agendas generally were more similar to the TV issue agendas than to the newspaper agendas. However, the reverse was not true. The high newspaper/low TV voters' agendas were not more similar to the newspaper agendas than to the television agendas. Apparently, heavy newspaper users were picking up their issue concerns from sources other than newspaper and television, such as personal experience, friends, acquaintances at work, and other media. Again, core panel data shed light on this phenomenon. By and large, heavy newspaper users ranked high in education and experience and felt competent to use their stored knowledge to make their own evaluations.

Those voters in our study who used both newspapers and television a great deal for political information had issue agendas during the summer campaign that were generally more similar to the combined television agendas than to the combined newspaper agendas. Heavy television exposure because of the conventions, combined with greater network sensitivity to voter issue concerns than was true of newspapers, is a possible explanation. As Table 5–2 shows, August was the month in which heavy newspaper reading lagged furthest behind heavy television watching during the election year. In the case of the intrapersonal issue agendas, the crosslagged correlations suggest, as was true for all voters combined, that the TV agenda was more responsive to the voter agenda (Rho = 0.27) than vice versa (Rho = 0.07). For the other two voter agendas (interpersonal and perceived community), the crosslagged correlations were nearly equal in strength, suggesting a possible reciprocal influence process between TV agendas and voter agendas.

In short, differing amounts of newspaper and television use for political information during the summer campaign had some influence on which issues were considered most important and which issues were discussed most often, but this influence was not as pronounced as would be expected if newspapers and television were the primary agenda-setters in the summer campaign. Those voters who relied mainly on television for political information during the summer tended to be concerned about, and to discuss, the same issues emphasized by television, but those voters who relied mainly on newspapers or on both newspapers and TV had aggregate issue agendas that were generally different from the media agendas.

Voters' Need for Orientation

As was true in the data analysis for the primary elections, the voters in this study of the summer campaign were also divided into three groups based on their level of political need for orientation—low, moderate, or high.[10] This was done because several recent studies of mass media uses and effects have suggested that a person's motives for using mass media may be just as important, if not more so, than his or her level of media exposure in predicting media effects.[11]

When the aggregate issue agendas of these three need-for-orientation groups were compared with the overall voter issue agendas in Tables 7–2, 7–3, and 7–4, fairly strong similarities were found for the intrapersonal agendas (Rhos ranged from 0.67 to 0.93) and for the interpersonal agendas (Rhos ranged from 0.58 to 0.95), but considerably less similarity was found for the perceived community agendas (Rhos ranged from 0.07 to 0.98). For the intra- and interpersonal agendas, these fairly strong correlations suggest that level of need for orientation did not have a major impact on which issues were of most personal concern or were discussed most often during the summer campaign. But the weak correlation of 0.07 for the perceived community agenda suggests that differing levels of need for orientation did have a major impact on which issues were perceived to be important to others in the community. Voters with high needs for orientation were most apt to talk with others during this period. In the process, they would form perceptions about community agendas that differed from those formed by people with less direct exposure to the community.

When the various need-for-orientation group agendas were compared with the newspaper and television agendas during June, July, and August, some of the same patterns were found as were illustrated in Figures 7–2 and 7–3 for all voters combined. Voter agendas tended to be more similar to the TV agendas than to the newspaper agendas, especially for voters with a high need for orientation. Voter and media agendas also tended to be more similar later in the summer.

Correspondence between voter and media agendas varied somewhat among groups. Voters with a low level of need for orientation generally showed greatest similarity to the media in their personal concerns. They also showed the greatest affinity in their intrapersonal agendas to newspaper agendas but not to television agendas. Correspondence between televison and intrapersonal agendas was similar for low and high need-for-orientation groups. The discussion agendas of voters with a high level of need for orientation resembled media issue agendas more than was true for voters with a low or moderate need for orientation.

In short, as in the primary season of the campaign, a voter's level of need for orientation did have some impact on which issues were perceived to be most important and which were discussed most often by the voters in our study during the summer campaign. These results offer some support for the hypothesis that a person's motives for using mass media are important in studying media effects.

Obtrusive and Unobtrusive Issues

Four issues, economic in nature, were clearly distinguished as unique among the major issues of the 1976 primary season. During the spring of that year, the mass media seemed to contribute only minimally to the public salience of such obtrusive topics as unemployment, inflation, taxation, and the economy in general. The unobtrusive issues, on the other hand, seemed to become more salient on the public agenda as a consequence of the emphasis and prominence given them by newspapers and television.

The correlations between the media and public agendas during the primary season suggest that the mass media were instrumental in bringing unobtrusive issues before the public and in telling their audiences which of these subjects and topics were most important. But the more obtrusive issues, those topics with which individuals have firsthand experience, seemed to reach high public salience as a consequence of personal experience. Voters seemed to hold no need to be told by newspapers and television that such issues were important.

The picture changed somewhat by the summer of 1976, however. Tables 7–5 and 7–6 show that, as in the primary period, few agenda-setting effects were evident when all 11 campaign issues were considered together. In fact, all but a single correlation in each table was negative in direction and all correlations were weak.

But what happened in the summer to the salience of those issues that were unobtrusive in the spring? Tables 7–7 and 7–8 show that in New Hampshire and in Illinois, but not in Indiana, the general agenda-setting pattern was preserved, especially for newspapers. That is, the correlations between the media agendas and voter agendas for unobtrusive issues indicate that an agenda-setting process is plausible in most cases. These

TABLE 7–5

Highest Obtained Correlations (Spearman's Rhos) Between the Media and Intrapersonal Voter Issue Agendas in August

Media	New Hampshire	Indiana	Illinois
Newspapers	0.27	−0.21	−0.01
Television	−0.23	−0.26	−0.10

Note: These are the highest obtained correlations among a multitude of tests using various time frames.

Source: Compiled by authors.

TABLE 7–6

Highest Obtained Correlations (Spearman's Rhos) Between the Media and Interpersonal Voter Issue Agendas in August

Media	New Hampshire	Indiana	Illinois
Newspapers	0.24	−0.30	−0.04
Television	−0.14	−0.13	−0.04

Source: Compiled by authors.

relationships, however, are somewhat weaker than the ones obtained in the spring. These findings suggest that in New Hampshire and Illinois there was a "fusion" effect in regard to issue obtrusiveness. As time went on and as the issues of the campaign became more familiar and more salient to the public, unobtrusive issues began to be more obtrusive. In other words, throughout the spring the mass media built up unobtrusive issues to a level of importance approaching that created by direct contact with obtrusive issues. In Indiana, it appears, this process was quicker. By summer, mass media emphasis seemed to have little or no impact on issue saliences of Indianapolis voters.

The explanation for the lower correlations in Indiana appears to lie with the Indiana voters rather than with the Indianapolis *Star*. The issue agenda of the *Star* was very similar to the agendas of the Chicago *Tribune* and the Lebanon *Valley News* in the summer period (average Rho = 0.84), but the Indianapolis voters in our study were more concerned about crime, government credibility, and government spending than were the other voters. In addition, the Indianapolis voters were less concerned about social problems, the environment/energy, and foreign affairs than were the other voters in our study. This difference in concerns among the Indianapolis voters seems to reflect the traditionally conservative political climate in Indiana rather than a difference in emphasis on issues by the *Star* and the three television network news programs. Whatever the cause, it is clear from the agenda correlations and from the Indiana voters' agenda of issues that during the summer season Indiana voters' concerns and topics of discussion differed from those of the other voters in our study.

Our findings suggest that as the campaign year rolls on and as the issues given prominence in the mass media gain salience among voters, a ceiling of salience is approached. It appears that such a ceiling, or level of salience saturation, is reached earlier with the obtrusive issues. And as the election date draws near, repeated emphasis on some issues by news-

TABLE 7-7

A Sample of Obtained Correlations Between the Media and Intrapersonal Voter Issue Agendas, Controlling for Issue Obtrusiveness

Media	New Hampshire			Indiana			Illinois		
	All Issues	Unobtrusive	Obtrusive	All Issues	Unobtrusive	Obtrusive	All Issues	Unobtrusive	Obtrusive
Newspapers	0.17	0.92	−0.80	−0.23	0.08	0.20	−0.01	0.62	0.95
Television	−0.23	0.40	0.21	−0.38	0.27	0.20	−0.23	0.43	0.32

Source: Compiled by authors.

TABLE 7–8

A Sample of Obtained Correlations Between the Media and Interpersonal Voter Issue Agendas, Controlling for Issue Obtrusiveness

Media	New Hampshire			Indiana			Illinois		
	All Issues	Unobtrusive	Obtrusive	All Issues	Unobtrusive	Obtrusive	All Issues	Unobtrusive	Obtrusive
Newspapers	0.18	0.76	−0.32	−0.33	−0.37	−0.39	−0.07	0.86	0.20
Television	−0.14	0.54	0.78	−0.33	−0.04	0.32	−0.19	0.70	0.32

Source: Compiled by authors.

papers and television seems to raise the public salience of unobtrusive issues to a point near salience saturation. Beyond this point, the mass media's role of agenda-setting becomes minimal or nonexistent.

Our summer data show this process occurring. In Indiana, newspapers and television have completed their election year agenda-setting role by August, whereas, in the other two sites, evidence of such impact was still present in August, although the magnitude of the relationship between the media and public agendas was on the decline.

SUMMING UP

The major conclusions from this analysis of mass communication and issues during the 1976 summer campaign follow.

Both newspapers and television continued to emphasize many of the same issues stressed during the 1976 primary season, with more changes in the TV ranking of issues than in the newspaper ranking from early to late summer. Many of the major changes in the TV issue agenda were in the direction of the more stable newspaper ranking of issues. Although this finding does not prove that newspapers were setting the issue agenda for television networks, it does suggest that newspaper editors were not being influenced to any noticeable degree by the more variable TV agenda or by other influences such as actual audience concerns. In fact, the voters in our study continued to be much more concerned about the economic issues than were the newspapers we studied.

As was true for the leading candidates in the primary elections, not all of the issues emphasized in the Democratic and Republican party platforms were also emphasized by newspapers and television, but some were. Two of the four issues ranked highest by both newspapers and TV during the summer campaign (foreign affairs and crime) seemed to be emphasized more strongly in the Republican party platform than in the Democratic platform. Although both party platforms emphasized economic issues such as tax reform, export controls, unemployment, and government spending, these issues were generally not ranked among the top four by the media we studied. Neither newspapers nor the TV networks apparently were particularly sensitive to the issue concerns of the two major political parties or to the concerns of the voters in the three communities we studied.[12]

The similarities between the intrapersonal and interpersonal voter issue agendas suggested that the voters in our study were personally concerned about the same issues that they discussed with others during the summer campaign, as was true during the primary season. But the ranking of issues perceived to be important to other voters in the community deviated considerably from the rankings of issues considered personally most important and discussed most often with others in early summer. By late summer, the perceived community agenda shifted to become more similar to the intra- and interpersonal voter agendas. There is thus no support for the hypothesis that the perceived community agenda was a major force in shaping the intrapersonal and interpersonal agendas. The shift does coincide with increased discussions about the election that might well have led to greater concensus.

The combined intra- and interpersonal voter agendas tended to be more similar to the television network issue agenda than to the combined newspaper agenda during the summer campaign, as was the case during the primary elections. But the perceived community issue agenda was quite dissimilar to both media agendas, suggesting again that appraisals of the general climate of opinion are more independent of media emphasis than are appraisals of voters' own concerns. Core panel data indicate that projections of community views are made on the basis of past experience with these views and on stereotypic projections of the reactions of average people in the community. They are not generally projections of the respondent's own views onto the community. In fact, respondents frequently set themselves verbally apart from the rest of the community: "I feel this way, but most people around here feel differently." When increased discussion brings more community interaction and when increased attention by members of the community to the media at election time brings about more shared experiences, personal agendas and perceived community agendas approximate each other more closely.

In both the primary elections and the summer campaign, the voter and media issue agendas generally became more similar from the beginning of each period until the end, with both TV and voter agendas moving generally in the direction of the more stable newspaper agenda. These findings indicate that even though the TV agenda more closely matched the voter agendas than did the newspaper agenda, newspapers may have been providing the baseline of issues for both the TV networks and the voters in our study.

Differing amounts of newspaper and television use for political information during the summer campaign had some influence on which issues were considered most personally important and which were discussed most often. But this influence was not as pronounced as might have been expected if newspapers and TV were the primary issue agenda-setters during the summer campaign. Those voters who relied mainly on TV for political information tended to be concerned about, and to discuss, the same issues emphasized by the TV networks. The generally more knowledgeable and independent voters who relied mainly on newspapers or on both newspapers and TV had aggregate issue agendas that were not particularly similar to the media agendas. From these findings one may conclude that other sources of influence besides newspapers and TV network news were helping to shape voter issue concerns during the summer campaign, such as personal experiences, conversations with others, and other media (magazines, radio, newsletters, and so on).

Differing levels of voter need for orientation (political interest and uncertainty) did have some impact on which issues were perceived to be most important and which were discussed most often by the voters in our study during the summer campaign. One set of findings was in the direction predicted by previous studies: The discussion agendas of voters with a high level of need for orientation were most similar to the media agendas. But another set of findings was opposite to what would be expected. The personal concern issue agendas of voters with a low level of need for orientation were most similar to media agendas. These findings support the view that those voters in our study who were highly interested and highly uncertain about which party to support were more likely to discuss the same issues emphasized by newspapers and television. Those who were not very interested but who were fairly sure about which party to support were more likely to consider personally most important the issues emphasized by the media, perhaps because they had not discussed these issues with others or thought much about them. Whatever the case, these findings offer some support for considering motives as well as media exposure patterns in studying media effects.

The nature of the issues under study seemed to make less difference during the summer season than during the primary campaign. The unobtrusive issues—those with which voters had minimal direct experience—appeared to become more obtrusive or more independent of media emphasis. Whatever the case, newspaper and television emphasis on these issues was not as strongly associated with voter concern and discussion of them as was true in the primary period of the campaign.

Taken together, the findings suggest less support for an agenda-setting function of newspapers and television during the summer campaign than had been the case during the primary elections of 1976. Not only are the correlations between the media agendas and the voter agendas noticeably lower in the summer campaign than during the primaries, but the directions of influence as measured by the crosslagged correlations and the changes in issue rankings over time are less clear. These trends may well reflect the fact that campaigns are periods of stepped-up political learning from the media. But once the initial set of lessons has been absorbed, people feel more competent to draw their own conclusions about the salience of issues. Hence the potency of media suggestions declines as the campaign moves on.

NOTES

[1]Mary E. Clifford, Raymond Hill, and Stephen Orlofsky, *1976 News Dictionary* (New York: Facts on File, 1977), p. 263.

[2]Ibid., p. 264.

[3]Ibid., p. 265.

[4]Ibid.

[5]Ibid., p. 267.

[6]The underlying assumption behind crosslagged correlation is that a cause should be more strongly correlated with its subsequent effect than vice versa. By comparing the two crosslagged correlations, it is possible to see if one measure (X) is more closely associated with another (Y) over time, whether the reverse is true (Y is more closely associated with X), or whether the two measures are equally correlated with each other over time. The Rozelle-Campbell Baseline estimates what the crosslagged correlations would be if there were no causal relationship between the two measures being considered. The general procedure for calculating the baseline is to average the synchronous (same-time) correlations between the measures at each of the two points in time and to average the autocorrelations (over-time correlations) between the same measure over time. This provides a baseline estimate of the diagonal correlation that one should expect to observe if there were no causal relationship between one variable at Time 1 and changes in the other between Time 1 and Time 2. For a more detailed discussion of crosslagged correlation and the Rozell-Campbell Baseline, see R. M. Rozelle and D. T. Campbell, "More Plausible Rival Hypotheses in the Cross-Lagged Panel Correlation Technique," *Psychological Bulletin* 71 (1969): 74–80, and D. R. Heise, "Causal Inference from Panel Data," in *Sociological Methodology 1970*, ed. E. F. Borgatta (San Francisco: Jossey-Bass, 1970), pp. 3–27.

[7]C. Richard Hofstetter, *Bias in the News: Network Television News Coverage of the 1972 Election Campaign* (Columbus: Ohio State University Press, 1976), pp. 39–40.

[8]Sharon Dunwoody, "Science Journalists: A Study of Factors Affecting the Selection of News at a Scientific Meeting," Ph.D. dissertation, Indiana University, December 1978.

[9]See Chapter 6, footnote 23, for the actual wording of the questions asked to measure newspaper and television use for political information.

[10]See Chapter 6, footnote 28, for the actual wording of the questions used to measure political relevance and political uncertainty. See the section, "Voters' Need for Orientation," in Chapter 6 for a discussion of how these measures were combined.

[11]See, for example, Jack M. McLeod and Lee B. Becker, "Testing the Validity of Gratification Measures Through Political Effects Analysis," in *The Uses of Mass Communications: Current Perspectives on Gratifications Research*, eds. Jay G. Blumler and Elihu Katz (Beverly Hills: Sage, 1974), and Jay G. Blumler, "The Role of Theory in Uses and Gratifications Studies," *Communication Research* 6 (January 1979): 9–36.

[12]Considering the nature of party platforms, this is not surprising. They represent a mixture and compromise of major current concerns with an accommodation to the special

interests of nearly every sizable group that might be wooed into the camp of the party. Moreover, they are generally regarded as symbolic rather than working documents, designed to express the party's concerns for its constituents rather than its blueprint for action. For a view that this reputation may be undeserved see Gerald M. Pomper, *Elections in America: Control and Influence in Democratic Politics* (New York: Dodd, Mead, 1968), pp. 158–59, 185–89. If the media look to the platforms as cues for issues that ought to be discussed—and we have no evidence that they do—one would expect that they would pick and choose with the choice dictated by their own appraisals of the salience of various issues and their suitability for media presentations. The rather eclectic pattern of media and platform correspondence supports the belief that media do not pattern their priorities on those of party platforms.

eight

MASS COMMUNICATION
AND ISSUES IN THE
FALL CAMPAIGN

Taken together, the findings from the summer campaign provide less support for an agenda-setting function of newspapers and television than was true during the primaries. Is the same true for the fall campaign? Which issues were being stressed by newspapers and television as the 1976 presidential campaign drew to a close? Which issues were of concern to the voters in our study as they watched the presidential and vice-presidential televised debates and speculated on who would win the election on November 2? And what was the strength of the relationships between media agendas and voter agendas during this fall campaign period from August 22 through November 2?

THE FALL CAMPAIGN SETTING

After the Republican national convention ended on August 19, the fall campaign (defined as August 22 through the November 2 election day) began rather slowly. The pace picked up after September 1, however, when representatives of Gerald Ford and Jimmy Carter reached agreement on the basic format for three nationally televised debates between the candidates. This agreement was announced by the League of Women Voters after the Federal Election Commission had ruled on August 30 that League financing of the debates would not constitute a violation of the federal ban on private campaign contributions in general elections financed by public subsidy.[1]

Before the first presidential debate on September 23, however, an interview with Carter, published in the November issue of *Playboy* magazine and made public September 20, stirred considerable controversy about Carter's personal fitness for office. In this interview, Carter was quoted as saying that he had "looked on a lot of women with lust" and had "committed adultery in my heart many times," but that "God forgives me for it."[2] After the interview was made public, adverse reaction to it began to spread, particularly through the religious community. The Reverend W. A. Criswell, pastor of the nation's largest Baptist church, the First Baptist Church of Dallas, said, "I am highly offended by this. I think he's mixed up in his moral values, and I think the entire church membership will feel the same way."[3] Carter's own pastor, Bruce Edwards, said, "I do wish he would have used different words."[4]

The first presidential debate, which focused on domestic issues, took place at the Walnut Street Theater in Philadelphia the evening of September 23. As Table 8–1 indicates, there were many references to economic matters, with taxes and government spending getting the most mentions. This first televised debate between presidential candidates involving an incumbent president was marred by a 27-minute loss of sound with only 9 minutes left in the 90-minute debate. During this time, the candidates remained standing behind lecterns before an estimated audience of some 90 million.[5]

Two days before the second debate, Agriculture Secretary Earl L. Butz resigned from President Ford's cabinet, acknowledging that he had been guilty of "gross indiscretion" in a remark about blacks made after the Republican convention to John Dean III, who had been covering the convention for *Rolling Stone* magazine, and to singer Pat Boone.[6] After submitting his resignation to Ford, Butz appeared in the White House press room on October 4 and said that he was resigning "to remove even the appearance of racism as an issue in the Ford campaign. President Ford is a decent man with high moral values who insists that every American be treated equally and with dignity. Every member of his Administration must and does subscribe to the same values."[7]

Butz' concern over racism becoming an issue in the campaign may have been unnecessary, if the debates are a barometer for public concerns. Table 8–1 indicates that racism was not mentioned in the second debate, which focused on foreign affairs and took place on October 6 in the Palace of Fine Arts in San Francisco. Even in the third debate, which had an open format and took place on October 22 at the College of William and Mary in Williamsburg, Virginia, racial issues were not emphasized. Nor were they emphasized during the fall campaign by the newspapers, television network news shows, or the voters in our study, as later analyses will show (see Tables 8–1, 8–2, 8–3, 8–4, and 8–5). This may reflect an emerging

TABLE 8–1

Issues Covered in the Presidential Debates (in percentages)

Issues	Debate One	Debate Two	Debate Three	Total	Carter	Ford
Unemployment	8.9	2.4	12.3	7.0	8.6	5.7
Inflation	4.4	0.0	6.2	3.0	3.6	2.5
Taxes	22.2	0.0	2.5	7.4	6.5	8.2
State of the economy	6.7	0.8	7.4	4.4	5.0	3.8
Crime	2.2	0.0	1.2	1.0	0.7	1.3
Racial issues and busing	0.0	0.0	3.7	1.0	0.7	1.3
Social problems	8.9	0.8	7.4	5.0	6.5	3.8
Environment and energy	6.7	1.6	6.2	4.4	6.5	2.5
Credibility of government and leaders	8.9	9.5	18.5	11.8	13.7	10.1
Government spending and size	22.2	3.2	2.5	8.7	6.5	10.8
Foreign affairs and defense	0.0	77.0	12.3	36.0	30.2	41.1
Other	8.9	4.8	19.8	10.1	11.5	8.9
(N)	(90)	(126)	(81)	(297)	(139)	(158)

Note: Each question, answer, rebuttal comment, and closing statement was coded according to issues mentioned. Any given question, answer, rebuttal, or closing statement could be coded into up to three issue categories. Entries tabled here are the percentages of coded items for each of the issue categories.

Some columns do not add to exactly 100.0 percent due to rounding errors.

Source: Compiled by authors.

political trend to steer clear of arousing racial animosities in political campaigns for fear that racial polarization hurts all candidates.

In the first debate, Carter and Ford expressed opposing views on economic policy, with Carter charging that the federal tax structure was "a disgrace" and "a welfare program for the rich."[8] Ford said that he believed in "tax equity for the middle-income taxpayers, increasing the exemption," and that Carter had "indicated publicly in an interview that he would increase the taxes for roughly half of the taxpayers."[9] Carter also pledged to reorganize the executive branch of the government, if elected, in such a way as to shift administrative jobs into the delivery of services. Ford countered that in the four years of Carter's administration the state of Georgia's expenditures had gone up more than 50 percent, government employment had gone up more than 25 percent, and the state's bonded indebtedness had gone up more than 20 percent.

The second debate featured sharp attacks by Carter on Ford's foreign policy and a strong defense by Ford of his record. Table 8–1 indicates that by far the majority of statements focused on the issue of foreign affairs and national defense, with some of the questions and answers dealing with the credibility of the government. Carter charged that the United States was not strong and not respected any more, and that it had no leadership in foreign affairs. Ford replied that Carter had advocated defense budget cuts of $15 billion, from $8 billion to $9 billion, and from $5 billion to $7 billion, and that there was "no way you can be strong militarily and have those kinds of reductions."[10] But Ford hurt his image as a foreign policy expert by the unfortunate remark that Eastern Europe was currently free from Soviet domination.[11]

Between the second and third presidential debates, Senators Robert Dole and Walter Mondale met in a debate, televised nationally from the Alley Theater in Houston, on October 15. Economic issues dominated this debate. Dole laced his responses with attacks on Jimmy Carter and the Democratic Party. Mondale said that new leadership and initiatives in social programs were needed. The candidates' contrasting styles came into focus near the end of the debate, when Dole ridiculed Carter as having "three positions on everything—that's why they're having three TV debates." Mondale responded in a composed vein that Carter stood for jobs, "a government that fights inflation," tax reforms, health programs, housing programs, senior citizens' programs, and "a foreign policy that operates in the public and on the basis of the belief of the American people."[12]

In the third presidential debate, Carter and Ford ranged over a fairly wide variety of topics, with government credibility, foreign affairs/defense, and unemployment leading the list of issues discussed (see Table 8–1). Although the tone of this last debate was rather subdued, with no flamboyant statements by the candidates, the questioning by the panel of prominent journalists was harsh and probing. Ford was asked about his role in blocking a House of Representatives probe of Watergate in 1972 and about his "rotten" economic and "hopeless" environmental records. Carter was asked why the electorate seemed turned off, how he had lost his large lead in the public opinion polls, and whether he would bring people with the "necessary background" into a Carter administration. The questioning also focused on the problems of the cities, blacks and other minorities, gun control, government spending, and crime.

Table 8–1 shows that, taken together, the three presidential debates focused most heavily on foreign affairs/defense and the combined economic issues (unemployment, taxes, inflation, and the general state of the economy). Government credibility was the third most frequently addressed subject in the presidential debates. But what issues were being emphasized by the three commercial television networks and the newspapers we studied during the fall campaign?

MEDIA EMPHASIS ON ISSUES

Table 8–2 indicates that foreign affairs/defense, government credibility, and social problems were the issues most emphasized by the newspapers in our study during the 1976 fall campaign. These were largely the same issues emphasized during the primaries and the summer campaign. The three television networks also stressed foreign affairs and government credibility, but they covered the issue of crime considerably more and social problems considerably less than did the newspapers.

Neither the newspapers nor the TV networks put especially heavy emphasis on the economic issues, however, in spite of the fact that these issues were stressed in the presidential debates and were of major concern to the voters in our study. Taxes, unemployment, and inflation ranked near or at the bottom of the newspaper and television issue agendas throughout the fall (see Table 8–2).

For the first time during the election year, the combined television issue agenda changed less than the combined newspaper agenda, as illustrated by the across-time correlations in Figure 8–1. The newspaper and television issue agendas became more similar to each other from August to November, as illustrated by the same-time correlations in Figure 8–1. In general, though, there were very few changes in either the newspaper or television combined issue agendas during the fall campaign. It seemed that, after many months of the campaign, the media had finally settled on the array of issues that ought to be the focus of attention during the closing weeks of the presidential contest. The television agenda was

TABLE 8-2

Issues Emphasized by Selected Newspapers and the Three Commercial Television Networks During the 1976 Fall Campaign

Issues	August 22–September 14 Newspapers Per-cent	Rank	Television Per-cent	Rank	September 15–October 25 Newspapers Per-cent	Rank	Television Per-cent	Rank	October 26–November 2 Newspapers Per-cent	Rank	Television Per-cent	Rank
Foreign affairs, defense	10.6	1.5	29.6	1	10.9	1	21.1	1	10.4	1	16.1	1
Government credibility	10.6	1.5	14.0	2	9.2	2	10.2	3	7.8	2	7.4	3
Crime	6.7	4	11.0	3	6.9	4	12.5	2	3.1	5	13.8	2
Social problems	10.3	3	6.5	5	7.4	3	4.4	5	6.5	3	1.2	5
General economy	5.7	5	6.8	4	5.4	5	7.9	4	5.2	4	5.8	4
Environment and energy	4.7	6	2.0	7	2.0	6	2.5	6	1.1	6.5	0.9	6
Government spending and size	2.0	7	0.2	11	1.4	7	0.2	10.5	1.1	6.5	0.2	8.5
Race relations and busing	1.2	9	2.3	6	1.3	8	1.4	7	0.4	9.5	0.2	8.5
Taxes	1.3	8	0.6	8.5	1.1	9	0.6	8	0.7	8	0.5	7
Unemployment	0.8	10.5	0.6	8.5	0.6	10	0.3	9	0.4	9.5	0.0	10.5
Inflation	0.8	10.5	0.3	10	0.3	11	0.2	10.5	0.2	11	0.0	10.5
(N)	(1,695)		(1,241)		(3,518)		(2,209)		(538)		(585)	

Notes: The rankings of issues by the three newspapers included in this study (Indianapolis *Star*, Lebanon [N.H.] *Valley News*, and Chicago *Tribune*) were combined into one newspaper ranking because they were positively correlated (Spearman's Rhos = 0.49 to 0.88 for the three time periods used in this table).

The rankings of issues by the three TV network evening news broadcasts (ABC, CBS, and NBC) were combined into one television ranking because they were positively correlated (Spearman's Rhos = 0.88 to 0.99 for the three time periods used in this table).

Each newspaper article three column inches or longer and each television network evening news story was coded into one, two, or three of 65 issue categories. More than one category was used for a news story only if it equally emphasized more than one issue. The 31 most common issue categories were condensed into the 11 general issue categories used here. Stories referring to the other 34 issue categories comprised less than 10 percent of all stories coded and of all issues mentioned by our panel members in response to open-ended survey questions.

Source: Compiled by authors.

143

FIGURE 8–1

Crosslagged Correlational Analysis (Spearman's Rhos) Between Newspaper and Television Issue Agendas
During the 1976 Fall Campaign

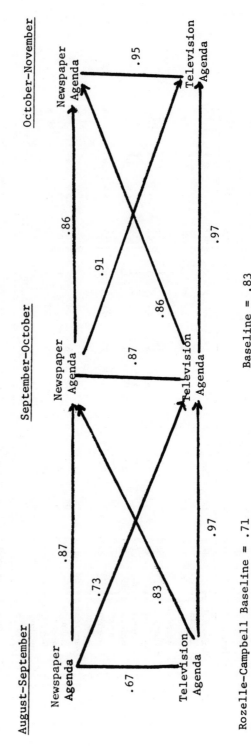

Source: Compiled by authors.

noticeably more stable during the fall campaign than during the spring or summer campaigns.

VOTER CONCERN WITH ISSUES

Even though the newspaper and television issue agendas were becoming more similar during the fall campaign, the voter agendas were not becoming more similar to these media agendas during this time. Tables 8–3, 8–4, and 8–5 show the intrapersonal, interpersonal, and perceived community voter agendas, and a quick look at these tables reveals that the voters in our study were far more concerned about the economic issues than were the newspapers and TV news shows we studied. Whereas the voters tended to place the more obtrusive economic issues (except taxes) near the top of their agendas, the media tended to place them in the middle or near the bottom of theirs.

The intrapersonal and interpersonal voter agendas were very similar during the fall campaign (Spearman's Rho was 0.97 in September, 0.90 in October, and 0.98 in November), indicating that the voters in our study evidently were personally concerned about the same issues that they were discussing most often with others. And, in the wake of consensus building through increased public discussion, for the first time during the 1976 election year, the perceived community agenda (measured only in October) was very similar to the intrapersonal (Rho = 0.81) and the interpersonal agendas (Rho = 0.98), indicating that the issues perceived to be important to others in the community were essentially the same as the issues discussed most often with others and of most personal concern. In other words, near the end of the 1976 election campaign, there was a convergence of all three kinds of voter issue agendas, much in the same manner as there was a convergence of the newspaper and television issue agendas.

Although the two media agendas became more similar to each other near the end of the campaign, as did the three voter agendas, the media agendas and voter agendas were generally more dissimilar to one another near the end of the campaign (especially in September/October) than at any other time during the campaign. With daily life experiences keeping alive the voters' concerns about inflation, unemployment, and the economy in general, the media's different priorities made few converts. In fact, just as the media had settled on a definite array of campaign issues as the fall focus, so the voters appeared to have settled on their own array of crucial concerns, with the more obtrusive economic issues at the top of the list.

TABLE 8-3

Intrapersonal Salience During the 1976 Fall Campaign

Issues	September		October		November	
	Percent	Rank	Percent	Rank	Percent	Rank
Foreign affairs, defense	11.7	3.5	7.0	4.5	7.1	5
Government credibility	2.6	9	3.5	7.5	5.3	6.5
Crime	7.1	5.5	3.5	7.5	4.4	8.5
Social problems	7.1	5.5	7.0	4.5	5.3	6.5
General economy	20.4	1.5	12.8	3	13.8	3
Environment and energy	4.1	8	2.9	9	4.4	8.5
Government spending and size	1.0	11	1.2	11	2.2	11
Race relations and busing	2.0	10	1.8	10	2.7	10
Taxes	5.1	7	5.2	6	7.6	4
Unemployment	11.7	3.5	16.9	2	17.3	2
Inflation	20.4	1.5	34.3	1	25.8	1
(N)	(125)		(117)		(126)	

Source: Compiled by authors.

TABLE 8-4

Interpersonal Salience During the 1976 Fall Campaign

Issues	September Percent	September Rank	October Percent	October Rank	November Percent	November Rank
Foreign affairs, defense	10.8	3	4.6	6	5.8	5
Government credibility	4.5	8	2.6	8.5	5.2	6
Crime	9.9	5	5.3	5	3.5	8
Social problems	9.9	5	3.3	7	4.7	7
General economy	30.6	1	15.9	2.5	14.5	2.5
Environment and energy	3.6	9	2.6	8.5	2.3	9.5
Government spending and size	2.7	10	1.3	10.5	2.3	9.5
Race relations and busing	1.8	11	1.3	10.5	1.2	11
Taxes	8.1	7	6.6	4	8.7	4
Unemployment	9.9	5	15.9	2.5	14.5	2.5
Inflation	20.7	2	32.4	1	25.0	1
(N)	(111)		(103)		(115)	

Source: Compiled by authors.

147

TABLE 8–5

Perceived Community Salience During the 1976 Fall Campaign

	October	
Issues	Percent	Rank
Foreign affairs, defense	0	11
Government credibility	1.9	6.5
Crime	1.9	6.5
Social problems	2.8	5
General economy	24.3	2
Environment and energy	0.9	9
Government spending and size	0.9	9
Race relations and busing	0.9	9
Taxes	15.0	4
Unemployment	15.9	3
Inflation	33.6	1
(N)	(107)	

Source: Compiled by authors.

MEDIA EMPHASIS ON ISSUES AND VOTER CONCERN WITH ISSUES

All Voters

Figures 8–2 and 8–3 reveal the extent of the dissimilarity between the voters' agendas and the media agendas during the fall campaign. Unlike the primary and summer campaigns, the voter and media agendas generally became more dissimilar as the fall campaign progressed. The most similarity between media agendas and voter agendas (for both newspapers and television) occurred in the predebate August/September time period for the interpersonal (discussion) voter agenda, but even at this point the media and voter agendas were only weakly correlated with each other (Spearman's Rhos were 0.26 for the newspaper agenda and 0.29 for the television agenda).

Figures 8–2 and 8–3 also suggest that the few changes occurring in the newspaper and television issue agendas during the fall campaign brought them more in line with voter concerns (especially between September and November) than vice versa. One of the most notable changes in the newspaper and TV agendas, for example, was the decrease in emphasis on the race relations issue from September/October to October/November (see Table 8–2). This issue had had very low salience for voters throughout the fall campaign, suggesting that the media were following the lead of the voters rather than vice versa (see Tables 8–3, 8–4, and 8–5).

FIGURE 8–2

Crosslagged Correlational Analysis (Spearman's Rhos) Between Newspaper Issue Agendas and Voter Issue Agendas During the 1976 Fall Campaign

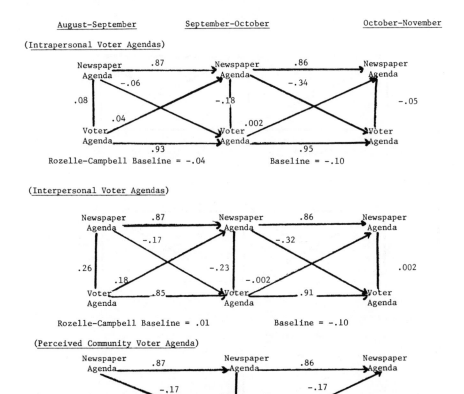

Source: Compiled by authors.

FIGURE 8–3

Crosslagged Correlational Analysis (Spearman's Rhos) Between Television Issue Agendas and Voter Issue Agendas During the 1976 Fall Campaign

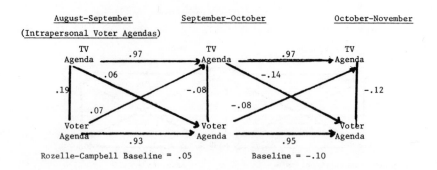

August–September   September–October   October–November
(Intrapersonal Voter Agendas)

Rozelle–Campbell Baseline = .05   Baseline = –.10

(Interpersonal Voter Agendas)

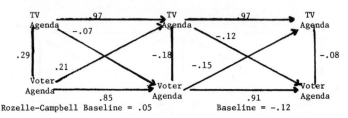

Rozelle–Campbell Baseline = .05   Baseline = –.12

(Perceived Community Voter Agenda)

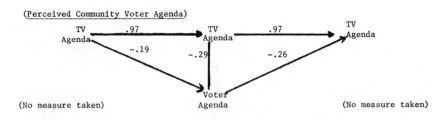

(No measure taken)   Voter   (No measure taken)
                         Agenda

Source: Compiled by authors.

The shifts in overall media and voter issue agendas during the fall campaign and the lack of similarity between media and voter agendas contain a clear message. Newspapers and television, in the fall, failed to set the agenda for relative salience of all issues combined. In addition, Table 8–6 offers no support for an aggregate agenda-setting effect of the three presidential debates.[13] Only the third debate agenda is consistently similar to the voter issue agendas, probably because an open format of topics was used. Moreover, the correlations after the debates are not noticeably stronger than the correlations before the debates The sole exception is the October intrapersonal (personally most important) voter agenda, for which the correlation is 0.49 compared with 0.31 before the debates. The rank order correlations in Table 8–6, like other analyses presented throughout these chapters, are, of course, aggregate analyses. As such, they test the views of groups of voters, rather than individual voters.

TABLE 8–6

Correlations (Spearman's Rhos) between Presidential Debate Agendas and Respondent Agendas

Measures	Debate One	Debate Two	Debate Three	Total
Intrapersonal				
August	−0.18	−0.07	0.34	−0.12
September	−0.20	−0.10	0.31	−0.05
Debates held				
October	0.07	−0.14	0.49	−0.01
November	0.05	−0.12	0.37	0.05
Interpersonal				
August	−0.13	0.12	0.30	0.03
September	−0.18	−0.10	0.36	0.00
Debates held				
October	0.15	−0.45	0.12	0.33
November	0.00	−0.13	0.40	0.04
Perceptual				
August	0.21	−0.56	0.07	−0.33
Debates held				
October	0.12	−0.53	0.06	−0.38

Note: The N's for these correlations are all 11.
Source: Compiled by authors.

Newspaper Readers and Television Viewers

As mentioned in earlier chapters, if newspapers and television have a substantial impact on what issues are considered important and discussed most often with others in a presidential campaign, we would expect to find that the issue agendas of more regular users of newspapers would be more similar to the newspapers' issue agendas than would the agendas of those voters who are less regular users of newspapers. The same should hold true for television.

When the issue agendas of the high newspaper/low television, low newspaper/high television, and high newspaper/high television groups were compared with the issue agendas for all voters combined, the correlations (Spearman's Rhos) ranged from 0.64 to 0.97 for the intrapersonal agendas in the fall campaign (September, October, and November), from 0.69 to 0.95 for the interpersonal agendas, and from 0.87 to 0.98 for the perceived community agendas.[14] These generally strong correlations indicate that the overall voter issue agendas displayed in Tables 8–3, 8–4, and 8–5 are fairly accurate summaries of the issue agendas of the three media use groups. Obviously, different patterns of media exposure did not substantially alter which issues were perceived as important (and the relative salience of these issues) by the voters in our study.

When the issue agendas of the three media use groups are compared with the newspaper and television agendas during the fall campaign period, many of the same patterns as illustrated in Figures 8–2 and 8–3 for all voters are evident. The voter and media issue agendas become noticeably dissimilar from September to October for all three media use groups, just as they do for all voters combined. There is not as much difference between the strength of the newspaper and television correlations for all three media use groups as there was in the spring and summer campaigns, which is also true of all voters combined.

The strongest correlations occurred between the TV issue agenda in August/September and the high TV/low newspaper group intrapersonal agenda in September (Rho = 0.43) and between both media agendas in August/September and the high newspaper/high TV group interpersonal agenda in September (Rhos = 0.36 and 0.35). These correlations indicate a television agenda-setting effect for the intrapersonal issue agenda of heavy users of television news in September. Similarly, heavy users of both newspapers and TV for political information had an interpersonal issue agenda that was more similar to both the newspaper and TV agendas than did light users of one medium (Rhos = from −0.11 to 0.01). But in the October and November interviews, as unobtrusive issues were made more obtrusive, the voter agendas are all negatively correlated with the media agendas with few differences between the media use group agendas, suggesting no support for a media agenda-setting effect.

In short, differing amounts of newspaper and TV use for political information during the early fall campaign (September) did have an influence on the relative salience of various issues—both in terms of personal concern and frequency of discussion—but this influence did not carry through to the months of October and November, probably because the issue agenda in the campaign was already set by that time.

Voters' Need for Orientation

When the aggregate issue agendas of the low, moderate, and high need-for-orientation groups were compared with the overall voter issue agendas in Tables 8–3, 8–4, and 8–5, the similarities were not nearly as strong as during the spring and summer campaigns (Spearman's Rhos ranged from 0.26 to 0.98 for intrapersonal agendas, from 0.33 to 0.96 for the interpersonal agendas, and from 0.53 to 0.69 for the perceived community agendas). These widely fluctuating correlations suggested that different levels of voter need for orientation were having a substantial impact on which issues were considered most important, and discussed most often, during the fall campaign.[15]

And, indeed, when the various need-for-orientation group agendas were compared with the newspaper and television agendas during September, October, and November, there were some considerable deviations from the patterns illustrated for all voters combined in Figures 8–2 and 8–3. Differing levels of need for orientation did not make much difference in the correlations between voter agendas and media agendas in September, but in October those voters with a high level of need for orientation, and hence a strong motivation to seek media information, had an intrapersonal agenda that was somewhat more similar to the newspaper and television agendas (Rhos = 0.06 and 0.14) than was the intrapersonal agenda for all voters combined (Rhos = −0.18 and −0.08) and that was markedly more similar to the newspaper and TV agendas than was the agenda of those with a low level of need for orientation (Rhos = −0.54 and −0.48).

But it is in November that need for orientation has its greatest effect on what issues are considered personally most important and what issues are discussed most often. Although intrapersonal issue salience for all voters combined is negatively correlated with the newspaper issue agenda in November (−0.05), intrapersonal issue salience for those voters with a high level of need for orientation is positively correlated (0.51) with the newspaper agenda. And, although the intrapersonal issue agenda for all voters combined is negatively correlated with the television issue agenda in November (−0.12), the intrapersonal agenda for the high need-for-orientation voters is positively correlated (0.40) with the TV agenda. The same is true for the interpersonal agendas (Rho = 0.002 with the newspaper agenda for all voters and 0.46 for those voters with a high level of need for orientation; Rho $= -0.08$ with the television agenda for all voters, and 0.32 for those with a high level of need for orientation).

In short, there is evidence in the fall campaign, especially in the late fall campaign, that differing levels of voter need for orientation did make a difference in which issues were considered important and which issues were discussed most often. This evidence is consistent with several earlier studies which show that higher levels of need for orientation (political interest and uncertainty) are associated with increased media agenda-setting during a political campaign.[16] In both September and November, the issue agendas of voters with a high level of need for orientation were consistently more similar to both newspaper and television agendas than was true for voters with a low level of need for orientation. In November, the high need-for-orientation voters also had issue agendas that were consistently and markedly more similar to the media issue agendas than those of all voters combined. These findings support earlier studies that suggest that personal motives for using mass media are just as important, if not more so, than are amounts of media exposure in predicting media effects.[17] Personal motives come into play most strongly at the end of a campaign when the need for information is greatest because of the impending voting choice and increased opportunities to participate in discussions of the upcoming election.

Obtrusive and Unobtrusive Issues

As we have seen, the distinction between obtrusive and unobtrusive campaign issues in the spring and summer periods suggested a variable agenda-setting influence of the mass media. Especially during the primary season, and to a lesser extent in the summer of 1976, newspapers and television seemed to be instrumental in setting the public agenda of such unobtrusive issues as crime, the environment, social problems, foreign affairs, and the like. The obtrusive issues on the other hand—those with which people generally have direct and regular experience, such as inflation and unemployment—seemed to have gained in public salience as a consequence of direct contact, and the mass media's role of highlighting such topics for their audiences seemed minimal. By November, very shortly before the actual presidential election date, the original distinction between obtrusive and unobtrusive issues all but faded away. Applying controls for the two issue types provided no significant improvement in the level of association between the media and public agendas.

Over time, the unobtrusive issues had become akin to the obtrusive ones in the public mind. Thus, over the presidential election year, we have witnessed a transition in the impact of newspapers and television on the public salience of issues. Early in the campaign, during the primary season, the mass media were particularly instrumental in pointing out the importance of new issues with which their audiences had, generally, little direct contact. Later in the campaign year, as these new and unobtrusive issues gained in public familiarity and salience, the potency of agenda-setting declined.

What overall picture emerges from the yearly trends in agenda-setting? People experience issues in many guises and learn about issues from many sources. Long before the oratory and discussion of the election year, such "bread-and-butter" issues as inflation and taxes were the concerns of many Americans. People did not have to be told about inflation and taxes to be concerned about them. But the beginning of the election year, with its many primaries, brought a set of less obtrusive issues into the media spotlight. The media coverage of the more unobtrusive issues had the potential for a novelty effect because the media seemed to be largely alone in their role of teacher and communicator for these issues. The results of this media teaching—the results of this learning by voters from the media—were seen in the spring comparisons of voter agendas with press agendas. The dominant pattern there was one of strong correlations between voter and press concerns for the unobtrusive issues but a much weaker relationship for the obtrusive issues with which voters had had considerable personal experience.

Such a limited-effects model of agenda-setting should not be surprising during the early portion of the election year. Public interest in politics was just beginning its quadrennial buildup, and one should expect personal experience to outweigh the secondhand reality of the mass media. In the summer, the agenda-setting effect was even more limited than in the spring, with only the unobtrusive issues of the spring continuing to show a close match between the agendas of the voters and the mass media. Media influence was diminished in the summer months because fewer significant events occurred then, making news less important, and because voters were more preoccupied with outdoor activities and vacations. Only the party conventions provided major news pegs for political coverage. Much of this coverage was riveted on the horserace and hoopla aspects of the campaign. As we moved into the fall of the election year, formerly unobtrusive issues became obtrusive so that the agenda-setting power of the media was further weakened.

SUMMARY AND CONCLUSIONS: PATTERNS THROUGHOUT THE YEAR

The findings presented in these three chapters on issues indicate that the agenda-setting function of the mass media with regard to issues varies according to these clusters of factors: period of the campaign, nature of the issues, orientations of voters, and kind of medium.

The period of the campaign has a major impact on the agenda-setting influence of newspapers and television, especially with regard to the more unobtrusive issues. Our data show the influence of both newspapers and television to be greatest during the primaries in the spring, somewhat less during the summer, and least during the final few months of the election campaign. This general trend of less media influence later in the campaign seemed to hold for all eleven issues considered together and especially for the seven more unobtrusive issues of foreign affairs, government credibility, crime, social problems, environment and energy, government spending and size, and race relations. Three of the four more obtrusive economic issues were of generally high concern to voters throughout the election year, regardless of the treatment of these issues by newspapers and the television network news shows. This suggests that personal experience is a more powerful teacher of issue salience than are the mass media, at least with regard to those issues that have a direct impact on the daily lives of voters.

There is also evidence that discussions with other people are important in setting an agenda of issues in an election campaign. As the 1976 campaign wore on and as discussion of politics increased among the voters we studied, the intrapersonal and perceived community agendas became more similar to the interpersonal agenda. By the last month of the campaign, these three issue agendas were nearly identical, with the perceived community salience rankings becoming more similar to the intra- and interpersonal salience rankings.

The nature of the issues was especially important in the early spring period. During the primaries, the more unobtrusive issues were ranked by voters in almost exactly the same order as they had been by newspapers and television during the previous two months or so. By contrast, the more obtrusive economic issues were ranked as considerably more important by voters than by either newspapers or television. By the summer season, the distinction between unobtrusive and obtrusive issues was less clear. After six months of rather consistent media emphasis, unobtrusive issues apparently had become established concerns of the voters we studied and less dependent upon media rankings. The voters seemed to have made up their minds about the relative importance of issues, regardless of their amount of coverage by newspapers and television.

In contrast to the declining importance of newspapers and television as issue agenda-setters and to the decreased significance of the nature of the issues later in the year, the orientations of the voters (at least their motivation to follow the campaign) seemed to become more important as the campaign drew to a close. Although patterns of newspaper and television news exposure and levels of motivation to follow the campaign had fairly minor effects on voter agendas during the spring and summer seasons, this was not true during the fall period. As in spring and summer, media exposure patterns made little difference in voter agendas during the fall, but motivation to follow the campaign became significantly more important. Those voters with a high need for orientation (high interest and high uncertainty about whom to support) had overall issue agendas that were substantially more similar to the media agendas than did other voters. This may be because those voters who were still undecided but who were highly interested had not engaged in as much discussion of issues with others earlier in the campaign and had not been as personally troubled by the economic issues as other voters had been.

Whatever the case, it was clear that motivation to follow the campaign was more important in the agenda-setting process near the end of the campaign when the need for information was greatest. An analysis of which factors were most important in vote choice after the election also revealed that voters with high motivation to follow the campaign were substantially more likely to cite issues as more important than candidate images or political party affiliation than were the other voters we studied.[18] This finding suggests that voters with a high need for orientation, who were following and absorbing the issue-related content of the media more closely than were others, would be likely to have issue agendas more similar to the media's agendas.

The distinctions between newspapers and television as issue agenda-setters became less pronounced as Election Day approached. During the primary elections in the spring, we had found evidence of a sort of "two-step flow" of issue agenda-setting, with the combined newspaper agenda remaining very stable over time, the television issue agenda changing in the direction of the newspaper agenda, and the voter agenda becoming more similar to the television issue agenda. But after the summer party conventions, the newspaper and television agendas became nearly identical and changed little. The few changes that did occur were in the direction of the voter agendas, offering no support for media agenda-setting during the fall period of the campaign. It should be remembered, however, that in the spring and summer periods, many of the changes in the television and voter agendas were in the direction of the more stable newspaper agenda, suggesting that newspapers were the primary agenda-setters of unobtrusive issues for the entire election campaign.

What can we conclude about the role of newspapers and television with regard to issues in a presidential campaign from these trends across the entire election year of 1976? Neither newspapers nor television have much agenda-setting influence on obtrusive issues. Instead, personal experiences and discussions with others are likely to determine which of these issues are considered most important by individual voters. For the unobtrusive issues, however, newspapers and television appear to be the major agenda-setters, especially during the early stages of the campaign.

This media agenda-setting influence varies with the substance of the issues (an important foreign event may supersede a less important event based on personal experience), the frequency and repetition of media coverage over time, the motivations of individual voters to follow the election campaign, and, to a lesser extent, their media exposure patterns. The television network news programs seem to take their cues on coverage of issues mainly from newspapers and voters. When newspapers present issues that voters find important or that television news personnel think voters will consider important, television news focuses on these issues. But by the final week of the campaign, the issue agendas of both voters and media are set, barring any major and unexpected events. This happens as a result of the more unobtrusive issues becoming more similar to the obtrusive ones over time in the minds of voters and because of the increased discussion among voters that leads to more community consensus on which issues are of major importance in the election.

The various trends reported in these chapters on issue agenda-setting suggest that newspaper coverage of issues is especially important early in a presidential campaign in determining which of the unobtrusive issues will play a major role in the election. Newspaper editors appear to have considerable discretion in choosing certain issues and neglecting others. Because there is limited space and time for media messages, editors must make choices about which issues to play up and which to play down. For instance, during the 1976 election year, many issues stressed by the leading candidates or the major political parties were not heavily covered by newspapers and television. The choices of newspaper editors were remarkably consistent over time in 1976 and appeared to have a major impact on the formation of television and voter issue agendas during the spring and summer periods of the campaign.

In light of the increasing importance of issues in U.S. presidential elections,[19] the decreasing importance of political party identification,[20] and the increased reliance on issue stands for making voting choices (at least by undecided and interested voters),[21] the issue coverage of newspapers and television may become an even more important factor in determining the outcome of future presidential races in this country. This places a great responsibility on newspapers and television to cover as many issues as clearly, completely, and fairly as possible, without regard to partisan considerations. In fulfilling this role, the major mass media of this country (especially the newspapers) may be doing far more than reinforcing partisan voters' predispositions, as claimed in earlier studies.[22]

They may be playing an important role in determining the outcome of presidential elections.

NOTES

[1] Mary E. Clifford, Raymond Hill, and Stephen Orlofsky, *1976 News Dictionary* (New York: Facts on File, 1977), p. 271.

[2] Clifford, Hill, and Orlofsky, *1976 News Dictionary*, p. 268; Jules Witcover, *Marathon: The Pursuit of the Presidency, 1972–1976* (New York: Viking, 1977), p. 566.

[3] Witcover, *Marathon*, p. 567.

[4] Ibid.

[5] Clifford, Hill, and Orlofsky, *1976 News Dictionary*, p. 271.

[6] Ibid., pp. 268–69.

[7] Ibid., p. 269.

[8] Ibid., p. 272.

[9] Ibid.

[10] Ibid., p. 276.

[11] Frederick T. Steeper, "Public Response to Gerald Ford's Statements on Eastern Europe in the Second Debate," in *The Presidential Debates: Media, Electoral, and Policy Perspectives*, eds. George F. Bishop, Robert G. Meadow, and Marilyn Jackson-Beeck (New York: Praeger, 1978), pp. 81–101.

[12] Clifford, Hill, and Orlofsky, *1976 News Dictionary*, p. 279.

[13] Lee B. Becker, David H. Weaver, Doris A. Graber, and Maxwell E. McCombs, "Influence on Public Agendas," in *The Great Debates: Carter vs. Ford, 1976*, ed. Sidney Kraus (Bloomington: Indiana University Press, 1979), pp. 418–28.

[14] See Chapter 6, footnote 23, for the actual wording of the questions asked to measure newspaper and television use for political information.

[15] See Chapter 6, footnote 28, for the actual wording of the questions used to measure political relevance and political uncertainty. See the section, "Voters' Need for Orientation," in Chapter 6 for a discussion of how these measures were combined.

[16] David H. Weaver, "Political Issues and Voter Need for Orientation," in *The Emergence of American Political Issues: The Agenda-Setting Function of the Press*, eds. Donald L. Shaw and Maxwell E. McCombs (St. Paul: West, 1977), pp. 107–19, and David H. Weaver, Maxwell E. McCombs, and Charles Spellman, "Watergate and the Media: A Case Study of Agenda-Setting," *American Politics Quarterly* 3 (October 1975): 458–72.

[17] See, for example, Jack M. McLeod and Lee B. Becker, "Testing the Validity of Gratification Measures Through Political Effects Analysis," in *The Uses of Mass Communications: Current Perspectives on Gratifications Research*, eds. Jay G. Blumler and Elihu Katz (Beverly Hills: Sage, 1974), and Jay G. Blumler, "The Role of Theory in Uses and Gratifications Studies," *Communication Research* 6 (January 1979): 9–36.

[18] See David H. Weaver and Maxwell E. McCombs, "Voters' Need for Orientation and Choice of Candidate: Mass Media and Electoral Decision Making," Paper presented at the

annual conference of the American Association for Public Opinion Research, Roanoke, Virginia, June 1978.

[19]Arthur Miller, "Election Study Notes New Trends in Voter Behavior, Attributes Close Race to Well-Run Campaign," *ISR Newsletter* 5 (1977, Ann Arbor, University of Michigan Institute for Social Research): 4–5, and Warren Miller and Teresa Levitin, *Leadership and Change* (Cambridge, Mass.: Winthrop, 1976).

[20]Robert D. Cantor, *Voting Behavior and Presidential Elections* (Itasca, Ill.: F. E. Peacock, 1975).

[21]Weaver and McCombs, "Voters' Need for Orientation and Choice of Candidate"; C. Anthony Broh, "Toward a Theory of Issue Voting," Sage Professional Papers in American Politics, vol. 1, series no. 04-011, 1973, pp. 6–10; Samuel A. Kirkpatrick, William Lyons, and Michael R. Fitzgerald, "Candidates, Parties, and Issues in the American Electorate," *American Politics Quarterly* 3(July 1975): 35–71; Norman H. Nie, Sidney Verba, and John P. Petrocik, *The Changing American Voter* (Cambridge, Mass.: Harvard University Press, 1976).

[22]For a discussion of some of these studies, see Elihu Katz, "Platforms & Windows: Broadcasting's Role in Election Campaigns," *Journalism Quarterly* 48 (Summer 1971): 304–14.

nine

IMAGES THROUGHOUT
THE CAMPAIGN

The word image, the dictionaries tell us, means a reproduction, imitation, or representation of a person or thing or a mental picture of something. As such, an image may be highly similar to the actual object or person or extremely different from the reality it seeks to represent. Political candidates see as an important goal the creation of a self-image that, they hope, will be perceived publicly in a positive and favorable way.

Arthur Krock, the newspaper columnist, refers to the image as a candidate's "acquired personality." Such a personality is created "through circumstances which made him famous before he entered politics, or through the opportunity to overshadow a rival that the Presidency supplies" (in the case of presidential politics).[1] The image of an office-seeker hinges, to a great extent, on the degree of similarity between the perceivers' and candidate's reality perception. "Our image of a candidate," according to Hahn and Gonchar, "is determined by the interaction of his personality and orientation to the world with ours."[2] Other definitions of the concept include those by Nimmo and Savage, "A human construct imposed on an array of perceived attributes projected by an object, event or person," and by Bowes and Strentz, who view a candidate's image as "his or her publicly perceived attributes."[3]

These views of a candidate's image as arrays of perceived attributes are closely related to the theory of agenda-setting. We argue that the relative salience of certain attributes of a candidate is basic to that candidate's image. By concentrating on certain attributes of a candidate and downplaying or ignoring other attributes, the mass media play an important agenda-setting role with regard to that candidate's image. In other words, the media provide an agenda of attributes from which voters' images of the candidates are formed. Such an agenda of attributes for each candidate in a campaign constitutes a major portion of the raw material from which images are formed by voters. But the knowledge and attitudes of the individual voters are also important sources of material for image construction, as will be indicated.

ORIGINS OF IMAGES

Sigel suggests that images originate from two sources: stimulus determinants, such as the perception of candidates' personalities or appearances, and perceiver determinants, arrived at through the perceiver's examination of the candidates' positions on political issues.[4] Graber has elaborated on the contribution of the mass media to the origins of images:

Although we do not know the precise influence of the press on public perception, we do know that political stories in the mass media are significant in furnishing raw material for the formation of political images. Most people do not invent political images out of thin air. Rather, they combine current political data supplied by the mass media with existing knowledge and attitudes and then weave these into a plausible and pleasing GESTALT.[5]

Thus, public images of candidates originate with the emergence of the candidates themselves in the public light. Exposure before the public reveals the candidates' physical features and mannerisms. Their behavior and activities reveal their positions on issues, their styles of operation, conduct, and reactions to others and others' ideas.

These bits of information are transmitted mostly via the mass media, but an important role is played by interpersonal networks. The entire set of perceptions about a candidate passes through attitudinal and personal filters and predispositions held by each member of the public. The overall result is "a picture in the head" of the perceiver, or an image, that may be favorable or unfavorable to the candidate, similar or dissimilar to some "objective" reality, and shared by many or few members of the public.

ISSUES VERSUS IMAGES

The question of whether image perceptions are more influential for voting decisions than are perceptions of candidates' stands on issues has not been resolved, nor is it likely to be, given the variations in different elections. But it emerges anew during each election campaign, with both laypeople and scholars split in their support of one or the other. Many, however, agree that a combination of the two contribute to the overall evaluation of candidates by the public, and that the two are often inseparable.

Katz and Feldman, for example, reviewed research conducted on the 1960 Nixon-Kennedy debates and concluded that the debates changed few opinions on the campaign issues because people focused more on such matters as personalities and presentation styles.[6] Images of the debaters dominated the event, and the messages they offered to the viewers did not alter the voters' stands on issues. Similarly, Leuthold, analyzing congressional elections, found that two-thirds of the voters decided on the basis of candidates' personalities rather than on their positions on specific issues.[7]

Andersen and Kibler found that source valence, defined as candidates' credibility, attraction, and homophily, was a significant predictor of voter preferences. Of these components of source valence, homophily was the best predictor. As they put it, "Persons appear to assess candidates' attitudes in relation to their own and tend to vote for a candidate perceived as attitudinally similar."[8] Such candidate-voter similarity transcends both issues and images. It is a more general determination of preference in terms of resemblance, comparability, likeness, and similarity.

In 1968 voters were asked by the American Institute for Political Communication:

If you had to name just one factor or thing which most influenced your voting decision in the presidential race, what would that one thing be?

While respondents tended to stress the importance of issues, the institute reported that:

41% of the respondents said one of the Presidential candidates or CHARACTER-ISTICS of that candidate was the factor "which most influenced" their Presidential vote. Some 25% said an issue or issues was most important. About 13% opted for party affiliation and another 13% for the desire for a change in national leadership, and 8.5% specifically referred to one or more of the media (a TV appearance, an editorial, a series of articles, etc.)[9]

IMAGES IN CONTEMPORARY POLITICS

In his re-analysis of the studies conducted by the University of Michigan's Survey Research Center (SRC) in the 1950s, Natchez asserts that "the preeminence of candidate imagery... emphasizes the shallow, nonpolitical implications of American elections."[10] He explains that individuals who are informed about political issues and who are cognizant of the implications of their decisions have usually been committed to particular parties. Political rhetoric appears to have greatest influence on individuals who are most poorly informed and most deficient in political allegiance. "Moved by the sound and fury of campaign propaganda, the decisions of these people contribute disproportionately to that segment of the electorate which defines the margin crucial to political victories (and defeats)."[11]

The recent decline in party affiliation and the corresponding decline in partisan voting have focused the interest of many researchers on candidate images as an increasingly important factor in voting by all segments of the population. Bowes and Strentz, for example, conclude that "while ties to traditional party and class loyalties have waned, the persona of the candidate has waxed in explanations of what sways voter preferences."[12] Greenstein observed that when individuals were asked to state what they liked or disliked about the president, their typical responses were about his personal image. He adds, "There are, of course, some references to his policy positions and his leadership qualities, but together these references are less frequent than statements about the President's personal qualities."[13] But Natchez concluded from his review of the SRC studies:

It is clear that candidate image has been the most volatile of the components identified by the SRC. What has not been so convincingly demonstrated is its relative magnitude.... Candidate image is only one of a number of forces operating at any given time. Its predictive power changes from candidate to candidate and election to election.[14]

VOTERS' IMAGES OF CANDIDATES IN THE 1976 CAMPAIGN

In our 1976 study, voters were asked, "Suppose you had some friends who had been away for a long time and were unfamiliar with the Presidential candidates. What could you tell them about (*CANDIDATE X)?*" Consistently, each time this question was asked (March, July, August, and October), voters in our study referred to the image characteristics of the two main candidates (Carter and Ford) much more often than to their policies and stands on political issues (see Table 9–1).

In general, the ratio of image to issue references about President Ford remained constant over time, while the percentage of image references to Carter was somewhat lower in March than during the rest of the year. Because he was relatively unknown to the electorate, Carter's image was

TABLE 9–1

Voters' Descriptions of the Leading Candidates Throughout the Election Year in Terms of Issues and Images (in percentages)

Candidates	March		July		August		October	
	Image-related	Issue-related	Image-related	Issue-related	Image-related	Issue-related	Image-related	Issue-related
Jimmy Carter	67.1	32.9	81.8	18.2	80.4	19.6	79.0	21.0
Gerald Ford	89.5	10.5	88.1	11.9	88.8	11.2	86.7	13.3

Source: Compiled by authors.

not well established, and it fluctuated during the year, as will be shown in more detail later.

The pattern of stressing image qualities rather than issues was more apparent among those who were highly interested in the presidential campaign than among those not very interested. We found no significant relationship between amount of media use for politics and reference to images, although the findings reported in Chapter 5 show that more interested voters used the media, especially television, to follow politics more than less interested voters. Increased media use means more exposure to mass media candidate images. This may explain the heightened awareness of candidate images found in well-informed voters.

But it is also plausible that individuals who are highly interested in the presidential campaign care more about images and personalities than issues and candidate positions on these issues, regardless of media exposure habits. As we learned from our intensive interviews, there are many reasons for high concern about images. First of all, personality is indeed crucial to a president's performance in office. Experts and laypeople alike agree that it is important to know whether a president is "an honest man, capable, and experienced." As one respondent put it when asked to state her ultimate criteria for choosing a president, "It has to get down to personalities—how they will react to various situations." Given the impossibility to know precisely what these situations will be in the future, the need to select a strong, trustworthy person becomes pressing. "I'll vote for the candidate I think is the better person, the better mind, the more honest."

Heavy reliance on personality appraisals is not particularly troublesome for the average voter, quite in contrast to issue appraisal. The average person is used to making personality appraisals from physical clues. "You are able to judge a person to some extent by watching his facial expression, his tone of voice, his appearance on T.V.," one respondent commented. Another, after complaining about the difficulty of understanding issues, noted that character was easy to detect: "Personality differences were so strong you didn't have to think about them." And a third one pointed to the fact that an appraisal of trustworthiness was a precondition for even considering the candidates' issue stands. "I was kind of in favor of Carter until his acceptance speech. He promised too much.... There's not much you can believe."

While personality assessments are made readily on the basis of past experiences, issue assessment is difficult because of the complexity of issues, the haziness of the candidates, conflicting appraisals, and a general feeling that promises of future performance are untrustworthy. Commenting on the difficulty of understanding an issue of close personal concern, such as inflation, one woman voiced a frequent complaint, "I don't like to read about inflation; too many figures turn me off. I'm not mathematical. I really don't understand economics." Another echoed the confusion when candidates contradict each other, "I want to know more about where the candidates stand on the military. Reagan says we're second best—Ford says we're not. So I don't know." Still others explained puzzlement about deciding their own stands on issues because the decision varied depending on the perspective from which they viewed the problem. No single stand had a monopoly on merits or faults.

The haziness of candidates was mentioned by nearly all respondents as a bar to their understanding issues and issue positions. "The majority of candidates are wishy washy, ambivalent, mealy mouthed. Problems are given attention but mostly just in rhetoric" was a typical comment. There was widespread suspicion that candidates were deliberately vague to appeal to people of different persuasions and that they avoided difficult issues. A college-educated young man commented about the presidential debates, "I didn't think they discussed issues much; just a lot of political jargon, blanket statements. When they get into specifics they spout off statistics—how do you know they're right?"

Another respondent noted that the taxation issue was shunned by the candidates, "It's political suicide for anyone to talk about taxes." Still others commented on the difficulties faced by any president in carrying out his promises, even when he made sincere efforts to live up to them.

Sincerity, of course, was not taken for granted. "He may not govern the way he talks," commented one respondent, who saw this as a particularly serious problem for new and untried contenders for the office. Another noted, "There are so many examples of big government being well-intentioned in programs. If they accomplished what they intended, they'd be fine. But it doesn't seem to work out that way."

A frequent comment was that the candidates were really quite close on issues: "I get the feeling that they're trying to make big issues where there really aren't many differences. I haven't got the time to sift through things where there's only a hair of difference.

Given the widespread feelings that image characteristics are important and the despair about understanding issues and being able to use them to decide among the candidates, what sorts of image characteristics were important for the voters in our study?

Types of Images

Voter's candidate descriptions fell into five general categories: cognitive—references to candidates' knowledge, understanding, wisdom, and so on, affective—descriptions of candidates in terms of liking and emotional preference, behavioral—comments regarding candidates' past activities and abilities to act, personal—statements about physical, demographic, and other attributes of "fact," and issue-related—remarks about candidates' ideologies, stands on specific issues, and general issue orientations.

Table 9–2 displays the distribution of voters' references to Carter and Ford along these five dimensions at four points during 1976. The voters in our study were most likely to refer to behavioral characteristics of Ford and to personal characteristics of Carter. This was not surprising, considering that President Ford was a better-known candidate, who had served many years in public office. Carter, on the other hand, generally received more personal and issue-related comments than did Ford. This is probably a reflection of voters' curiosity and uncertainty about the "new face," his personal characteristics and style, and, to a lesser extent, his stands on various issues. It also reflects voters' feeling that their "friends," whom they were presumably helping, would want to know about these matters.

Examining the shifts in public perceptions over time reveals similar trends for the two presidential candidates along the cognitive, behavioral, and issue-related dimensions (see Table 9–2). On the cognitive level, references to both candidates' knowledge and wisdom increased until August and dropped dramatically by October. On the behavioral level, the pattern of responses about past and present activities suggests a steady increase over time for Carter and an almost monotonic, but slower, increase for Ford.

Issue-related comments declined for both candidates until they sharply increased, one month before the election, especially for Carter. A sizeable shift from descriptions of Carter in cognitive and personal terms to issue-related attributions in October accounted for the drastic increase in the issue-related area. The increase in issue-related comments about Ford, on the other hand, is attributable to a shift from the cognitive and affective dimensions.

Apparently, as Election Day drew near, the candidates' issue orientations and political positions became clearer and better known and were perceived by voters as more important than they had been earlier in the campaign. The emerging picture is one of voters highly interested in the personal characteristics of the candidates throughout the campaign period. Shortly before the election date, however, these voters appeared to stress important issue positions of the office seekers in describing them to their friends. We cannot tell whether this change reflected voters' own judgments of what was important in voting, the feeling that others were interested in these matters, or a normative sense that issues ought to be important.

TABLE 9–2

Voters' Descriptions of the Leading Candidates Throughout the Election Year in Terms of Issues and General Image Dimensions (in percentages)

| | Carter | | | | Ford | | | |
	March	July	August	October	March	July	August	October
Cognitive	21.3	21.7	27.0	13.4	15.9	18.0	26.0	16.2
Affective	18.8	24.1	11.2	13.4	36.3	28.1	21.9	13.1
Behavioral	22.5	22.9	29.2	32.0	37.2	43.8	40.6	44.4
Personal	25.0	19.3	30.3	20.6	3.5	3.4	7.3	16.2
Issue-related	12.5	12.0	2.2	20.6	7.1	6.7	4.2	10.1
Total	100.0°	100.0	99.9°	100.0	100.1°	100.0	100.0	100.0

°Does not total to 100.0 percent because of rounding error.
Source: Compiled by authors.

Voters' Education

The level of education of voters was related to their comments about the candidates. Highly educated (some college or more) persons' references to Carter shifted from an emphasis on affective attributes in March to cognitive and behavioral characteristics in July, to personal references in August, and, finally, in October, to behavioral references again. Respondents with less education (high school graduate or less) were similarly unable to hold a consistent and stable image of Carter, shifting from personal emphasis in March to affective comments in July and to behavioral attributions in August and October.

When asked about Jimmy Carter, highly educated individuals tended to mention issue-related attributes more often than did less educated people. For Ford, the trend was reversed—less educated individuals were more likely to describe him in issue-related terms than were highly educated voters.

The overall picture is one of significant similarities as well as differences between the two educational levels in comments about the two candidates. In general, both groups stress behavioral characteristics. But highly educated people emphasized cognitive attributes as well, while less educated respondents mentioned affective characteristics more readily. Intellect, knowledge, and wisdom are of prime importance for individuals with higher education. Those with lower levels of education are more apt to think and comment about the candidates in affective and emotional terms.

Voters' Sex

Being male or female also influenced voters' evaluations of Carter, but less so for Ford, the incumbent candidate. With the exception of the fall (October) period, the modal female response differed from the male response. In March, almost a third of the men mentioned affective characteristics of Carter, compared with 7.7 percent of the women, whose most frequent response referred to the personal dimension (30.8 percent). In July, the number of males who mentioned behavioral attributes of Carter (31.1 percent) was more than double the size of the parallel female group (14 percent). Almost a third of the female respondents (30.2 percent), on the other hand, referred to Carter's affective characteristics in July, as compared with only 20 percent of the males.

The differences between men and women lessened in the fall period, as Carter became better known. In August, most males mentioned personal characteristics, while most females mentioned behavioral aspects of Carter. By October, just before the elections, all respondents tended to mention behavioral attributes more frequently than any other image type.

For President Ford, no clear distinction between men's and women's attributions was evident. With the exception of the March period, the modal response for all respondents stressed behavioral attributes. While the references to Ford appeared to be fairly stable over time, there were two discernible trends. For males and females, references to personal attributes increased as time went on—slightly in the spring and summer and somewhat more dramatically from August to October; for females, affective descriptions decreased sharply, dropping from a high of 44 percent in March to 13.7 percent in October. At the same time, affective references to Carter fluctuated within a range between 7.7 percent and 30.2 percent.

These findings lend support to the previously mentioned view that voters held an unclear and unstable image of Carter throughout the campaign year. The image of the incumbent president was far more stable and better established in the voters' minds, with a fair degree of agreement between men and women.

Graber has suggested that voters do not usually judge leaders on the basis of political criteria because the mass media fail to supply the necessary facts, or they provide such information in a form that is difficult to use.[15] She concludes that information availability, rather than intrinsic public preferences, may thus explain the public's choice of appraisal criteria. Our findings show that, in 1976, the public's preference was indeed the personal domain rather than the substantive area of political issues.

Illinois Voters' Images

In addition to studying the general types of candidate images held by all voters in our study, we looked at more-specific voter image dimensions for the Illinois voters and compared these more-specific voter image qualities with specific image dimensions as presented in Chicago *Tribune* stories. Time and monetary constraints prevented us from making the same comparisons between Indiana and New Hampshire voters and the media they used. Based on our analyses of the relationships between media and voter issue agendas in the three communities, however, we suspect that the relationships we found in Illinois between newspaper and voter image agendas are fairly representative of what we would find in the other two communities.

Tables 9–3 through 9–6 show the distributions of the Illinois voters' specific image references to the two leading candidates, Carter and Ford. The overall distribution for each candidate is divided into three major categories, indicating the nature of the voter descriptions: "normative" refers to qualities the candidates ought to have; "positive" refers to

TABLE 9–3

Illinois Voters' Descriptions of the Leading Candidates During March in Terms of Issues and Specific Image Dimensions (in percentages)

	Carter				Ford			
	Normative	Positive	Negative	Total	Normative	Positive	Negative	Total
Man of principles	0.0	18.4	7.7	14.1	0.0	22.7	0.0	10.0
Inspires confidence	0.0	0.0	19.2	7.8	0.0	0.0	7.1	4.0
Holds leadership qualities	0.0	2.6	3.8	3.1	0.0	0.0	3.6	2.0
Appealing manner	0.0	23.7	3.8	15.6	0.0	4.5	3.6	4.0
Compassionate	0.0	0.0	0.0	0.0	0.0	0.0	0.0	0.0
Forthright	0.0	2.6	7.7	4.7	0.0	0.0	10.7	6.0
Uses restraint	0.0	2.6	0.0	1.6	0.0	4.5	0.0	2.0
Strong	0.0	2.6	0.0	1.6	0.0	0.0	7.1	4.0
People's person	0.0	5.3	0.0	3.1	0.0	4.5	0.0	2.0
Competent	0.0	18.4	0.0	10.9	0.0	18.2	21.4	20.0
Versatile	0.0	0.0	0.0	0.0	0.0	4.5	0.0	2.0
Uses own judgment	0.0	0.0	0.0	0.0	0.0	0.0	14.3	8.0
Other image references	0.0	18.4	34.6	25.0	0.0	36.4	25.0	30.0
Issue-related references	0.0	5.3	23.1	12.5	0.0	4.5	7.1	6.0
Total	0.0	99.9[a]	99.9[a]	100.0	0.0	99.8[a]	99.9[a]	100.0
(N)	(0)	(38)	(26)	(64)	(0)	(22)	(28)	(50)

[a]Does not total 100.0 percent because of rounding error.
Source: Compiled by authors.

172

desirable qualities the candidates are said to possess; and "negative" refers to desirable qualities the candidates are said to lack.

Table 9–3 shows that in March, early in the campaign year, the Illinois voters perceived Carter as possessing more desirable image dimensions than he lacked. But just the opposite was true for Ford; when one balances positive against negative qualities, he was perceived as predominantly deficient in desirable image traits. There were no references by voters to qualities either candidate should possess in March or throughout the rest of the campaign. Carter's strongest positive image attributes in March were being a man of principles, having an appealing manner, and being competent. His weakest attributes were inspiring confidence and his issue stands (or lack of them). Ford's strongest image dimension in March was being a man of principles, according to the Illinois voters in our study. He was perceived as weakest in inspiring confidence, being forthright, being strong, and using his own judgment.

Later in the campaign, as Table 9–4 shows, the Illinois voters perceived Carter as lacking more desirable dimensions than he possessed. Ford, by contrast, rose in the public's esteem. By July, Illinois voters thought that he had more positive than negative traits. Carter's strongest perceived attributes in July were similar, but not identical, to those noted in March: a man of principles, an appealing manner, a people's persons, and competent. His weakest attributes were inspiring confidence, holding leadership qualities, and his approach to issues. Ford's strongest perceived attributes in July were being a man of principles, holding leadership qualities, and having an appealing manner. His weakest image attributes were inspiring confidence, being forthright, being competent, and his stands on issues.

One month later, the Illinois voters perceived Carter as possessing an equal number of positive and negative image attributes. Ford was credited with possessing even more positive attributes than he had been in July. As Table 9–5 shows, Ford's strongest perceived image dimensions were the same as in July, and his weakest dimensions were narrowed from four to two; being competent and issue approaches. Inspiring confidence and being forthright, characteristics Ford was seen to lack in March and July, were evaluated more neutrally in August by the Illinois voters.

Carter's strongest image attributes were the same as in July, except that he was not perceived in August as a people's person. His weakest image characteristics in August differed from those in July, except for the view that he lacked the ability to inspire confidence. He was perceived in August as stronger in leadership qualities than in July, but as less forthright. And his approaches to issues were rated considerably more positively in August than in July (see Table 9–5).

TABLE 9–4

Illinois Voters' Descriptions of the Leading Candidates During July in Terms of Issues and Specific Image Dimensions (in percentages)

	Carter				Ford			
	Normative	Positive	Negative	Total	Normative	Positive	Negative	Total
Man of principles	0.0	17.2	2.6	8.8	0.0	31.0	0.0	17.1
Inspires confidence	0.0	6.9	15.4	11.8	0.0	0.0	11.8	5.3
Holds leadership qualities	0.0	3.4	10.3	7.4	0.0	9.5	2.9	6.6
Appealing manner	0.0	13.8	7.9	10.3	0.0	7.1	0.0	3.9
Compassionate	0.0	0.0	2.6	1.5	0.0	4.8	2.9	3.9
Forthright	0.0	3.4	5.1	4.4	0.0	0.0	11.8	5.3
Uses restraint	0.0	0.0	0.0	0.0	0.0	4.8	0.0	2.6
Strong	0.0	3.4	0.0	1.5	0.0	2.4	2.9	2.6
People's person	0.0	13.8	2.6	7.4	0.0	0.0	0.0	0.0
Competent	0.0	20.7	2.6	10.3	0.0	14.3	23.5	18.4
Versatile	0.0	3.4	0.0	1.5	0.0	0.0	5.9	2.6
Uses own judgment	0.0	0.0	0.0	0.0	0.0	0.0	0.0	0.0
Other image references	0.0	3.4	25.6	16.2	0.0	14.3	14.7	14.5
Issue-related references	0.0	10.3	25.6	19.1	0.0	11.9	23.5	17.1
Total	0.0	99.7°	100.3°	100.2°	0.0	100.1°	99.9°	99.9°
(N)	(0)	(29)	(39)	(68)	(0)	(42)	(34)	(76)

°Does not total 100.0 percent because of rounding error.

Source: Compiled by authors.

TABLE 9-5

Illinois Voters' Descriptions of the Leading Candidates During August in Terms of Issues and Specific Image Dimensions (in percentages)

	Carter				Ford			
	Normative	Positive	Negative	Total	Normative	Positive	Negative	Total
Man of principles	0.0	15.2	3.1	9.2	0.0	24.4	0.0	14.5
Inspires confidence	0.0	0.0	12.5	6.2	0.0	6.6	3.2	5.3
Holds leadership qualities	0.0	6.1	9.4	7.7	0.0	8.9	0.0	5.3
Appealing manner	0.0	15.2	6.3	10.8	0.0	11.1	0.0	6.6
Compassionate	0.0	3.0	0.0	1.5	0.0	0.0	3.2	1.3
Forthright	0.0	0.0	6.3	3.1	0.0	2.2	0.0	1.3
Uses restraint	0.0	3.0	0.0	1.5	0.0	2.2	0.0	1.3
Strong	0.0	0.0	0.0	0.0	0.0	2.2	6.5	3.9
People's person	0.0	0.0	0.0	0.0	0.0	0.0	0.0	0.0
Competent	0.0	12.1	6.3	9.2	0.0	15.6	32.3	22.4
Versatile	0.0	0.0	0.0	0.0	0.0	0.0	3.2	1.3
Uses own judgment	0.0	0.0	0.0	0.0	0.0	0.0	0.0	0.0
Other image references	0.0	18.2	31.3	24.6	0.0	15.6	29.0	21.1
Issue-related references	0.0	27.3	25.0	26.2	0.0	11.1	22.6	15.8
Total	0.0	100.1°	100.2°	100.0	0.0	99.9°	100.0	100.1°
(N)	(0)	(33)	(32)	(65)	(0)	(45)	(31)	(76)

°Does not total 100.0 percent because of rounding error.
Source: Compiled by authors.

175

By October of the 1976 election year, Carter was perceived by the Illinois voters in our study as lacking nearly twice as many positive image qualities as he possessed, and Ford was perceived in just the opposite manner (see Table 9–6). In March, the reverse had been true—Ford was perceived as lacking more positive image attributes than he possessed, and Carter was seen as possessing more than he lacked (see Table 9–3). During the campaign, then, the Illinois voters changed their images of the two candidates—in a positive direction for Ford and in a negative direction for Carter. But it is interesting to note that Carter was perceived by the voters more frequently and positively in terms of issues by the end of the campaign—which Ford lacked throughout.

The strengths and weaknesses of the two candidates, in terms of specific image dimensions, varied somewhat during the campaign but not greatly. Near the end of the election campaign, Ford was still perceived as strongest on principles but weakest on competence. The percentage of voter descriptions of Ford identifying him as competent fell from about 18 percent in March to about 6 percent in October. Carter, on the other hand, was characterized more as possessing competence than as lacking it throughout the campaign, and by October this was his strongest image dimension. Throughout the campaign, Carter was perceived as most lacking in the ability to inspire confidence (see Tables 9–3 through 9–6).

Thus, throughout the campaign, the Illinois voters' overall images of the two candidates changed, but the specific strengths and weaknesses in the images of the candidates remained moderately stable. Although these voters were much more likely by the end of the campaign to describe Ford in terms of image attributes he possessed and Carter in terms of those attributes he lacked, they still viewed Carter as more competent than Ford and Ford as more able to inspire confidence and to lead than Carter. And they were much more likely by October to describe Carter in terms of issues than they were Ford.

What images of the two leading candidates were presented in the newspaper read most frequently by these Illinois voters, the Chicago *Tribune*? Were the same changes in candidate images occurring in the *Tribune* during the election campaign?

CANDIDATE IMAGES IN THE CHICAGO *TRIBUNE*

During 1976, the Chicago *Tribune* published a total of 19,068 stories about the political process, the issues, the candidates, the election campaign, and related topics. Of these, 1,998, or about 10 percent, dealt with candidate images—426 stories about President Gerald Ford, 599 about

TABLE 9–6

Illinois Voters' Descriptions of the Leading Candidates During October in Terms of Issues and Specific Image Dimensions (in percentages)

	Carter				Ford			
	Normative	Positive	Negative	Total	Normative	Positive	Negative	Total
Man of principles	0.0	10.7	6.0	7.7	0.0	15.4	0.0	10.3
Inspires confidence	0.0	7.1	28.0	20.6	0.0	11.5	0.0	7.7
Holds leadership qualities	0.0	0.0	14.0	9.0	0.0	11.5	0.0	7.7
Appealing manner	0.0	3.6	2.0	2.6	0.0	0.0	0.0	0.0
Compassionate	0.0	3.6	0.0	1.3	0.0	1.9	0.0	1.3
Forthright	0.0	0.0	10.0	6.4	0.0	3.8	3.8	3.8
Uses restraint	0.0	0.0	0.0	0.0	0.0	3.8	0.0	2.6
Strong	0.0	7.1	0.0	2.6	0.0	0.0	3.8	1.3
People's person	0.0	3.6	0.0	1.3	0.0	0.0	11.5	3.8
Competent	0.0	10.7	4.0	6.4	0.0	5.8	26.9	12.8
Versatile	0.0	3.6	0.0	1.3	0.0	0.0	0.0	0.0
Uses own judgment	0.0	3.6	0.0	1.3	0.0	3.8	3.8	3.8
Other image references	0.0	3.6	8.0	6.4	0.0	26.9	30.8	28.2
Issue-related references	0.0	42.9	28.0	33.3	0.0	15.4	19.2	16.7
Total	0.0	100.1°	100.0	100.2°	0.0	99.8°	99.8°	100.0
(N)	(0)	(28)	(50)	(78)	(0)	(52)	(26)	(78)

°Does not total 100.0 percent due to rounding error.

Source: Compiled by authors.

Jimmy Carter, 516 about the other candidates, and 457 "image-type" stories about none of the candidates in particular.

Within these stories, the *Tribune* made 731 references to Ford, of which 182 (24.9 percent) dealt with his issue orientation. Carter recieved 887 image references, of which 181 (20.4 percent) were issue-related. Table 9–7 shows the distribution of the newspaper's image-related references to the two candidates.

The overall description of Ford appears balanced between the positive and negative categories. Of all comments, 51.0 percent were positive, 46.4 percent were negative, and the remaining 2.6 percent were normative. The yearly picture of Carter is not so balanced. Overall, 40.1 percent of the image references were positive, compared with 57.8 percent negative, and 2.1 percent normative.

Of the thirteen image categories (including "other"), Ford received more positive than negative comments on five: a man of principles, holding leadership qualities, an appealing manner, using his own judgment, and "other." Carter was presented as more positive than negative along six dimensions: holding leadership qualities, an appealing manner, compassionate, a people's person, versatile, and "other."

On the other hand, Ford's image was presented by the *Tribune* as more negative than positive along the dimensions of inspiring confidence, being compassionate, being forthright, using restraint, and being strong. Carter's image was presented in more negative than positive terms with regard to his ability to inspire confidence, to be forthright, to use restraint, and to be strong. Ford's strongest image attributes during the election year, according to the Chicago *Tribune*, were his appealing manner and his issue-related positions. Carter's strongest image attributes were his appealing manner, compassion, "people's person" aura, and issue-related stands.

The yearly summary of *Tribune* attribution, however, tells us very little about the dynamic nature of the "image-conferral" process. This summary is somewhat diluted because the early part of the year saw a multitude of candidates and contenders, including an unknown, Jimmy Carter. Only later in the year, following several months of coverage, did candidates Ford and Carter emerge as the finalists in the presidential race. This dilution is not as marked as might be expected, however. Between January 15, 1976, and June 30, 1976—three weeks after the last primary—70 percent of the total information supply about candidate images referred to Ford, Carter, and Reagan, leaving the seven other serious contenders (Wallace, Brown, Humphrey, Udall, Bayh, Jackson, and Church) with a scant 30 percent of the coverage.[16]

Tables 9–8, 9–9, and 9–10 show the distribution of the *Tribune's* image- and issue-related references to the two candidates during the

TABLE 9-7

Chicago *Tribune* Coverage of the Leading Candidates for the Entire Election Year in Terms of Issues and Specific Image Dimensions (in percentages)

	Carter				Ford			
	Normative	Positive	Negative	Total	Normative	Positive	Negative	Total
Man of principles	0.0	5.9	6.6	6.2	10.5	5.4	3.5	4.6
Inspires confidence	22.2	14.6	22.2	19.2	10.5	16.4	19.8	17.8
Holds leadership qualities	0.0	6.2	6.0	6.0	0.0	11.3	10.0	10.4
Appealing manner	0.0	4.8	1.9	3.0	5.3	4.3	1.8	3.1
Compassionate	0.0	5.9	2.3	3.7	0.0	4.3	6.5	5.2
Forthright	16.7	3.7	17.3	11.8	5.3	2.1	7.4	4.6
Uses restraint	0.0	0.8	8.2	5.1	0.0	1.3	3.5	2.3
Strong	0.0	4.8	6.4	5.6	10.5	3.8	5.3	4.6
People's person	5.6	5.6	1.0	2.9	0.0	1.3	2.1	1.6
Competent	11.1	1.4	2.7	2.4	15.8	6.2	6.2	6.4
Versatile	5.6	0.8	0.2	0.6	0.0	1.6	2.4	1.9
Uses own judgment	0.0	0.0	0.0	0.0	0.0	0.5	0.3	0.4
Other image references	11.1	19.9	8.4	13.1	26.3	14.2	8.6	11.9
Issue-related references	27.8	25.6	16.6	20.4	15.8	27.3	22.7	24.9
Total	100.1°	100.0	99.8°	100.0	100.0	100.0	100.1°	99.7°
(N)	(18)	(356)	(513)	(887)	(19)	(373)	(339)	(731)

°Does not total 100.0 percent because of rounding error.
Source: Compiled by authors.

179

TABLE 9–8

Chicago *Tribune* Coverage of the Leading Candidates During the 1976 Primary Season in Terms of Issues and Specific Image Dimensions (in percentages)

	Carter				Ford			
	Normative	Positive	Negative	Total	Normative	Positive	Negative	Total
Man of principles	0.0	7.8	5.3	6.6	0.0	6.8	6.8	6.6
Inspires confidence	0.0	14.1	21.1	17.2	0.0	10.2	16.2	13.1
Holds leadership qualities	0.0	7.8	7.0	7.4	0.0	10.2	12.2	10.9
Appealing manner	0.0	7.8	3.5	5.7	0.0	5.1	0.0	2.2
Compassionate	0.0	6.3	0.0	3.3	0.0	5.1	8.1	6.6
Forthright	0.0	1.6	17.5	9.0	0.0	0.0	2.7	1.5
Uses restraint	0.0	1.6	0.0	0.8	0.0	0.0	0.0	0.0
Strong	0.0	3.1	12.3	7.4	0.0	8.5	13.5	10.9
People's person	0.0	6.25	1.8	4.1	0.0	3.4	1.4	2.2
Competent	0.0	4.7	0.0	2.5	50.0	5.1	5.4	6.6
Versatile	0.0	1.6	0.0	0.0	0.0	1.7	4.1	2.9
Uses own judgment	0.0	0.0	0.0	0.0	0.0	0.0	0.0	0.0
Other image references	100.0	21.8	17.5	20.5	25.0	11.9	4.1	8.0
Issue-related references	0.0	15.6	14.0	14.8	25.0	32.2	25.7	28.5
Total	100.0	100.0	100.0	99.3°	100.0	100.2°	100.2°	100.0
(N)	(1)	(64)	(57)	(122)	(4)	(59)	(74)	(137)

°Does not total 100.0 percent because of rounding error.

Source: Compiled by authors.

three main periods of the election year; the early campaign period, from January 1 to April 30; the summer period from May 1 to August 31; and the fall period, from September 1 to November 2, Election Day.

Images in the Primaries

Overall, Ford and Carter received about an equal number of references in the Chicago *Tribune* during the winter and spring of 1976. The incumbent president received more negative than positive references (54.0 percent and 43.1 percent respectively), while the former Georgia governor was portrayed in a more favorable light (52.5 percent positive and 46.7 percent negative references). This pattern is opposite to the overall yearly pattern.

Ford's somewhat unfavorable image in the *Tribune* was due to image attributes, while issue-related references to him were more positive than negative. Carter, on the other hand, was presented in a balanced manner (equally negative and positive) in relation to his issue orientation. Only three image attributes of Ford received predominantly positive comments: appealing manner, people's person, and "other." The most frequent negative reference to Ford related his ability to inspire confidence. Carter was praised more than he was denounced for the following image dimensions: man of principles, leadership qualifications, appealing manner, compassion, restraint, people's person, competence, versatility, and "other." The *Tribune* was most critical about Carter's ability to inspire confidence and his forthrightness.

Clearly, in the early part of the campaign year, the Chicago *Tribune* offered a rather positive image of the new man from the South. The president, on the other hand, was presented less favorably in terms of his personal image but more positively in terms of issue-related references.

Images in the Summer

A shift in the picture of the candidates painted by the Chicago *Tribune* began to emerge in the summer of 1976. While the overall comments about Carter were slightly more positive than negative, the difference between the two was reduced: 49.1 percent positive and 48.0 percent negative (see Table 9–9). Carter was mentioned much more frequently than Ford, but Ford was presented more positively in the summer than he had been in the previous months: 55.5 percent of the references to the incumbent president were positive compared with only 40.1 percent negative references.

The differential treatment of the two candidates by the *Tribune* was even more striking for just the pure image references: Ford received 55.5 percent positive and only 39.0 percent negative mentions, whereas Carter was mentioned favorably in 44.6 percent and unfavorably in 52.5 percent of the image references. Both candidates were presented more positively than negatively along the issue-related image dimension, with Ford receiving 55.4 percent positive and 43.2 percent negative comments, while references to Carter were 61.4 percent positive and 35.6 percent negative.

More specifically, Ford was presented in the *Tribune* as having more positive than negative attributes in most of the image categories, with the exception of the confidence, people's person, and "other" image dimensions. In most cases, the differences between the "positive" (possessed by candidate) and the "negative" (lacking) image references were very small for Ford, suggesting balanced coverage.

Jimmy Carter, in contrast, received more positive than negative references with regard to holding leadership qualities, having an appealing manner, being compassionate, being the people's person, and in the "other" category. But he was presented overall as lacking the ability to inspire confidence and as lacking forthrightness. These negative issue references contributed greatly to an overall decline in Carter's image as presented by the *Tribune* in the summer.

Images in the Fall

By the fall of 1976, our data show that the Chicago *Tribune* presented a highly favorable image of the president and a rather negative picture of the Democratic contender. During the two and a half months prior to the presidential elections, positive and negative image references to Ford were about even (50.6 percent and 48.4 percent respectively); during the same period, Carter was referred to positively in only 27.3 percent of the mentions by the *Tribune* and negatively in 71.1 percent (see Table 9–10). *Tribune* references to Carter were especially negative with regard to his forthrightness, restraint, and ability to inspire confidence. In addition, for the first time during the campaign year, negative issue-related references to Carter outnumbered positive references more than two to one. Positive issue-related comments about Ford constituted 60.9 percent of all such references to the president in the fall, while only 37.7 percent of these 69 references were negative. In contrast to earlier periods in the year, however, the purely image references to Ford tended to be slightly more negative than positive (47.8 percent positive and 51.4 percent negative). Ford, during this period, was presented as more positive than negative along six of the thirteen image dimensions. This was also true for Carter.

TABLE 9–9

Chicago *Tribune* Coverage of the Leading Candidates During the 1976 Summer Campaign in Terms of Issues and Specific Image Dimensions (in percentages)

	Carter				Ford			
	Normative	Positive	Negative	Total	Normative	Positive	Negative	Total
Man of principles	0.0	5.9	9.3	7.4	16.7	5.9	3.6	5.5
Inspires confidence	18.2	10.7	18.0	14.4	16.7	15.8	16.4	16.1
Holds leadership qualities	0.0	5.9	4.4	5.0	0.0	12.5	11.8	11.7
Appealing manner	0.0	3.2	1.6	2.4	8.3	4.6	3.6	4.4
Compassionate	0.0	2.7	2.2	2.4	0.0	4.6	4.5	4.4
Forthright	27.3	6.4	21.3	14.2	8.3	2.6	2.7	2.9
Uses restraint	0.0	1.1	3.8	2.4	0.0	2.0	0.0	1.1
Strong	0.0	6.4	8.7	7.4	16.7	4.6	4.5	5.1
People's person	9.1	5.3	1.6	3.7	0.0	1.3	2.7	1.8
Competent	9.1	0.5	1.6	1.3	8.3	6.6	6.4	6.6
Versatile	0.0	0.5	0.5	0.5	0.0	1.3	0.9	1.1
Uses own judgment	0.0	0.0	0.0	0.0	0.0	0.0	0.9	0.4
Other image references	9.1	18.2	7.1	12.6	16.7	11.2	12.7	12.0
Issue-related references	27.3	33.2	19.7	26.5	8.3	27.0	29.1	27.0
Total	100.1°	100.0	99.8°	100.2°	100.0	100.0	99.8°	100.1°
(N)	(11)	(187)	(183)	(381)	(12)	(152)	(110)	(274)

°Does not total 100.0 percent because of rounding error.
Source: Compiled by authors.

TABLE 9–10

Chicago *Tribune* Coverage of the Leading Candidates During the 1976 Fall Campaign in Terms of Issues and Specific Image Dimensions (in percentages)

	Carter				Ford			
	Normative	Positive	Negative	Total	Normative	Positive	Negative	Total
Man of principles	0.0	4.8	5.1	4.9	0.0	4.3	1.9	3.2
Inspires confidence	33.3	21.9	25.3	24.5	0.0	19.1	23.9	21.3
Holds leadership qualities	0.0	5.7	7.0	6.5	0.0	10.5	7.7	9.1
Appealing manner	0.0	5.7	1.8	2.9	0.0	3.7	1.3	2.5
Compassionate	0.0	11.4	2.9	5.2	0.0	3.7	7.1	5.3
Forthright	0.0	0.0	14.7	10.4	0.0	2.5	12.9	7.5
Uses restraint	0.0	0.0	12.8	9.1	0.0	1.2	7.7	4.4
Strong	0.0	2.9	3.7	3.4	0.0	1.2	1.9	1.6
People's person	0.0	5.7	0.4	1.8	0.0	0.6	1.9	1.2
Competent	16.7	1.0	4.0	3.4	0.0	6.2	6.5	6.2
Versatile	16.7	1.0	0.0	0.5	0.0	1.9	2.6	2.2
Uses own judgment	0.0	0.0	0.0	0.0	0.0	1.2	0.0	0.6
Other image references	0.0	21.9	7.3	11.2	66.7	17.9	7.7	13.4
Issue-related references	33.3	18.1	15.0	16.1	33.3	25.9	16.8	21.6
Total	100.0	100.1°	100.0	99.9°	100.0	99.9°	99.9°	100.1°
(N)	(6)	(105)	(273)	(384)	(3)	(162)	(155)	(320)

°Does not total 100.0 percent because of rounding error.
Source: Compiled by authors.

184

Throughout the year, then, the Chicago *Tribune* references to the two leading candidates painted a picture of two different men. In the early primary period there appeared to be a less-than-qualified president facing a more charismatic and favorable, yet little known, contender. Later, however, the *Tribune*'s picture changed. Like the painter who abruptly changes the stroke while introducing new hues into the picture, the Chicago daily began to favor re-electing Gerald Ford in its image references.

The differential treatment of the two candidates should have been clearly evident to the regular readers of the *Tribune*. Overall, our image data indicate that President Ford was treated evenly, with about equal positive and negative image references. Jimmy Carter, on the other hand, did not enjoy the same balance; the ratio of positive to negative treatment of Carter went from about 1.0:1.0 in the primary and summer periods to 1.0:2.5 in the fall, resulting in a yearly average of about 1.0:1.4.

This differential treatment of the two candidates parallels to some extent the changes that occurred in the Illinois voters' images of these same candidates. As pointed out in the previous section of this chapter, these voters were more likely by the end of the campaign to describe Gerald Ford in terms of the image attributes he possessed and Jimmy Carter in terms of those attributes he lacked. In other words, the voters appeared to change their images of Ford in a positive direction and their images of Carter in a negative direction during the campaign, just as the Chicago *Tribune* had.

But did the image changes in the *Tribune* precede, coincide with, or follow the changes in the voters' images? The next section considers the relationship over time between Illinois voter and Chicago *Tribune* specific agendas.

TRIBUNE IMAGES AND VOTER IMAGES

Total Image Agendas

Figure 9–1 shows that the total image agendas of the *Tribune* and the Illinois voters were generally similar throughout the campaign for both Carter and Ford, except in the spring primary period for Ford, probably because Ford's image was already fairly well-established from his stint as president. And there is evidence to suggest that the Illinois voters were taking their cues on Carter's image from the *Tribune* rather than vice versa. It also appears likely that the *Tribune* portrayal of Ford in the spring had more influence on voter images of him in the summer than vice versa. But from summer to fall, voter and newspaper images of Ford seemed to

FIGURE 9–1

Crosslagged Correlational Analysis (Spearman's Rhos)
Between Chicago *Tribune* Total Image Agendas and Illinois Voters'
Total Image Agendas During the 1976 Campaign

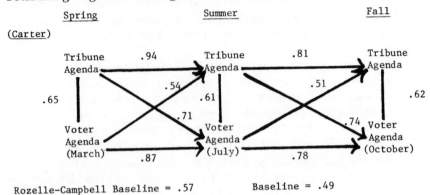

Rozelle–Campbell Baseline = .57   Baseline = .49

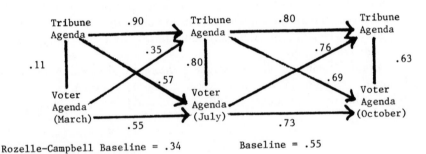

Rozelle–Campbell Baseline = .34   Baseline = .55

Source: Compiled by authors.

reinforce each other. Throughout the campaign, the *Tribune* image agendas for both candidates were more stable than were the Illinois voters', as was true for the issue agendas of all voters and all three newspapers, suggesting again that the newspaper was having more influence on the voters than vice versa. This conclusion is further supported by examining the crosslagged correlations from spring to fall. In Ford's case, the correlation of the spring *Tribune* total image agenda with the fall voter total image agenda is 0.47, whereas the correlation of the spring voter image agenda with the fall *Tribune* image agenda is only 0.21, below the baseline of 0.24.[17] In Carter's case, the correlation of the spring *Tribune* image agenda with the fall voter agenda is 0.77, as compared with a correlation of 0.44 between the spring voter agenda and the fall *Tribune* agenda (baseline = 0.46).

With regard to Ford's and Carter's total images, then, there is evidence from the Illinois site of our study that the Chicago *Tribune* played an important agenda-setting role for the voters who regularly read this newspaper. This evidence supports the idea that mass media agenda-setting is not limited to issues, but that it takes place for candidate images as well.

Positive Image Agendas

From spring to summer, the same newspaper agenda-setting seems to have occurred for the positive images (those the candidates are said to possess) as for the total images of the two leading candidates (Figure 9–2). But it is less clear in the summer-to-fall period whether changes in images in the *Tribune* led or followed changes in voter images of Carter and Ford. When the spring-to-fall crosslagged correlations are compared, however, it is apparent that the spring *Tribune* images are more closely associated with the fall voter images than vice versa for both Carter (0.39 versus 0.18, with a baseline of 0.28) and Ford (0.58 versus 0.21, with a baseline of 0.29). The correlations for positive images tend to be somewhat weaker than those for the total images, suggesting that media image qualities as such have more impact on voters' images of candidates than whether these qualities are pictured in a positive or negative vein. In other words, the media appear to be better at telling voters what to think about in forming their images of the candidates than what to think regarding the pluses and minuses of these candidates.

Figure 9–2 also supports the view that the Illinois voters' perceptions of the image qualities possessed by Ford were more influenced by the *Tribune*'s description of these qualities than was true for Carter, especially as the campaign drew to a close. This probably reflects the *Tribune*'s tendency to say more about Ford's desirable attributes than Carter's as the election drew nearer.

Negative Image Agendas

As expected, Figure 9–3 indicates that the Illinois voters' perceptions of desirable qualities lacked by Carter were more closely associated with the *Tribune*'s description of such near the end of the campaign than was true for Ford. This most likely reflects the *Tribune*'s increasing emphasis on Carter's image deficiencies and its decreasing emphasis on Ford's

FIGURE 9–2

Crosslagged Correlational Analysis (Spearman's Rhos) Between Chicago *Tribune* Positive Image Agendas and Illinois Voters' Positive Image Agendas During the 1976 Campaign

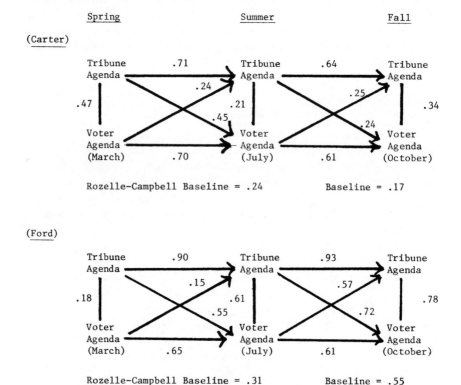

Source: Compiled by authors.

shortcomings as the election drew nearer. But the direction of influence is much less clear for the negative image agendas than it is for the positive or total image agendas. The crosslagged correlations in Figure 9–3 suggest a mostly reciprocal influence over time between the *Tribune* and the Illinois voters' negative image agendas, especially for Carter. This may be partially due to the stability of the negative image agendas of voters and of the *Tribune* over the campaign period. In terms of the ranking of image qualities Carter was said to lack, neither the *Tribune* nor the Illinois voter panel changed much from spring to fall (see Figure 9–3). Both empha-

FIGURE 9–3

Crosslagged Correlational Analysis (Spearman's Rhos) Between Chicago *Tribune* Negative Image Agendas and Illinois Voters' Negative Image Agendas During the 1976 Campaign

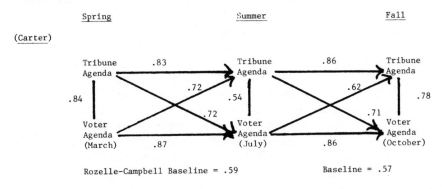

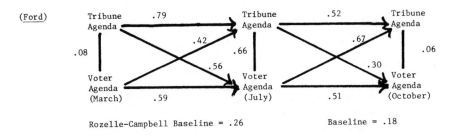

Source: Compiled by authors.

sized Carter's lack of ability to inspire confidence and his lack of forthrightness (see Tables 9–3 through 9–10). In short, although there is a surprising amount of agreement between the *Tribune* and the Illinois voters on which image dimensions Carter lacked (and which ones Ford lacked during the summer), there is less convincing evidence on the direction of influence than there is for the positive and total image agendas.

Normative Image Agendas

No correlations were possible between the *Tribune* and voter normative image agendas (those image dimensions the candidates ought to possess) because the Illinois voters, when asked to describe the candidates to friends, did not dwell on these dimensions (see Tables 9–3 through 9–6). But the *Tribune* did describe both Carter and Ford occasionally in normative terms (see Tables 9–7 through 9–10). Not surprisingly, the *Tribune* described Carter as needing to acquire the same qualities he was said to lack—the ability to inspire confidence and to be more forthright. Ford's normative image agenda was not so highly correlated with his negative image agenda as was Carter's. This lack of correlation may have contributed to the generally low correlations between the *Tribune* negative image agenda and the Illinois voters' negative image agenda for Ford.

Whatever the case, Figures 9–1, 9–2, and 9–3 suggest that the Illinois voters were more influenced by the Chicago *Tribune*'s description of those desirable qualities that Carter lacked than by those he possessed, and by the *Tribune*'s coverage of those favorable qualities Ford possessed rather than those he lacked. This pattern paralleled the *Tribune*'s increasing emphasis on the negative image attributes of Carter and the positive image attributes of Ford. The pattern lends support to the idea that media agenda-setting applies to images as well as issues and that media emphasis or neglect of certain kinds of image dimensions contributes to voter evaluations of candidates as well as to voter images of such candidates.

SUMMING UP

This chapter on mass media and candidate images leads to the following major conclusions.

The image of a political candidate can be viewed as an array of perceived attributes, an agenda of image dimensions. The ranking of these perceived attributes or dimensions appears to be influenced by newspaper (and probably by other media) emphasis on certain attributes and de-emphasis of others. By concentrating on certain attributes of a candidate and downplaying others, the Chicago *Tribune* appeared to play an important image agenda-setting role for the Illinois voters in our study.

Although mass media are important sources of raw material for the formation of candidates' images, interpersonal communication networks also play an important role, as do the knowledge and attitudes of individual voters. Whereas the mass media are more likely to provide information about candidates, interpersonal contacts and individual attitudes are likely to be most important in the evaluation of the media-originated information about the candidates.

It is not clear from previous studies whether candidate images are more important than candidate issue stands in voting decisions, but there is general agreement that both images and issue stands are important determinants of the overall evaluation of political candidates and that issues and images are often inseparable. Declines in political party affiliation and class loyalties have heightened the importance of candidate images and issue positions in voting.

In the 1976 election campaign, Jimmy Carter's image was less well-established than was Gerald Ford's, especially at the beginning of the year, and it tended to fluctuate during the campaign more than did Ford's. Most voters in our study consistently referred to images rather than issues in their descriptions of Carter and Ford, especially those who were highly interested in the presidential campaign and who were heavier users of the media, particularly television, to follow politics. Voters in our study, especially those in the Evanston core panel, seemed to be able to learn about candidate images more easily than about issue positions. The complexity of issues and the haziness of the candidates were mentioned most often as barriers to understanding. But references to issues did increase as the election drew near, primarily in descriptions of Carter, suggesting that issues played a more important role in the evaluation of the candidates later in the campaign when voting decisions were more pressing for more voters.

The candidates' past activities and abilities to act became more important to the voters in our study as the campaign progressed, as did their orientations to issues. Apparently as Election Day drew near, the candidates' issue orientations and political positions became clearer and better known and were perceived by voters as more important than they had been earlier in the campaign. The more highly educated voters in our study tended to emphasize the behavior and knowledge of the candidates, whereas the less educated voters described the candidates more in terms of emotional preferences and behavior.

During the campaign, the Illinois voters in our study changed their images of both Carter and Ford—in a positive direction for Ford (emphasizing desirable qualities he possessed) and in a negative direction for Carter (emphasizing desirable qualities he lacked). But Carter was described by these voters in terms of issues more than Ford, especially near the end of the campaign, confirming the earlier conclusion that issues became more important in the voting decisions of those who waited until late in the campaign to decide.

In nearly 2,000 news stories dealing with candidates images, the Chicago *Tribune* (the newspaper relied on by most of the Illinois voters in our study) changed its descriptions of the candidates during the campaign to emphasize the favorable image qualities that Carter lacked and Ford possessed, paralleling the shifts in Illinois voters' images of the two candidates. Crosslagged correlational analysis suggests that the *Tribune* descriptions of the candidates were having more influence on the Illinois voters than vice versa throughout the campaign. These findings support the idea that media agenda-setting (at least newspaper agenda-setting) extends to candidate images as well as to issues and that media emphasis or de-emphasis of certain image attributes contributes to voter evaluations of candidates as well as to overall voter images of those candidates.

This newspaper agenda-setting influence on voters' candidate images is not a simple and direct process, any more than it is for issues. Obviously, it varies according to a number of factors such as media exposure patterns of voters, interpersonal communication patterns, prior knowledge and attitudes, levels of motivation to follow the campaign, levels of uncertainty in making voting decisions, and so on. But our data establish that, overall, the Chicago *Tribune*'s image agendas for Carter and Ford did have an influence on the image agendas of the Illinois voters in our study during the 1976 presidential election. We suspect that the same is true for other newspapers—and for television—in other communities.

NOTES

[1]Arthur Krock, "'The Man Who'—Not 'The Issue Which,' " New York *Times*, October 16, 1960, p. 19.

[2]Dan F. Hahn and Ruth M. Gonchar, "Political Myth: The Image and the Issue," *Today's Speech* 20 (Summer 1972): 57–65, p. 61.

[3]Dan Nimmo and Robert L. Savage, *Candidates and Their Images* (Pacific Palisades: Goodyear, 1976), p. 8; and John E. Bowes and Herbert Strentz, "Candidate Images: Stereotyping and the 1976 Debates," in *Communication Yearbook II*, ed. Brent Ruben (New Brunswick, N.J.: Transaction Books, 1978), p. 391.

[4]Roberta S. Sigel, "Effects of Partisanship on Perception of Political Candidates," *Public Opinion Quarterly* 28 (Fall 1964): 483–96, pp. 484–85.

[5]Doris A. Graber, "Personal Qualities in Presidential Images: The Contribution of the Press," *Midwest Journal of Political Science* 16 (February 1972): pp. 50–51.

[6]Elihu Katz and Jacob J. Feldman, "The Debates in Light of Research: A Survey of Surveys," in *The Process and Effects of Mass Communication*, eds. Wilbur Schramm and Donald F. Roberts (Urbana: University of Illinois Press, 1971), pp. 701–53.

[7]D. A. Leuthold, *Electioneering in a Democracy: Campaigns for Congress* (New York: John Wiley, 1968).

[8]Peter A. Andersen and Robert J. Kibler, "Candidate Valence as a Predictor of Voter Preference," *Human Communication Research* 5 (March 1978): p. 11.

[9]American Institute for Political Communication, *The 1968 Campaign: Anatomy of a Crucial Election* (Washington, D.C.: American Institute for Political Communication, 1970), pp. 71–72.

[10]Peter B. Natchez, "Images of Voting: The Social Psychologists," *Public Policy* 18 (Summer 1970): 576.

[11]Ibid, p. 577.

[12]Bowes and Strentz, "Candidate Images," p. 391.

[13]Fred I. Greenstein, "Popular Images of the President," *American Journal of Psychiatry* 122 (November 1965): p. 526.

[14]Natchez, "Images of Voting," pp. 580–81.

[15]Graber, "Personal Qualities in Presidential Images," p. 47.

[16]During the primaries, 77 percent of all *Tribune* news stories dealing with individual candidates, 84 percent of editorials, 69 percent of all columns, 83 percent of poll reports, and 71 percent of cartoons also dealt with the three frontrunners.

[17]A Spearman's Rho of $+1.0$ indicates a perfect correlation between two sets of rankings. A Rho of 0.0 indicates no correlation, and a Rho of -1.0 indicates that one ranking is just the opposite of the other (a perfect inverse correlation). As explained in Chapter 5, crosslagged correlation is used to check on the relationships of variables across time. The logic underlying crosslagged correlation is that if X is the cause of Y or influences the value of Y, then the correlation of X at time one with Y at time two should be stronger than the correlation of Y at time one with X at time two. In other words, a cause at time one should correlate with its subsequent effect more strongly than an effect at time one with its cause at time two. The Rozelle-Campbell Baseline is an estimate of what the diagonal (crosslagged) correlations would be if there were no causal relationship between the two variables. Thus, if one crosslagged correlation is substantially above the baseline and one is substantially below it, one can conclude that the first crosslagged correlation indicates an influence of the first variable on the second over time. For the formula for calculating the Rozelle-Campbell Baseline, see R. M. Rozelle and D. T. Campbell, "More Plausible Rival Hypotheses in the Cross-Lagged Panel Correlation Technique," *Psychological Bulletin* 71 (1969): 74–80, and Leonard P. Tipton, Roger D. Haney, and John R. Baseheart, "Media Agenda-Setting in City and State Election Campaigns," *Journalism Quarterly* 52 (Spring 1975): 15–22.

ten

ISSUES, IMAGES, INTEREST: THE ELECTION YEAR IN REVIEW

What have we learned in this yearlong study of the influence of newspapers and television news on voters during the 1976 presidential election campaign? What can we say about voters' learning during this election, based on more than 1,100 interviews with them in three different communities, analysis of thousands of newspaper and television news stories during the entire year, and careful study of the daily diaries and in-depth conversations of a core panel of voters in Evanston, Illinois?

To what extent do the media set agendas of issues, candidates, and candidate images? Under what circumstances and over what periods of time does this transfer of salience take place? How is it accomplished? Do the media concentrate their coverage on a few key issues and a few key attributes of a few key candidates perceived to be the leaders of the race? Do they raise the salience of politics in general on a much broader agenda of concerns? Are newspapers and television equal partners in the agenda-setting process? Is learning of the relative importance of various issue and image qualities accompanied by learning of more detailed information about public issues and events and personalities of the day? Or is agenda-setting a comparatively mindless form of rote learning in which voters memorize media priorities and emphases without absorbing much of the information on which these priorites are based? Finally, what are the implications of media agenda-setting for press performance and for our political system?

These are the key questions that guided our study in Evanston, Ill.; Lebanon, N.H.; and Indianapolis, Ind. The answers to these questions are discussed and summarized below. Even though many of them are not as simple, unqualified, and final as one might hope, they contribute substantially to our understanding of voters' learning from the mass media and the mass media agenda-setting process. In addition, they speak to the question of the performance of newspapers and television in a presidential election and to the impact of this performance on presidential politics in the United States.

ISSUE AGENDA PATTERNS

Our findings throughout the 1976 election year suggest that the agenda-setting function of the mass media with regard to issues varies according to these clusters of factors: period of the campaign, kind of news medium, nature of the issues, and orientation and characteristics of voters.

Time Periods

The period of the campaign has a major impact on the agenda-setting influence of newspapers and television, especially with regard to more obtrusive (less directly experienced) issues. Our data indicate that the influence of both newspapers and television is greatest during the primaries in the spring, somewhat less during the summer, and least during the final months of an election campaign. This pattern generally held for all three communities in our study (but especially for the voters of higher socioeconomic status in Evanston), signifying that the issue agenda-setting process is not static but varies as the campaign progresses.

This general trend of declining media influence on the perceived importance of various issues was confined mainly to the seven unobtrusive issues of foreign affairs, government credibility, crime, social problems, environment and energy, government spending and size, and race relations. For obtrusive issues, media agenda-setting appeared to be minimal at all times. Three of the four more obtrusive economic issues remained of generally high concern to voters throughout the election year, regardless of their treatment by newspapers and television network news shows. This indicates that personal experience is a more powerful teacher of issue salience than are the mass media when the issues have a direct impact on voters' daily lives. Absence of media agenda-setting for obtrusive issues can have major political consequences when these issues play an important role in voting choices, as happened in 1976. Wides' analysis of sample data collected by the University of Michigan's Center for Political Studies shows that evaluations of economic competency of parties and candidates—obtrusive issues in 1976 as well as in other presidential elections—directly influenced voting decisions.[1]

Our study also provides evidence that discussions with other persons are important over time in setting an agenda of issues in an election campaign. As the 1976 campaign wore on and as political conversations increased among the voters we studied, the personal concern and perceived community issue agendas became more similar to the personal discussion agendas. By the last month of the campaign, these three issue agendas were nearly identical. Thus both direct personal experiences and conversations with others serve to mediate the agenda-setting influence of newspapers and television with regard to campaign issues.

We should not belittle media influence, however. All three voter issue agendas, it must be remembered, generally became more similar over time to earlier newspaper agendas. Newspapers thus had a major influence on which issues were discussed with others and which were considered important by voters.

Newspapers and Television.

The distinctions between newspapers and television as issue agenda-setters became less pronounced as the election drew nearer. During the primaries in the spring, we found evidence of a "two-step flow" of media agenda-setting, with the combined newspaper issue agenda remaining very stable over time, the television agenda changing to become more similar to the stable newspaper agenda, and the voter agendas becoming more similar to the television network issue agenda. This sequence suggests that newspapers were the primary agenda-setters of unobtrusive issues during the election campaign. After the summer conventions, the newspaper and television issue agendas became nearly identical and changed little. The few changes that did occur were in the direction of the voter agendas, offering no support for media agenda-setting during the fall period of the campaign.

When the differences between newspaper and television issue agenda-setting were examined for each community separately, similar patterns emerged. Newpapers exerted an influence on unobtrusive issue salience over a longer period of time—about two months—compared with television's influence span of about one month. This amounted to an *agenda-setting* role for newspapers versus a *spotlighting* role for television, especially apparent during the August to October period of the campaign and in Indiana and New Hampshire, where voters tended to be less educated and were more likely to be blue-collar workers than in Illinois. The higher educational and occupational levels of the voters in Evanston seemed to work against distinct agenda-setting roles for newspapers and television, perhaps because higher-status voters rely more on other sources of information, including interpersonal discussion, for establishing their issue agendas than do less well educated and lower-status voters.

Unobtrusive and Obtrusive Issues

The nature of the issues was especially important in the early spring period of the campaign. During the primaries, the more unobtrusive issues (those less likely to be directly experienced by voters) were ranked by voters in nearly the same order as they had been by newspapers and television during the previous two months or so, whereas the more obtrusive economic issues were ranked considerably more important by voters than by either newspapers or television. By the summer season, the distinction between obtrusive and unobtrusive issues was less clear. The unobtrusive issues seemingly had become more obtrusive after six months of rather consistent media emphasis. This made them more established concerns of the voters in our study and less dependent upon media rankings. By this time, apparently, voters had made up their minds about the relative importance of issues, without reference to current newspaper and television coverage.

Voters' Orientation

In contrast to the declining importance of newspapers and television as issue agenda-setters and to the decreased significance of the nature of the issues later in the year, the orientations and characteristics of voters seemed to become more important as the campaign drew to a close. Although levels of motivation to follow the campaign had fairly minor effects on voter issue agendas during the spring and summer seasons, this was not true during the fall period. Those voters with a high need for orientation (high interest and high uncertainty about whom to support) had issue agendas in the fall that were substantially more similar to the media agendas than did other voters. Thus motivation to follow the campaign was most important in the agenda-setting process near the end of the campaign when the need for information was greatest for unde-cided voters. After the election, voters with a high need for orientation were more likely than other voters to cite issues as more important than either candidate images or political party affiliation in deciding for whom to vote.[2] This finding suggests that voters with a great deal of motivation to follow the campaign (a high need for orientation) were paying more attention to the issue-related content of the mass media near the end of the campaign than were other voters. Accordingly, they were more likely to have issue agendas similar to the media agendas.

Learning which issues are important from the mass media is not the same as learning detailed information about candidate positions on these issues. In other words, issue agenda-setting does not equal understanding of issues and knowledge of the differences in approaches to issues by the various candidates. Our data on learning, especially from the core panel of voters in Evanston, suggest that most learning from the media is confined to awareness—the ability to recognize both issues and images without the ability to recall related facts spontaneously. Only a few of our respondents were able to define the positions taken by both leading candidates on any particular issue. Thus many voter judgments about the salience of various issues appear to be founded on rote learning from the media rather than carefully considered choices.

Nevertheless, the importance of media agenda-setting should not be underestimated just because many voters do not learn detailed information about the issues stressed by the media. The first stage in the public opinion process is increased salience of an issue or issues.[3] Without initial awareness of and concern about certain issues, it is highly unlikely that voters will increase their knowledge of such issues or develop opinions about them. The media, especially newspapers early in the election year, appear to be major issue agenda-setters, at least for the more unobtrusive issues. Although beyond the personal experience of most voters, these issues encompass important public policies in such areas as foreign affairs, government spending, and government credibility, which are crucial to the welfare of every citizen.

Media agenda-setting influence varies in potency, of course. It hinges on the substance of the issues (a significant foreign event may supersede a less significant event based on personal experience), the frequency or repetition of media coverage over time, the motivations of individual voters to follow the election campaign, their levels of education and lifestyles, and their media exposure patterns. But in spite of such variations, media influence on issue salience of unobtrusive issues remains important for most of the groups of voters we studied.

The voters least likely to be influenced by media issue agenda-setting are those with more education, higher-status jobs, more prior political knowledge, and more interest in the campaign. Great knowledge and more sources of information permit greater freedom to form independent judgments about the importance of various issues. But for the majority of less well informed voters, issue agenda-setting occurs quite commonly. Our data suggest that newspaper emphasis of issues is especially significant early in a presidential campaign for determining which unobtrusive issues voters will deem most important and will discuss most often.

Media Influence

It also appears that reporters and editors exercise considerable discretion in choosing certain issues to emphasize over time. This means that not all of the issues stressed by the leading candidates or the major political parties will be heavily covered by newspapers and television. In fact, political scientist Thomas Patterson, in another yearlong study of the 1976 election, reports that the issues the candidates stressed most heavily were not the same as those displayed most prominently in the news.[4] Patterson found that in their campaign speeches and television political advertising, the candidates talked mostly about "diffuse" issues: broad policy proposals, such as the commitment to maintain a healthy economy. By contrast, the media stressed what Colin Seymour-Ure has called "clear-cut" issues—those which neatly divide the candidates, provoke conflict, and can be stated in simple terms, usually by reference to shorthand labels such as "busing" and "detente."[5]

One of Patterson's major conclusions regarding issues in the 1976 presidential campaign is that the issue news reflected the interests of the press more than the candidates' interests.[6] This conclusion is consistent with our finding that the media, particularly newspapers, are major issue agenda-setters early in the campaign.

In light of the decreasing importance of political party identification,[7] the increasing importance of issues in U.S. presidential elections,[8] and the increased reliance by undecided and interested voters on issue stands for making voting choices,[9] the issue coverage of newspapers and television may play an increasingly more important role in the outcome of future presidential races. Hence media emphasis and de-emphasis of certain issues may have far-reaching effects on issues and problems dealt with by the president and the congress after the election. This places a great responsibility on the media, especially newspapers, to put an early spotlight on public policy issues likely to have the greatest long-term significance for the society at large and to make as clear as possible the various candidates' positions on these issues. In doing so, the major mass media of this country (especially the newspapers) are doing far more than reinforcing partisan voters' predispositions, as earlier studies have suggested.[10]

IMAGE AGENDA PATTERNS

It seems that the neglect of image agenda-setting in nearly all of the previous media agenda-setting studies has been a serious oversight.[11] Our study shows that the press plays a major role in setting the agenda of candidate image qualities or attributes. In fact, this image agenda-setting function of the media probably has more pervasive influence on the voters' early perceptions of the campaign and the final choices available at election time than does issue agenda-setting.

Candidate Recognition

The most basic dimension of a candidates' image is name recognition or awareness. If the voters have not heard of a candidate or do not recognize his or her name, they are not likely to have a politically useful image of him or her. Therefore, the most fundamental image agenda-setting role performed by the media is simply to familiarize voters with candidates' names.

In this process it is crucial how much coverage is given to the various contenders before and during the first primaries of the election campaign. Our analysis of the Chicago *Tribune*'s coverage of the candidates showed that between January 15 and June 30—three weeks after the last primary—70 percent of the total information referred to Ford, Carter, and Reagan, leaving the seven other serious contenders (Wallace, Bayh, Brown, Harris, Udall, Jackson, and Church) with a scant 30 percent of the coverage. And Patterson found in his study of 1,200 voters in Erie, Pa., and Los Angeles, Cal., that before the first primary in New Hampshire, the Democratic candidates were largely unknown to the voters. Only 20 percent felt they "knew" Carter, Udall, Harris, Bayh, Brown, Church, or Jackson. After subsequent news coverage focused heavily on Carter, he was the sole Democrat to become dramatically more familiar to the voters.[12] The percentage of the voters who felt that they "knew" Carter rose to more than 80 percent, a 60 percent increase from the preprimary level. Comparable figures in our three communities were a 16 percent vote for Carter as frontrunner in February, rising to 80 percent in March. In contrast, recognition levels rose by only 14 percent for Udall, Brown, and Jackson and by only 9 percent for Church, remained fairly constant for Harris, and even declined for Bayh. Patterson concludes that these differences did affect the outcome of the Democratic primaries because voters limited their choices to familiar candidates.

Using data from our study, along with those from another study of 335 registered Democrats in Onondaga, N.Y., and national poll data gathered by the Gallup Organization, Becker and McCombs likewise found that from February to March, voters went from being unsure of who was leading the crowded Democratic field of candidates to placing Jimmy Carter at the top of the list—or agenda—of candidates.[13] Based on content analysis of *Newsweek* magazine and correlations of media use patterns of voters with levels of recognition of the candidates, Becker and McCombs concluded that the media were at least partially responsible for these shifts in voter perceptions.

Thus there is evidence from the 1976 election to support the conclusion that the press is a powerful influence in setting the agenda of candidates early in the primaries by focusing coverage on only one or two perceived frontrunners in each party. But what of the images of individual candidates? Does the press also help to set the agenda of image attributes for individual politicians?

Image Attributes

The image attributes stressed in Chicago *Tribune* coverage and in descriptions used by Illinois voters to acquaint their friends with the leading candidates run along parallel lines. This suggests that the *Tribune* did play an important agenda-setting role for the Illinois voters in our study by concentrating on certain Carter and Ford attributes and downplaying others. In nearly 2,000 news stories dealing with candidate images, the *Tribune* (the newspaper read most heavily by the Illinois voters in our study) changed its descriptions of the candidates during the election year so that the Carter image became increasingly unfavorable while the Ford image improved. The Illinois voters in our study changed their images of the two candidates in the same manner. Furthermore, crosslagged correlational analysis suggests that, for the most part, the *Tribune* descriptions of Carter and Ford influenced the Illinois voters rather than vice versa. These findings support the idea that media agenda-setting (at least newspaper agenda-setting) extends to specific image dimensions as well as to issues and to an agenda of candidates. These findings also signify that media emphasis or de-emphasis of certain image dimensions can contribute to overall voter evaluations of candidates as well as to their images of such candidates.

We also found that the voters in our study thought it easier to learn about candidate images than about issues, enhancing the chances for image agenda-setting. In fact, voters consistently referred to images three or four times as often as to issues in their descriptions of Carter and Ford. This was especially true of voters who were above average in interest in the campaign and in their use of television to follow politics. Although the media presented ample information of all kinds during the 1976 campaign, they emphasized personal qualities of the candidates and campaigning activities. The voters learned accordingly. Image dimensions pertaining to personality traits and styles of the candidates were better remembered than those pertaining to job qualifications and ideology, a finding duplicated in Patterson's study.[14]

Voters seemed to ignore much of what was presented, especially details about the candidates' stands on public policy issues. Although the complexity and dullness of issues and the haziness and repetitiveness of the candidates with regard to issue positions were often mentioned as barriers to understanding, references to issues did increase in candidate descriptions as the election drew near, primarily in descriptions of Carter. This conveys the impression that issues played a more important role in the evaluations of the candidates later in the campaign when voting decisions were more pressing.[15]

In addition to their issue positions, the candidates' past activities and perceived abilities to act also became more important to the voters in our study as the campaign progressed. While all voters stressed the importance of the candidates' actions, possibly because they became clearer and better known, the more highly educated voters tended to emphasize the candidates' intellectual capacities more than did less well educated voters. The latter described the candidates more in terms of emotional preferences. Prior knowledge, high interest, and high media exposure were all linked positively to learning. Obviously, knowledge-rich voters learned at accelerated rates, leaving knowledge-poor voters further behind as the campaign rolled on.[16]

In light of these trends throughout the campaign, we conclude that candidate and image agenda-setting are major effects of newspaper and television coverage of a presidential election, perhaps more pervasive and important than issue agenda-setting. Voters seem to be able to learn about candidates and their images more easily than about issues and issue positions, and the media devote considerable time and space to discussion of personal qualities of individual candidates and their campaign activities.

Like issue agenda-setting, image agenda-setting is neither simple nor direct. It varies according to a number of factors, such as media exposure patterns of voters, interpersonal communication patterns, prior knowledge and attitudes, levels of motivation to follow the campaign, and levels of uncertainty in making voting decisions. Our data show that, overall, newspapers and television did play a major role in setting the agenda of candidates in the primaries and setting the agenda of images for Carter and Ford later in the campaign. This ability to influence voters' perceptions of the leading candidates in a presidential election places a great responsibility on the mass media to cover as many candidates as equally as possible early in the campaign and to focus heavily on their job qualifications and ideologies.

As it now stands, both issue and image agenda-setting largely involve acts of faith by voters in media judgments, rather than considered choices based on careful analysis of the wealth of information available from the mass media. This rather superficial learning on the part of many voters is unlikely to change drastically in the future, even if media coverage of presidential elections were to change. Nonetheless, improved media coverage is essential because it may contribute to gradual improvements in voter learning over the span of several elections. Hope for such improvements is slim, however, considering that there has been no substantial rise in voter information levels in recent years, judging by the quantity of answers to election questions. When one compares the number of responses given to open-ended questions about the likes and dislikes of parties and candidates in 1952 with the number of responses in 1976, the changes are minimal.[17]

INTEREST PATTERNS

In addition to issue and image agenda-setting, we also discovered that the media, especially television, had an important influence on a key variable in the early stages of the election: voter's levels of interest in the campaign. Our panelists' preprimary level of interest was positively related to levels of media use—especially use of television— to follow politics throughout most of the remainder of the year. However, media effects were also considerable. In line with agenda-setting theory, frequent use of television to follow politics during the primaries played a significant role in stimulating subsequent voter interest in the campaign. For the remainder of the election period, there was a mostly reciprocal relationship between use of mass media to follow politics and interest in the campaign.

Thus there is evidence that media exposure—particularly use of television— to follow politics is most important in the spring primary period for stimulating subsequent interest in the campaign. This supports the view that the media can be instrumental in spurring voter interest in the campaign that is needed for learning about candidates, their images, and the issues. In light of our finding that news stories must be interesting to be remembered, this places an obligation on the media to make their campaign news as interesting as possible in order to stimulate subsequent interest in the campaign and increased learning of candidate-, image-, and issue-related information.

CONCLUSIONS

Our findings show that the influence of newspapers and television is greatest during the preprimary and early primary period of a presidential election campaign. This influence, which we have called agenda-setting, applies to issues, to candidates and their images, and to interest in the campaign. We found that newspapers seem to play the dominant role in establishing an agenda of issues early in the campaign, that television plays the dominant role in stimulating later voter interest in the campaign, and that both media are important in establishing an agenda of candidates—and an agenda of image dimensions of the leading candidates—early in the campaign.

We also found that most learning from the mass media is confined to *awareness*—the ability to recognize issues, candidates, and images without the ability to recall pertinent facts spontaneously. Only a few of the voters in our study could describe the positions taken by both leading candidates on any particular issue; both issue and image agenda-setting appear to be largely acts of faith in media judgments. Voters found it easier to learn about candidates and their images, especially their personalities and styles, than about issues and issue positions. Only those news stories considered "interesting" by voters were well-remembered.

If one subscribes to the prevailing view that voting decisions should involve comparative appraisals of the candidates' issue stands, these findings have important implications for the news media. The media, especially newspapers from which television news seems to take many cues, should make a concerted effort at the beginning of an election year, and even before that time, to cover as many issues as possible and to make the positions of the various political parties and candidates on these issues as clear as possible. This coverage should go beyond clear-cut issues to the more diffuse policy proposals as well.

The media should also try to cover as many candidates as equally as possible early in the campaign. By focusing on only one or two winners of early primaries, the choices of voters are unnecessarily restricted before the campaign has a chance to really begin. And there should be more coverage of candidates' job qualifications and ideologies, as well as of their personalities, styles, and campaign activities.

We agree with Patterson that the burden on the media is particularly severe during the early nomination phase of a presidential election campaign.[18] And our study has demonstrated that this is precisely when the media are likely to have their greatest influence on voters. But we do not agree with Patterson's contention that the news cannot be an adequate guide for informed political choice. The media do not have to narrow the field of contenders so early in the campaign; they do not have to concentrate on the clear-cut, conflict-laden issues and gloss over the positions of candidates on a wide range of more diffuse policy issues; they do not have to focus on the personalities and styles of campaign activities of candidates rather than on their job qualifications and political stances; and they do not have to present information on issues and job qualifications in an uninteresting and dull fashion. Even though we agree with Patterson that the major themes of the news are dictated more by journalistic values than by political ones, such journalistic values do include a commitment to accuracy, impartiality, and empirical evidence— values compatible with producing an informed electorate.

Patterson and other scholars contend that the real weakness of the presidential election system in the United States is the dismantling of the political party. Party leaders, they argue, are more adept than voters at selecting nominees who will meet the public's desire for leadership.[19] Parties are also credited with being ultimately more responsive than the media to the needs of voters because parties must win voter support in elections. This leads to the conclusion that the time has come to find ways to increase the party's influence in a nomination system that blends popular participation and party influence. But such a plan may well be unrealistic. It may be impossible to buck the trend of diminishing influence of political parties on voting choices in presidential elections. The voters are unlikely to abandon their heavy reliance on the mass media for political decision-making information as long as this permits them the maximum individual freedom of choice.

Our study reveals that media coverage of the 1976 presidential election was both functional and dysfunctional in providing voters with the information they needed to make intelligent choices on their own. We found that a great amount of information was available in the media, especially in newspapers, about issues and the personalities, past experiences, and job qualifications of the major candidates.[20] But we also found many deficiencies. For instance, many important stories that had appeared at the beginning of the election year were not repeated, and the agendas of candidates, images, and issues were set very early in the campaign. Thus the basic structure of the race was determined very quickly, long before most voters were highly attentive to the campaign or had had a chance to reflect and discuss the various issues and candidates that had emerged at the beginning of the campaign year.

It must be emphasized, however, that media deficiencies were made worse by voter shortcomings. Busy lifestyles and the low priority that many people place on politics contributed significantly to making political learning rather spotty and thin. In fact, data from the University of Michigan's 1976 election studies show that "how closely a citizen monitors his or her information environment appears to be more important than how rich a given information source is."[21] Even if media coverage of the campaign were consistently informative and fascinating, it is unlikely that audience attention and use patterns would shift radically. Nonetheless, by being so preoccupied with a few issues and a few candidates so early in the campaign and by being so reluctant to repeat "old" news, the media did contribute to unduly narrowing the voters' options very early in the presidential campaign. There is also the problem of simply reporting claims and counterclaims by candidates and their supporters, without attempting to evaluate the truth of such claims. Such reporting tends to leave the voters confused or encourages them to tune out to avoid confusion.

Thus the low levels of political learning associated with media agenda-setting in the 1976 election campaign are a product of both media coverage and voters' interest, attention, and media use patterns. Perhaps it is not realistic to expect voters to learn much more than the salience of various issues, candidates, and images during a complex campaign. But if most voter learning is confined to the awareness level of agenda-setting, this places a special responsibility on newspapers and television news to cover a broad range of issues, candidates, and images and to explain their importance simply and interestingly. Probably the media should make an effort to keep issue, candidate, and image agendas flexible and varied until the closing weeks of the campaign.

If the libertarian philosphy of the free marketplace of ideas is to prevail in U.S. presidential election campaigns, the words of the Hutchins Commission, published in 1947, speak to this need to avoid premature media agenda-setting:

Civilized society is a working system of ideas. It lives and changes by the consumption of ideas. Therefore it must make sure that *as many as possible* of the ideas which its members have are available for its examination.[22] (Emphasis ours.)

Thus far we have emphasized the significance of our findings in relation to future performance by the mass media. We now turn to the broad implications for the political system in general.

The discretion that newspeople enjoy in selecting issues to highlight or ignore gives them the potential to influence the outcome of presidential elections. For instance, in modern times, an emphasis on foreign policy issues has generally aided Republicans, while stress on economic concerns has helped to elect Democrats. By making choices among issues, often quite independently from the stated issue priorities of the candidates and even from the flow of real world events, the media may determine which candidate is shown in the best light and, hence, elected.

Additionally, issues that become the focus of media attention during an election often generate wide public debate and lead to promises of future public policy action by political leaders. These promises become political coin of the realm that can be converted into pressures for future performance. In this manner the media, particularly newspapers that help set the agenda patterns for television and the public, can set the stage for political action after the election.

However, the power of the media to shape the issue agenda for political leaders and the public is not unlimited. As we have seen, many important issues are matters of personal experience for the audience or matters in which saliences have already been shaped by past learning from a variety of media and personal information sources. Irrespective of media agenda-setting, these issues may assume major importance in an election if the public is greatly concerned about them. This is what happened with such issues as unemployment and inflation in 1976. Although the media gave them comparatively little coverage, public concern caused them to be major factors in tipping the balance from Ford to Carter.[23] Media agenda-setting power thus operates only in the space bounded by the audience's prior knowledge and by its past and current real world experiences. Of course, this leaves a vast array of crucial issues hitherto unknown to the public and beyond its personal experiences that may, through media activities, move to the center of the political stage.

However, it is in the realm of candidate images, even more than of issues, that the media appear to have their greatest and most immediate effects on election outcomes. The media, very early in the primary process, designate frontrunners and suggest the criteria by which success and failure are to be judged in the primary campaigns. This designation is particularly important in elections into which many little-known candidates have thrown their hats. To the victor of the coveted frontrunner designation then go most of the spoils of media publicity. In 1976 that designation was given to Jimmy Carter after less than 5 percent of the delegates had been selected. From then on, Carter, along with Ford and Reagan, the two Republican frontrunners, received the bulk of publicity, making it well-nigh impossible for other contenders to gain sufficient money, supporters, and the wide national following essential for viable presidential contenders. The fate of late entrants into the campaign is now virtually sealed—without the advantages of early media support, their chances for reaching the election finals are minimal.

It is thus no exaggeration to say that the media can make or break presidential hopefuls. Not only may they determine who will be nominated, but their ability to project advantageous or disadvantageous images for candidates and link them to suitable issues also may decide who will be elected. The candidates, knowing the power of the media over the life and death of their candidacies, have learned to adjust their campaigns accordingly. The quest for favorable media coverage determines where candidates campaign, what newsworthy activities they will undertake to gain television coverage in particular, and what issues they and their supporters will stress as likely media attractions. In this manner, campaigns, which are crucial political scenes in the electoral drama, are continually altered and adjusted to meet the media's needs and preferences.

The political consequences are profound. Costs of campaigning have escalated, making the need to raise money a dominant campaign concern. Candidates are selected for their skills as media performers rather than for their professional aptitudes. Campaigns have become more and more trivialized, through emphasis on horserace and hoopla characteristics. At first, this was a major idiosyncrasy of television, which needs pictorially interesting news. But it has become increasingly true of newspapers as well in recent elections.[24] Its pervasiveness is likely to be an important factor in the growing cynicism of the electorate and in the drop in turnout of eligible voters on Election Day.

The current emphasis on using the television medium extensively for campaigning in presidential elections also has lessened the dependence of candidates on political parties to introduce them to the public and to endorse them for election. It has therefore opened the presidential race more widely to people outside the circle of party favorites. If they win elections, such candidates are comparatively independent of party pressures and controls. For good or ill, their freedom of action is greatly enhanced.

The media's ability to spur interest in the election, too, has important political consequences. Interest, as we have seen, stimulates learning and therefore leads to more-informed voters who can vote more intelligently. Interest, too, affects turnout in presidential elections, which may determine which party wins, especially in a close election.[25] Finally, interest in an election that focuses citizen attention on the governmental process may be an effective antidote to public cynicism and apathy. As long as citizens are interested in democratic processes, the advantages of a democratically governed society are within reach. It is only when citizens no longer care and ignore major political events, like presidential elections, that democracy is in danger.

On final major political question raised by our research needs to be examined. We have argued in this chapter that it is the responsibility of the media to use their agenda-setting power to alert voters to as broad a range of issues and images as possible. An unexpressed assumption behind this admonition is that newspeople should determine what the important issues are, what image qualities need to be stressed, and whose names should be made widely familiar to the electorate for its consideration. Media news people presumably act as surrogates of the voting public in making these decisions.

But are they, in fact, sound and valid surrogates? Can they be trusted with making the kinds of choices that best advance the interests of the

American public? The fact that public agendas differ substantially from media agendas for those issues with which the public is most familiar raises some serious doubts about the merits of media choices. So does the fact that the agendas of candidates, many of whom are publicly elected officials, also differ substantially in the choice of issues and images to be stressed. While our research does not provide answers for these questions, it does point to the need for examining the news-making process more closely to explain how media agendas are formed and to evaluate their merits.

These open questions also remind us, once more, about the many questions concerning agenda-setting that remain unanswered. With this book, we have advanced understanding of this important process further than others have done, but much exciting and important work still lies ahead.

NOTES

[1]Jeffrey W. Wides, "Perceived Economic Competency and the Ford/Carter Election," *Public Opinion Quarterly* 43 (Winter 1979): 535–43.

[2]David Weaver and Maxwell McCombs, "Voters' Need for Orientation and Choice of Candidate: Mass Media and Electoral Decision Making," Paper presented at the annual conference of the American Association for Public Opinion Research, Roanoke, Virginia, June 1978.

[3]Daniel Katz, "Attitude Formation and Public Opinion," in *Political Attitudes & Public Opinion*, eds. Dan D. Nimmo and Charles M. Bonjean (New York: David McKay, 1972), pp. 13–26.

[4]Thomas E. Patterson, *The Mass Media Election: How Americans Choose Their President* (New York: Praeger, 1980), pp. 31–42.

[5]Colin Seymour-Ure, *The Political Imact of Mass Media* (Beverly Hills: Sage, 1974), p. 223.

[6]Patterson, *The Mass Media Election*, pp. 41–42.

[7]Robert D. Cantor, *Voting Behavior and Presidential Elections* (Itasca, Ill.: F. E. Peacock, 1975).

[8]Arthur Miller, "Election Study Notes New Trends in Voter Behavior, Attributes Close Race to Well-Run Campaign," *ISR Newsletter* 5 (Ann Arbor: University of Michigan Institute for Social Research, 1977): 4–5; Warren E. Miller and Teresa E. Levitin, *Leadership and Change: The New Politics and the American Electorate* (Cambridge, Mass: Winthrop, 1976); C. Anthony Broh, "Toward a Theory of Issue Voting," Sage Professional Papers in American Politics, vol. 1, series no. 04-011, 1973, pp. 6–10; Samuel A. Kirkpatrick, William Lyons, and Michael R. Fitzgerald, "Candidates, Parties, and Issues in the American Electorate," *American Politics Quarterly* 3 (July 1975): 35–71; Gerald M. Pomper, "From Confusion to Clarity: Issues and American Voters, 1956–1968," *American Political Science Review* 66 (1972): 415–28; and David E. Repass, "Issue Salience and Party Choice," *American Political Science Review* 65 (1971): 389–400.

[9]Weaver and McCombs, "Voters' Need for Orientation"; Broh, "Toward a Theory of Issue Voting"; Kirkpatrick, Lyons, and Fitzgerald, "Candidates, Parties, and Issues"; and Norman H. Nie, Sidney Verba, and John P. Petrocik, *The Changing American Voter* (Cambridge, Mass.: Harvard University Press, 1976).

[10]For a discussion of some of these studies, see Elihu Katz, "Platforms & Windows: Broadcasting's Role in Election Campaigns," *Journalism Quarterly* 48 (Summer 1971): 304–14; Maxwell E. McCombs, "Mass Communication in Political Campaigns: Information, Gratification, and Persuasion," in *Current Perspectives in Mass Communication Research*, eds. F. Gerald Kline and Phillip J. Tichenor (Beverly Hills: Sage, 1972), pp. 169–94.

[11]For reviews of most of these studies, see Maxwell E. McCombs, "Agenda-Setting Research: A Bibliographic Essay," *Political Communication Review* (Summer 1976): 1–7; Donald L. Shaw and Maxwell E. McCombs, *The Emergence of American Political Issues: The Agenda-Setting Function of the Press* (St. Paul: West, 1977); and Maxwell E. McCombs and Donald L. Shaw, "An Up-to-Date Report on the Agenda-Setting Function," Paper presented to the 30th annual conference of the International Communication Association, Acapulco, Mexico, May 1980.

[12]Patterson, *The Mass Media Election*, pp. 43–48, 107–14.

[13]Lee B. Becker and Maxwell E. McCombs, " U.S. Primary Politics and Public Opinion: The Role of the Press in Determining Voter Reactions," Paper presented to the 27th annual conference of the International Communication Association, Berlin, West Germany, May 1977; Lee B. Becker and Maxwell E. McCombs, "The Role of the Press in Determining Voter Reactions to Presidential Primaries," *Human Communication Research* 4 (Summer 1978): 301–07.

[14]Patterson, *The Mass Media Election*, pp. 134–38.

[15]Kessel points out that the most salient images and issues are not necessarily most decisive in voting decisions. In the seven presidential elections from 1952 to 1976, issues were most important for voting choices in all but the 1976 election, where they dropped slightly behind image qualities, according to Kessel. See John H. Kessel, *Presidential Campaign Politics: Coalition Strategies and Citizen Response* (Homewood, Ill.: Dorsey Press, 1980), pp. 205–07.

[16]Other research supports the conclusion that higher socioeconomic status people learn from increasing mass media information at faster rates than do lower socioeconomic status people, thus creating a widening "knowledge gap" between those who are well-educated and more attentive to mass media (especially printed media) and those who are less well-educated and less attentive to mass media. See Phillip J. Tichenor, George A. Donohue, and Clarice N. Olien, "Mass Media and Differential Growth in Knowledge," *Public Opinion Quarterly* 34 (Summer 1970): 158–70; Phillip J. Tichenor, Jane M. Rodenkirchen, Clarice N. Olien, and George A. Donohue, "Community Issues, Conflict, and Public Affairs Knowledge," in *New Models for Mass Communication Research*, ed. Peter Clarke (Beverly Hills: Sage, 1973) pp. 45–79; and George A. Donohue, Phillip J. Tichenor, and Clarice N. Olien, "Mass Media and the Knowledge Gap: A Hypothesis Reconsidered," *Communication Research* 2 (January 1975): 2–23.

[17]Kessel, *Presidential Campaign Politics*, p. 258.

[18]Patterson, *The Mass Media Election*, p. 173.

[19]Ibid., p. 180.

[20]In fact, there is evidence that the coverage of the "substance" of the 1976 campaign (defined as candidate qualities and issue-related material) by some metropolitan papers, such as the New York *Times*, the Chicago *Tribune*, and the Chicago *Sun-Times*, increased

from the 1968 campaign, whereas coverage of the "horserace" aspects decreased from 1968 to 1976. See John M. Russonello and Frank Wolf, "Newspaper Coverage of the 1976 and 1968 Presidential Campaigns," *Journalism Quarterly* 56 (Summer 1979): 360–64, 432.

[21] Kessel, *Presidential Campaign Politics*, p. 194.

[22] Commission on Freedom of the Press, *A Free and Responsible Press* (Chicago: University of Chicago Press, 1947), p. 6.

[23] Arthur H. Miller and Warren Miller, "Partisanship and Performance: 'Rational' Choice in the 1976 Elections," Paper presented to the annual convention of the American Political Science Association, Washington, D.C., 1977.

[24] Doris A. Graber, *Mass Media and American Politics* (Washington, D.C., Congressional Quarterly Press, 1980), pp. 178–79.

[25] Lyman Kellstedt, "Television Viewing Habits and Vote Turnout," Paper presented to the International Communication Association, Acapulco, Mexico, 1980.

BIBLIOGRAPHY

A. *Agenda-Setting References*

Becker, Lee B., and Maxwell E. McCombs. "The Role of the Press in Determining Voter Reactions to Presidential Primaries." *Human Communication Research* 4(Summer 1978):301–07.

_____."U.S. Primary Politics and Public Opinion: The Role of the Press in Determining Voter Reactions." Paper presented to the 27th annual conference of the International Communication Association, Berlin, West Germany, May 1977.

Becker, Lee B., Maxwell E. McCombs, and Jack M. McLeod. "The Development of Political Cognitions." In *Political Communication: Issues and Strategies for Research*, edited by Steven H. Chaffee, pp. 21–63. Beverly Hills: Sage, 1975.

Becker, Lee B., David H. Weaver, Doris A. Graber, and Maxwell McCombs. Influence on Public Agendas." In *The Great Debates: Carter vs. Ford, 1976*, edited by Sidney Kraus, pp. 418–28. Bloomington: Indiana University Press, 1979.

Benton, Marc, and P. Jean Frazier. "The Agenda-Setting Function of Mass Media at Three Levels of 'Information Holding.'" *Communication Research* 3 (July 1976): 261–74.

Bowers, Thomas A. "Candidate Advertising: The Agenda is the Message." In *The Emergence of American Political Issues: The Agenda-Setting Function of the Press*, edited by Donald L. Shaw and Maxwell E. McCombs, pp. 53–67. St. Paul: West, 1977.

Carey, John. "Setting the Political Agenda: How Media Shape Campaigns." *Journal of Communication* 26 (Spring 1976): 50–57.

Ebring, Lutz, Edie N. Goldenberg, and Arthur Miller, "Front-Page News and Real World Cues: A New Look at Agenda-Setting by the Media. "*American Journal of Political Science* 24 (February 1980): 16–49.

Eyal, Chaim H. "Time Frame in Agenda-Setting Research: A Study of Conceptual and Methodological Factors Affecting the Time Frame Context of the Agenda-Setting Process." Ph.D. dissertation, Syracuse (New York) University, 1979.

Eyal, Chaim H., James P. Winter, and William F. DeGeorge. "Time Frame for Agenda-Setting." Paper presented at the annual convention of the American Association for Public Opinion Research, Buck Hill Falls, Pennsylvania, May 1979.

Forth, Rodney, and Laurily Epstein. "Agenda-Setting Research: The Effects of Social Context on Individual and Group Behavior." Paper presented at the annual convention of the Midwest Association for Public Opinion Research, Chicago, November 1979.

Funkhouser, G. Ray. "The Issues of the Sixties: An Exploratory Study in the Dynamics of Public Opinion." *Public Opinion Quarterly* 37 (Spring 1973): 62–75.

————. "Trends in Media Coverage of the Issues of the '60s." *Journalism Quarterly* 50 (Autumn 1973): 533–38.

Glavin, William. "Political Influence of the Press." American Newspaper Publishers Association *News Research Bulletin* 4 (November 1976): 1–6.

Graber, Doris A. "Agenda-Setting: Are There Women's Perspectives?" In *Women and the News*, edited by Laurily Keir Epstein, pp. 15–37. New York: Hastings House, 1978.

Hilker, Anne K. "Agenda-Setting Influence in an Off-Year Election." American Newspaper Publishers Association *News Research Bulletin* 4 (November 1976): 7–10.

Hong, Kisun, and Sara Shemer. "Influence of Media and Interpersonal Agendas on Personal Agendas." Paper presented at the annual convention of the Association for Education in Journalism, Madison, Wisconsin, August 1977.

McClure, Robert D., and Thomas E. Patterson. "Setting the Political Agenda: Print vs. Network News." *Journal of Communication* 26 (Spring 1976): 23–28.

McCombs, Maxwell E. "The Agenda-Setting Function of the Press." Paper presented at a conference on Women and the News, Washington University, St. Louis, September 1977.

————. "Agenda-Setting Research: A Bibliographic Essay." *Political Communication Review* 1 (1976): 1–7.

————. "Elaborating the Agenda-Setting Influence of Mass Communication." Paper prepared for the bulletin of the Institute for Communication Research, Keio University, Tokyo, Japan, Fall 1976.

————. "Expanding the Domain of Agenda-Setting Research: Strategies and Theoretical Development." Paper presented at the annual convention of the Speech Communication Association, Washington, D.C., December 1977.

————. "Newspapers Versus Television: Mass Communication Effects Across Time." In *The Emergence of American Political Issues: The Agenda Setting Function of the Press*, edited by Donald L. Shaw and Maxwell E. McCombs, pp. 89–105. St. Paul: West, 1977.

McCombs, Maxwell E., and Donald L. Shaw. "The Agenda-Setting Function of Mass Media." *Public Opinion Quarterly* 36 (Summer 1972): 176–87.

————. "An Up-to-Date Report on the Agenda-Setting Function." Paper presented to the 30th annual conference of the International Communication Association, Acapulco, Mexico, May 1980.

McCombs, Maxwell E., and David Weaver. "Voters and the Mass Media: Information-Seeking, Political Interest, and Issue Agendas." Paper presented at the annual conference of the American Association for Public Opinion Research, Buck Hill Falls, Pennsylvania, May 1977.

————. "Voters' Need for Orientation and Use of Mass Media." Paper presented at the annual convention of the International Communication Association, Montreal, Canada, April 1973.

McLeod, Jack M., Lee B. Becker, and James E. Byrnes. "Another Look at the

Agenda-Setting Function of the Press." *Communication Research* 1 (April 1974): 131–66.

Mullins, L. Edward. "Agenda-Setting and the Young Voter." In *The Emergence of American Political Issues: The Agenda Setting Function of the Press*, edited by Donald L. Shaw and Maxwell E. McCombs, pp. 133–48. St. Paul: West, 1977.

Palmgreen, Philip, and Peter Clarke. "Agenda-Setting with Local and National Issues." *Communication Research* 4 (October 1977): 435–52.

Shaw, Donald L., and Thomas A. Bowers. "Learning from Commercials: The Influence of TV Advertising on the Voter Political 'Agenda.'" Paper presented at the annual convention of the Association for Education in Journalism, Fort Collins, Colorado, 1973.

Shaw, Donald L., and Maxwell E. McCombs. *The Emergence of American Political Issues: The Agenda-Setting Function of the Press*. St. Paul: West, 1977.

Stone, Gerald. "Cumulative Effects of the Media." Paper presented at the Conference on Agenda-Setting Research, Syracuse (New York) University, Fall 1974.

Tipton, Leonard P., Roger D. Haney, and John R. Baseheart. "Media Agenda-Setting in City and State Election Campaigns." *Journalism Quarterly* 52 (Spring 1975): 15–22.

Weaver, David H. "Political Issues and Voter Need for Orientation." In *The Emergence of American Political Issues: The Agenda Setting Function of the Press*, edited by Donald L. Shaw and Maxwell E. McCombs, pp. 107–19. St. Paul: West, 1977.

Weaver, David H., and Maxwell E. McCombs. "Voters' Need for Orientation and Choice of Candidate: Mass Media and Electoral Decision Making." Paper presented at the annual conference of the American Association for Public Opinion Research, Roanoke, Virginia, June 1978.

Weaver, David H., Maxwell E. McCombs, and Charles Spellman "Watergate and the Media: A Case Study of Agenda-Setting." *American Politics Quarterly* 3 (October 1975): 458–72.

Williams, Wenmouth, and David C. Larsen. "Agenda-Setting in an Off-Election Year." *Journalism Quarterly* 54 (Winter 1977): 744–49.

Zucker, Harold G. "The Variable Nature of News Media Influence." In *Communication Yearbook II*, edited by Brent D. Ruben, pp. 225–40. New Brunswick, N.J.: Transaction Books, 1978.

B. *General Election and Political Communication References*

American Institute for Political Communication. *The 1968 Campaign: Anatomy of a Crucial Election*. Washington, D.C.: American Institute for Political Communication, 1970.

Amundsen, Kirsten. *The Silenced Majority*. Englewood Cliffs: Prentice Hall, 1971.

Andersen, Peter A., and Robert J. Kibler. "Candidate Valence as a Predictor of Voter Preference." *Human Communication Research* 5 (March 1978): 4–14.

Arterton, F. Christopher. "The Media Politics of Presidential Campaigns: A Study of the Carter Nomination Drive." In *Race for the Presidency*, edited by James David Barber, pp. 26–54. Englewood Cliffs: Prentice Hall, 1978.

Atkin, Charles K., John Galloway, and Oguz B. Nayman. "News Media Exposure, Poltical Knowledge and Campaign Interest." *Journalism Quarterly* 53 (Summer 1976): 231–37.

Berelson, Bernard, Paul Lazarsfeld, and William McPhee. *Voting*. Chicago: University of Chicago Press, 1954.

Bowes, John E., and Herbert Strentz. "Candidate Images: Stereotyping and the 1976 Debates." In *Communication Yearbook II*, edited by Brent Ruben, pp. 354–406. New Brunswick, N.J.: Transaction Books, 1978.

Broh, C. Anthony. "Toward A Theory of Issue Voting." Sage Professional Papers in American Politics, vol. 1, series no. 04-011. Beverly Hills: Sage, 1973.

Campbell, Angus, Philip Converse, Warren Miller, and Donald Stokes. *The American Voter*. New York: John Wiley, 1964.

Cantor, Robert D. *Voting Behavior and Presidential Elections*. Itasca, Ill.: F.E. Peacock, 1975.

Graber, Doris A. *Mass Media and American Politics*. Washington, D.C.: Congressional Quarterly Press, 1980.

_____. "Personal Qualities in Presidential Images: The Contribution of the Press." *Midwest Journal of Political Science* 16 (1972): 46–76.

_____. "Press Coverage and Voter Reaction." *Political Science Quarterly* 89 (1974): 68–100.

_____. *Verbal Behavior and Politics*. Urbana: University of Illinois Press, 1976.

Greenstein, Fred I. "Popular Images of the President." *American Journal of Psychiatry* 122 (November 1965): 523–29.

Hahn, Dan F., and Ruth M. Gonchar. "Political Myth: The Image and the Issue." *Today's Speech* 20 (Summer 1972): 57–65.

Hofstetter, C. Richard. *Bias in the News: Network Television News Coverage of the 1972 Election Campaign*. Columbus: Ohio State University Press, 1976.

Katz, Elihu. "Platforms & Windows: Broadcasting's Role in Election Campaigns." *Journalism Quarterly* 48 (Summer 1971): 304–14.

Katz, Elihu, and Jacob J. Feldman. "The Debates in Light of Research: A Survey of Surveys." In *The Process and Effects of Mass Communication*, edited by Wilbur Schramm and Donald F. Roberts, pp. 701–53. Urbana: University of Illinois Press, 1971.

Kellstedt, Lyman. "Television Viewing Habits and Vote Turnout." Paper presented to the annual convention of the International Communication Association, Acapulco, Mexico, 1980.

Kessel, John. *Presidential Campaign Politics: Coalition Strategies and Citizen Response*. Homewood, Ill.: Dorsey Press, 1980.

Kirkpatrick, Samuel A., William Lyons, and Michael R. Fitzgerald. "Candidates, Parties, and Issues in the American Electorate." *American Politics Quarterly* 3 (July 1975): 35–71.

Krock, Arthur. "'The Man Who'—Not 'The Issue Which.'" New York *Times*, October 16, 1960, p. 19.

Lamb, Karl A. *As Orange Goes: Twelve California Families and the Future of American Politics*. New York: W.W. Norton, 1975.

Lane, Robert E. *Political Ideology: Why the American Common Man Believes What He Does*. New York: Free Press, 1962.

Lazarsfeld, Paul, Bernard Berelson, and Hazel Gaudet. *The People's Choice*. New York: Columbia University Press, 1944.

Leuthold, D.A. *Electioneering in a Democracy: Campaigns for Congress*. New York: John Wiley, 1968.

McCombs, Maxwell E. "Mass Communication in Political Campaigns: Information, Gratification, and Persuasion." In *Current Perspectives in Mass Communication Research*, edited by F. Gerald Kline and Phillip J. Tichenor, pp. 169–74. Beverly Hills: Sage, 1972.

McCombs, Maxwell E., and L. Edward Mullins. "Consequences of Education: Media Exposure, Political Interest and Information-Seeking Orientation." *Mass Comm Review* 1 (August 1973): 27–31.

McLeod, Jack M., and Lee B. Becker. "Testing the Validity of Gratification Measures Through Political Effects Analysis." In *The Uses of Mass Communications: Current Perspectives on Gratifications Research*, edited by Jay G. Blumler and Elihu Katz, pp. 137–64. Beverly Hills: Sage, 1974.

Mehling, Reuben, Sidney Kraus, and Richard D. Yoakam. "Pre-Debate Campaign Interest and Media Use." In *The Great Debates*, edited by Sidney Kraus, pp. 224–31. Bloomington: Indiana University Press, 1962.

Miller, Arthur. "Election Study Notes New Trends in Voter Behavior, Attributes Close Race to Well-Run Campaign." *IRS Newsletter* 5 (1977, Ann Arbor, University of Michigan Institute for Social Research): 4–5.

Miller, Arthur H., and Warren Miller. "Partisanship and Performance: 'Rational' Choice in the 1976 Elections." Paper presented to the annual convention of the American Political Science Association, Washington, D.C., 1977.

Miller, Warren E., and Teresa E. Levitin. *Leadership and Change: The New Politics and the American Electorate*. Cambridge, Mass.: Winthrop, 1976.

Natchez, Peter B. "Images of Voting: The Social Psychologists." *Public Policy* 18 (Summer 1970): 553–88.

Nie, Norman H., Sidney Verba, and John P. Petrocik. *The Changing American Voter*. Cambridge, Mass.: Harvard University Press, 1976.

Nimmo, Dan, and Robert L. Savage. *Candidates and Their Images*. Pacific Palisades: Goodyear, 1976.

Patterson, Thomas E. *The Mass Media Election: How Americans Choose Their President*. New York: Praeger, 1980.

Patterson, Thomas E., and Robert D. McClure. *The Unseeing Eye: The Myth of Television Power in National Elections*. New York: G.P. Putnam, 1976.

Pomper, Gerald M. *Elections in America: Control and Influence in Democratic Politics*. New York: Dodd, Mead, 1968.

_____. "From Confusion to Clarity: Issues and American Voters, 1956–1968." *American Political Science Review* 66 (1972): 415–28.

_____. *Voter's Choice: Varieties of American Electoral Behavior*. New York: Dodd, Mead, 1975.

Repass, David E. "Issue Salience and Party Choice." *American Political Science Review* 65 (1971): 389–400.

Russonello, John M., and Frank Wolf. "Newspaper Coverage of the 1976 and 1968

Presidential Campaigns." *Journalism Quarterly* 56 (Summer 1979): 360–64, 432.

Seymour-Ure, Colin. *The Political Impact of Mass Media*. Beverly Hills: Sage, 1974.

Sigel, Roberta S. "Effects of Partisanship on Perception of Political Candidates." *Public Opinion Quarterly* 28 (Fall 1964): 483–96.

Steeper, Frederick T. "Public Response to Gerald Ford's Statements on Eastern Europe in the Second Debate." In *The Presidential Debates: Media, Electoral, and Policy Perspectives*, edited by George F. Bishop, Robert G. Meadow, and Marilyn Jackson-Beeck, pp. 81–101. New York: Praeger, 1978.

Weaver, David H., and G. Cleveland Wilhoit. "News Media Coverage of U.S. Senators in Four Congresses, 1953–1974." *Journalism Monographs* 67 (April 1980): 1–34.

Wides, Jeffrey W. "Perceived Economic Competency and the Ford/Carter Election." *Public Opinion Quarterly* 43 (Winter 1979): 535–43.

Witcover, Jules. *Marathon: The Pursuit of the Presidency, 1972–1976*. New York: Viking, 1977.

C. *Other Related References*

Andersen, Kenneth, and Theodore Clevenger, Jr. "A Summary of Experimental Research on Ethos." *Speech Monographs* 30 (1963): 59–78.

Atkin, Charles. "Instrumental Utilities and Information Seeking." In *New Models for Mass Communication Research*, edited by Peter Clarke, pp. 205–42. Beverly Hills: Sage, 1973.

Blumler, Jay G. "The Role of Theory in Uses and Gratifications Studies." *Communication Research* 6 (January 1979): 9–36.

Blumler, Jay G., and Elihu Katz. *The Uses of Mass Communication: Current Perspectives on Gratifications Research*. Beverly Hills: Sage, 1974.

Brown, Steven R. "Intensive Analysis in Political Research." *Political Methodology* 1 (1974): 1–25.

Clifford, Mary E., Raymond Hill, and Stephen Orlofsky. *1976 News Dictionary*. New York: Facts on File, 1977.

Commission on Freedom of the Press. *A Free and Responsible Press*. Chicago: University of Chicago Press, 1947.

Comstock, George, Steven Chaffee, Natan Katzman, Maxwell McCombs, and Donald Roberts. *Television and Human Behavior*. New York: Columbia University Press, 1978.

Donohue, George A., Phillip J. Tichenor, and Clarice N. Olien. "Mass Media and the Knowledge Gap: A Hypothesis Reconsidered." *Communication Research* 2 (January 1975): 3–23.

Dunwoody, Sharon. "Science Journalists: A Study of Factors Affecting the Selection of News at a Scientific Meeting." Ph.D. dissertation, Indiana University, December 1978.

Epstein, Edward Jay. *News from Nowhere: Television and the News*. New York: Vintage Books, 1974.

Frank, R.S. *Message Dimensions of Televised News*. Lexington, Mass.: Lexington Books, 1973.

Graber, Doris A. *Crime News and the Public*. New York: Praeger, 1980.

Heise, D.R. "More Plausible Rival Hypotheses in the Cross-Lagged Panel Correlation Techniques." In *Sociological Methodology 1970*, edited by E.F. Borgatta, pp. 3–27. San Francisco: Jossey-Bass, 1970.

Hovland, Carl I., and Walter Weiss. "The Influence of Source Credibility on Communication Effectiveness." *Public Opinion Quarterly* 16 (1961): 635–50.

Katz, Daniel. "Attitude Formation and Public Opinion." In *Political Attitudes & Public Opinion*, edited by Dan D. Nimmo and Charles M. Bonjean, pp. 13–26. New York: David McKay, 1972.

Lippmann, Walter. *Public Opinion*. New York: Free Press, 1922.

Neuman, W. Russell. "Patterns of Recall among Television News Viewers." *Public Opinion Quarterly* 40 (1976): 115–23.

Noelle-Neumann, Elisabeth. "The Spiral of Silence: A Theory of Public Opinion." *Journal of Communication* 24 (Spring 1974): 43–51.

_____. "Turbulences in the Climate of Opinion: Methodological Applications of the Spiral of Silence Theory." *Public Opinion Quarterly* 41 (Summer 1977): 143–58.

Orum, Anthony M., Roberta S. Cohen, Sherri Grasmuck, and Amy W. Orum. "Sex, Socialization and Politics." *American Sociological Review* 39 (1974): 197–209.

Rosenberg, Morris. *The Logic of Survey Analysis*. New York: Basic Books, 1968.

Rozelle, R.M., and D.T. Campbell. "More Plausible Rival Hypotheses in the Cross-Lagged Panel Correlation Techniques." *Psychological Bulletin* 71 (1969): 74–80.

Sapiro, Virginia. "Socialization to Political Gender Roles Among Women." Midwest Political Science Association paper, Chicago, 1977.

Soule, John W., and Wilma E. McGrath. "A Comparative Study of Male-Female Political Attitudes at Citizen and Elite Levels." In *A Portrait of Marginality: The Political Behavior of the American Woman*, edited by Marianne Githens and Jewel Prestage, pp. 178–95. New York: David McKay, 1977.

Stroman, Carolyn. "Race, Public Opinion and Print Media Coverage." Ph.D. dissertation, Syracuse (New York) University, 1978.

Tannenbaum, Percy H. "The Indexing Process in Communication." In *The Process and Effects of Mass Communication*, edited by Wilbur Schramm and Donald F. Roberts, pp. 313–25. Urbana: University of Illinois Press, 1971.

Tichenor, Phillip J., George A. Donohue, and Clarice N. Olien. "Mass Media and Differential Growth in Knowledge." *Public Opinion Quarterly* 34 (Summer 1970): 158–70.

Tichenor, Phillip J., Jane M. Rodenkirchen, Clarice N. Olien, and George A. Donohue. "Community Issues, Conflict, and Public Affairs Knowledge." In *New Models for Mass Communication Research*, edited by Peter Clarke, pp. 45–79. Beverly Hills: Sage, 1973.

Tolman, E.C. *Purposive Behavior in Animals and Man*. New York: Appleton-Century, 1932.

Weiss, Walter. "Effects of the Mass Media of Communication." In *The Handbook of Social Psychology*, edited by Gardner Lindzey and Elliot Aronson, pp. 77–195. 2nd ed., vol. 5. Reading, Mass.: Addison Wesley, 1969.

Wilhoit, G. Cleveland, and David H. Weaver. *Newsroom Guide to Polls and*

Surveys. Washington, D.C.: American Newspaper Publishers Association, 1980.

Wright, Charles. "Functional Analysis and Mass Communication." *Public Opinion Quarterly* 24 (Winter 1960): 605–20.

INDEX

ABOUT THE AUTHORS

Chaim H. Eyal is on the faculty of the Communication Institute at the Hebrew University of Jerusalem. He earned his Ph.D. at Syracuse University and spent a year there as a postdoctoral fellow in the Communication Research Center, concentrating on agenda-setting research. His dissertation involves "Time Frame in Agenda-Setting Research: A Study of Conceptual and Methodological Factors Affecting the Time Frame Context of the Agenda-Setting Process."

Doris A. Graber is a professor of Political Science at the University of Illinois, Chicago Circle. She has combined a career of academic research and teaching with practical experience as a newspaper reporter and feature writer. Among her recent publications on the impact of the mass media on public attitudes and policies are *Verbal Behavior and Politics* (University of Illinois Press, 1976), *Mass Media and American Politics* (Congressional Quarterly Press, 1980), and *Crime News and the Public* (Praeger, 1980). Her Ph.D. is from Columbia University.

Maxwell E. McCombs is a John Ben Snow professor of Newspaper Research and director of the Communication Research Center at Syracuse University. This is the third consecutive presidential election study of agenda-setting in which he has participated. His extensive writings on agenda-setting include *The Emergence of American Political Issues: The Agenda Setting Function of the Press*, with Donald L. Shaw (West, 1977). Prior to joining the Syracuse faculty in 1973, McCombs was at the University of North Carolina and at the University of California, Los Angeles. His Ph.D. is from Stanford University.

David H. Weaver is an associate professor of Journalism at Indiana University-Bloomington and director of the Bureau of Media Research in the School of Journalism there. He has written several book chapters and articles on the role of the mass media in elections and is a regular contributor to *Journalism Quarterly* and the *ANPA News Research Bulletin* of the American Newspaper Publishers Association. His recent publications include *Newsroom Guide to Polls and Surveys*, with G. Cleveland Wilhoit (ANPA, 1980) and "News Media Coverage of U.S. Senators in Four Congresses, 1953–1974," with G. Cleveland Wilhoit (Journalism Monographs, 1980). He has worked as a reporter and editor on three Indiana daily newspapers, a North Carolina daily newspaper, and in the U.S. Army. His Ph.D. is from the University of North Carolina.